MY
DISAPPEARING
UNCLE

MY DISAPPEARING UNCLE

EUROPE, WAR *and the* STORIES *of a* SCATTERED FAMILY

KATHY HENDERSON

The History Press

First published 2023

The History Press
97 St George's Place, Cheltenham,
Gloucestershire, GL50 3QB
www.thehistorypress.co.uk

British Library Cataloguing in Publication Data.
A catalogue record for this book is available from the British Library.

ISBN 978 1 80399 122 1

Typesetting and origination by The History Press
Printed and bound in Great Britain by TJ Books Limited, Padstow, Cornwall.

Trees for LYfe

It is funny, but it strikes me that a person without anecdotes that they nurse while they live and that survive them, are more likely to be utterly lost not only to history but to the family following them. Of course this is the fate of most souls, reducing entire lives, no matter how vivid and wonderful, to those sad black names on withering family trees, with half a date dangling after and a question mark.

My father's happiness not only redeemed him, but drove him to stories, and keeps him even now alive in me like a second more patient and more pleasing soul within my poor soul.

The Secret Scripture by Sebastian Barry

Contents

A Simplified Family Tree

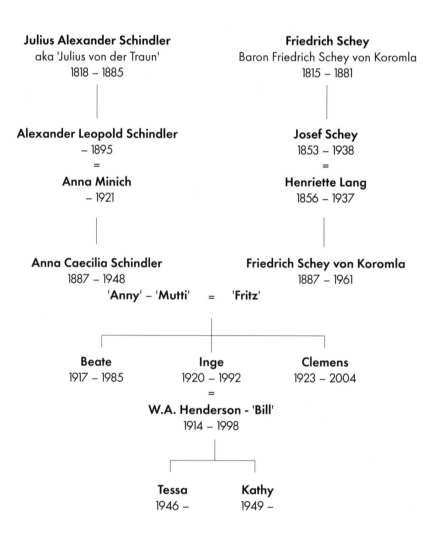

Julius Alexander Schindler
aka 'Julius von der Traun'
1818 – 1885

Friedrich Schey
Baron Friedrich Schey von Koromla
1815 – 1881

Alexander Leopold Schindler
– 1895
=
Anna Minich
– 1921

Josef Schey
1853 – 1938
=
Henriette Lang
1856 – 1937

Anna Caecilia Schindler
1887 – 1948
'Anny' – 'Mutti'   =   'Fritz'

Friedrich Schey von Koromla
1887 – 1961

Beate
1917 – 1985

Inge
1920 – 1992
=
W.A. Henderson - 'Bill'
1914 – 1998

Clemens
1923 – 2004

Tessa
1946 –

Kathy
1949 –

The Schey family was large. The first Baron Friedrich was one of five children, his son Josef was one of eight and his son Friedrich one of five. Almost all of them went on to have children of their own.

Introduction

Hungary, August 2011. The weather has turned cool and very wet when I look Koromla up on the map and wonder about a day trip. It looks tiny – on a white road not near anywhere. Part of the Csatka lands, a helpful archivist had told me. 'What's Csatka?' I ask the friend I'm staying with.

'I think it's a place,' he says, and there it is on the same map.

A long drive through slanting rain from the rolling hills and vineyards behind Lake Balaton across flat plains to the low hills and green river valleys of Estergom county. Cars give way to people in horse-drawn wagons with high seats. The windscreen wipers vie with Radio Bartok offering Bach's cantata *Nimmt von uns, Herr, du treuer Gott* and I am immediately at home in that universal language – the one that bridged countries and nationalities and bypassed the bitterness of wars and was the deepest, most formative part of my upbringing. It was one of those occasions where everything starts to resonate with meaning.

The only reason I'm driving to this utterly remote place is a vague curiosity about the origin of a name: my mother's Austrian surname – 'Schey von Koromla' (which always sounded rather sonorous and exotic). It's an excuse to visit somewhere unknown and invest the visit with purpose or meaning. I'm not asking why I need purpose or meaning, just enjoying the pretext to go where I wouldn't otherwise.

The road atlas I've borrowed shows Koromla well off the main and even secondary roads on a small, white track in an area with almost no other markings in it. In fact, there are almost no roads where Koromla is. I didn't know why. Maybe it was on a mountain (so much for my knowledge of Hungarian topography). Now, as a fan of white roads, I turn off onto the first of these and head off between flat fields. Abruptly, the tarmac surface ends and after a while bumping along a rutted track and turning this way and that across a great wide plain, the track runs out altogether and I come to a house in the middle of nowhere.

A woman hanging out washing looks surprised, suspicious.

'Koromla?' I'm smiling, lost.

She points back the way I have come, saying, 'Sure. Sure.'

Sure, she says, and I understand that's where I have to go back to – Súr, pronounced 'sure' – and we smile at each other, helpless in the face of a mutual lack of language. I turn round and bump back through the fields.

Súr is a small town with streams running either side of its wide, main street. There are no people to be seen and no cars either. I take the next turning to the left, signposted to Csatka Puszta, and drive into the empty space on the map.

It turns out to be not a mountain but a wide river valley, thick green with willow trees and dripping hedges and occasional stretches of gold, like patches on a quilt spread out in between. The sunflowers are hanging their heads in the rain but that doesn't stop their yellow fringes shining against the lush green. It is beautiful in an untouched way that I have rarely seen. And right on cue, Bartok Radio breaks into Handel in English:

Where e'er you walk, cool gales shall fan the glade;
Trees, where you sit, shall crowd into a shade:
Where'er you tread the blushing flow'rs shall rise;
       And all things flourish,
And all things flourish where'er you turn your eyes.

Koromla is the end of the road, an appendix to the loop from Súr so small it doesn't even have a sign. It sits on the slope of a rounded hay-field hill that curves down to the river winding through the fields below.

The road finishes. This must be it, a handful of houses sit spaced out on either side of a wide grass track: the main street.

I stop the car and walk. All around, the fields are full of flowers – pink clover, white, blue flax, yellow buttercups and more. The road leads down to the willow trees and alder that line the river and as I climb up the hill on the other side, I can see the valley winding into the distance, the hills there flanked with thick woods and more rolling hills. It is one of the most peaceful places I've ever been. I can hear birdsong, an occasional voice, a chicken clucking triumphantly over an egg, bees humming, a cat meowing in the long grass and each bite of the spade as a shirtless man in dungarees digs out the line of a boundary wall around a derelict house with a new roof at the bottom of the village.

I count. There are five houses, six with a bigger one, seven, eight (locked up, collapsing roof) and nine, a larger one painted white at the top of the hill. Even adding the three I passed on the drive from the crossroads, there are twelve at the most, four of them abandoned. There is no sign of a grand estate or a 'big house'. These are small farmhouses.

A horse is browsing in one backyard, others in a field. There's a not very big, not very new tractor parked in front of one, a green cart with a load of forgotten hay and, behind an iron gate, a wooden hay wagon and some spare wagon wheels sleeping in the long grass. There is no road sound. The birds are so loud you can hear their wings as they fly

Koromla, 2011.

11

past. The swallows are gathering on a single electric wire and it's raining again. Are they thinking about migration in the same way I am wondering about socks?

Koromla is a place where time and the world has passed by – or maybe just been gentle – and I am grateful to the accident of a name for the excuse to find it. It is hard to leave.

When I finally turn the car around and drive away, Bartok Radio celebrates with field recordings of the kind of Csárdás fiddle music that makes you want to dance for joy.

So, what was it with the name, I wonder? Why Schey von Koromla? There's no sign of a big house or estate here, of 'grand manner' living, or a parvenu's seat of power, not even a derelict one. Was it just a pleasing word perhaps? Lord So-and-So of Puddletown. 'Csatka', said the archivist, this Koromla was part of the Schey lands at Csatka, so maybe the big house would be there. When the sign for Csatka Puszta appears again it seems worth a look – the road map shows it as a white road leading, in turn, back to the main road.

Or perhaps not. A little further on, a turning to the right, complete with signpost, expires into a field of stubble. I carry on along the other little road, beside woodland and marsh meadow, until it is blocked by a metal barrier with ferocious signs, incomprehensible. The intention is clear enough: Keep Out! Go away! And from the gate, as far as the eye can see, the land ahead is enclosed by a high, wire fence. Inside it, a few animals from some ancient breed of white cattle graze in a field beside an observation tower and the fields slope up towards a wooded hill.

I am about to turn round and drive away when I notice some large buildings up there. They are very large, several storeys high, like a series of barracks or tenements, but clearly very old. Is this what I'm looking for?

I get out and walk up to the gate. It isn't locked. If I am careful to shut it behind me so there is no risk to any livestock. I wouldn't be trespassing, just following the road on the map – no need for me to get out of the car. I look at the signs again and decide I can't read Hungarian. A risk worth taking.

At the top of the hill the big buildings are even more impressive than I'd thought – though I have no idea what they were. I'm looking for the big house that surely had to go with them, but there is only a row of cottages, built low against the hill, and a paved courtyard.

The road turns sharp left past the last two and becomes a muddy track, getting muddier, the puddles deeper, the overhanging trees darker. Soon the hire car is out of its depth. This road isn't going anywhere either. It's time to turn round.

An engine roars. I look in the rear-view mirror and there are the glaring headlights of a Range Rover that is virtually touching the car, boxing me in. So, turning round might not be the thing either. Two dogs, each the size of a small pony, bound round the car barking and snarling at the windows. And a tall, handsome man shouts furiously at me in Hungarian.

I try German and he switches effortlessly.

I play the tourist, point at the map, the road back to Súr.

'Can't you read the signs?'

'Sorry, I can't read Hungarian. I thought they meant shut the gate.'

'People round here are not friendly. I have fifteen dogs roaming wild here.' It is a threat not a description.

I ask him about the buildings – mention the family and their name, the land at Csatka, play the innocent.

He mellows – an idiot tourist – and tells me about the estate being Zichy not Schey, built in the 1840s and already neglected when the Zichys went under and the buildings were sold in 1849. His cattle are special. People round here are not so friendly. He plans to build a visitors' centre in future so people can come and see them.

He gives me his website address. Escorts me off his land.

It was a thin cover story and I was no more convinced by it than he had been by my 'can't read'. We were a good match. We both pretended to believe each other. What was someone doing barricaded in on a remote hillside surrounded by dogs and deeply suspicious of the local people? And what would anyone want with those huge barracks buildings – bigger than barns, with no ground-floor windows? When I looked at his website, it included the word 'security'. Maybe they'd be useful for storing things in, large things maybe. You could put full-size missiles in there and nobody would be the wiser.

Vivid imaginings? Perhaps. But everywhere, like the damp rising from the ground I'd been walking on that day, there seemed to be a sense of things just below the surface, puzzles, histories not told – and always so much more to understand. And I am curious, tuned to it like an old habit.

This, I realise, is something I've always known: the lure of a tale, that sense of puzzlement and curiosity and a deep hunger to know, what happened? Because stories were what I'd grown up with. Among the assortment of things I'd inherited from the ancestors – the big forehead, height, double-jointed fingers, a tendency to sadness, a cupboard full of tins and the certainty of belonging to more than one place (or was it no place at all?) – stories were everywhere.

There was the one about the little boy brought from India in the 1830s to a remote boarding school in Yorkshire and left there by his parents, who were never heard of again. Or the young Jew from Hungary who, at around the same time, walked to Vienna without a penny to his name, made his fortune, built a palace, then lost it all again.

There were my father's Scottish grandfathers, who made their lives in Chile, trading the length of the Pacific coast in the days of sailing ships, and the one who rode across the Andes on a horse.

There was the love story of the young star of the Burgtheater among the writers and musicians of Vienna in the early 1900s. Or, in Ireland, the one about the red-headed girl on the staircase and the disobedient son who wouldn't marry the girl of his father's choice.

There was the telegram that slipped down behind a Dorset post office counter and the marriage that didn't happen.

There was the disappearing uncle.

And there were my sister and I in the 1960s, packed into my mother's small and overloaded car, trundling across Europe as if it belonged to us, to the accompaniment of more tales, like the one about her hitchhiking over the Brenner Pass in a fire engine with a drunken driver.

Then there's what happens when you listen to the stories and they start to tell themselves all over again. And the more you hear, the more questions there are, answers unpeeling like the layers of an onion.

Every family has tales like these: not heroic, not of victims in a politically correct cause, just themselves, a scattering of yarns from different places, a hotchpotch of the people who made us. Perhaps that's why I find them interesting. Fathers deserted, mothers died, wars scattered families, economies collapsed, people fell in love (and out again), children were born and grew up and finally we find ourselves here. But the more I heard, the more improbable it seemed that I should ever have been born.

Why the stories I grew up with survived across such distances of time and place is a good question. Maybe because they were the ones that hooked themselves into the experience of their listeners and stuck like burrs, remembered because they fitted. Maybe, in short, because of what happened next. Or was what happened next somehow influenced by the telling and retelling itself?

Whichever it was, in our family they seem to have got themselves told and retold from one generation on to the next without too much difficulty, until one day I woke up and realised that they seemed to have landed on me, and that, being oral stories, they were also as ephemeral as the rain falling outside (and as essential). With a cast of hundreds, all pulling in different directions, if I didn't write them down they might well disappear into the ether.

That's how it began. It was going to be straightforward. Here were good tales, full of energy and enjoyment and entertainment, a gift from the past to the future. All I had to do was get them down, like an anthology, a disparate collection with a slender common strand.

Of course, a bit of background might be necessary sometimes: an idea of surrounding events, historical context. And so I opened the history books – and nearly drowned. Here was the history of Europe: the twentieth century, the nineteenth, even the eighteenth …

How to contain all this? To tell these stories in chronological order would probably begin with a medieval myth and finish, for now, in the third decade of the twenty-first century. But as I wrestled with them, another order emerged – a second chronology. This was the sequence in which the stories were passed on or emerged in the course of my life, the way they were told (or not told) during my childhood and adolescence and since: the process of transmission. Bit by bit, this became an account of my growing up too, the story of how I learned the stories – a memoir – and a look at the complicated dance between the present and the past.

It's this order, this double chronology, that guides the telling, or should I say assembly, that follows. Because somehow what became more and more interesting is how and why things get shaped, told, remembered and told again – and, equally important, what is *not* told. How history emerges, creeps out of the woodwork.

As I went, unexpected parallels also appeared, sometimes alarmingly. Was there a connection? How is it that stories work on subsequent generations? Is it possible that the stories might even generate the parallels?

In childhood, the tales came in separate chunks, each one complete in itself and, in that matter-of-fact way that children have, my sister and I took them as they came. They didn't necessarily have to fit together. Over time, different parts of the narrative appeared, like stuff washed up on the shore. It was a slow, accumulative process that brought different pieces of the picture; we took on what we were ready for. Only as I grew up and grew older did I start to try and fit them together, ask questions. And then I noticed the gaps and enquired. This book is the result.

Looking behind the scenes has its own dangers. It's unsettling to find evidence that contradicts the narrative you've grown up with; it can shake you to the core. The narrative has become part of who you are. But then, like all history, these stories had a purpose. With real life far too big to be carried forward complete, they are a way of managing the past, wrestling it into a shape that contains it, makes it safe and usable, useful and, above all, portable. This is rocket fuel for the next generation. Where the facts diverge from the narrative there were reasons for it.

Two world wars stand sentinel here. My mother's parents married in the middle of the First World War, my mother and father at the beginning of the Second and, right on cue, I arrived smack in the middle of the twentieth century and took the rest of it and then some to even begin to understand.

I would have liked to weave the tales of my parents and their very different families into one narrative but the further I went, the bigger it grew until it proved more than I could handle. So, this is about my maternal inheritance, the stories from my mother's family. But they would never have become mine had it not been for my father's interest in and retelling of them.

It is not a work of genealogical research — record offices, censuses and certificates — though I've tried to include the essentials. Instead, it's based on oral narrative: stories, anecdotes and the cobwebs of memory stubbornly clinging to objects, books, even buildings.

Women of the past are famously harder to trace than men, elusive in the historical record. They change their names on marriage, seldom have publicly recognised careers — daughter of, sister of, mother of — and, judging by their presence in the obituaries, rarely die. Their records lie in other places, above all in stories like these that are handed down by word of mouth; these are one of the ways we learn ourselves.

So, this is also a tribute to the women who came before me: my mother, her mother and her mother before her, each one a woman on her own. It's a tale of to-hell-with-that mothers — matrilineal, a-historic, even without names sometimes, and full of unreliable sources but, in some essential way, true.

That it turned into an encounter with the history books and the relationship between conventional history and oral narrative was a surprise. But if there's one thing that stands out from these stories, which loop and thread and cross and knot like a tangled ball of string and have wound themselves around me for a lifetime, it's the richness of it all.

Part I

TRAVELS WITH MY MOTHER

Family stories are a kind of DNA, encoded messages about how things are and should be, passed from one generation to another.

The War After by Anne Karpf

1

Mist and Mirrors

The Family That Wasn't

Family was a big thing in our house when I was growing up. This was odd because there wasn't much of a family really. People at school had uncles and aunts and cousins and grandparents all around, but by the time I surfaced in London in the 1950s, all my grandparents were dead or gone and aunts, uncles and cousins far away. Still, or maybe because of that, family was a big thing.

From their rare appearances, relatives seemed to come in different flavours. There were the best-behaviour, smart ones (mainly Scots, Irish, English), who we saw on special occasions.

'Don't let us down.'

'Is your hair brushed? Skirt straight?' (This to me, who lived in trousers and up trees.)

'Let me have a look at you.' And my mother/father would spit on her/his handkerchief to wipe imagined smudges off my face.

There were people in assorted foreign languages and accents who blew in and out of the house from time to time on tides of music, food and talk and kissed us warmly on both cheeks. It wasn't always clear if they were actually relatives but it didn't matter. There were arty ones: painters, sculptors, singers, musicians, architects, some of them quiet and some who waved their arms and shouted and laughed. There were the complicated ones – mad, sad, worried, ill, divorcing – who were talked about in hushed voices above our heads. Then there were the ones who were very far away.

Loyal aunts sent us birthday and Christmas presents without fail and we grumbled about writing thank-you letters. And on one or two occasions we were got together with some cousins, a lot riding on it, and either hated each other on sight, or, even worse, actually liked each other and immediately provoked discussions about the dangers of 'too much' contact with cousins of the opposite sex, to our great embarrassment. This family thing was clearly complicated.

Strange names floated through their talk: Tantes and Onkels (my mother), Tios and Tias (my father). My mother's sister – slender, beautiful, of the dramatic gestures – went by the name of Beetle. My father's elderly aunt was Tyranny. There was another old lady too, unimaginably strange and ancient to our eyes, who we occasionally went to see. (Remember this one, reader.) Who was she? Goodness knows. In a dark, red house in Hampstead we would climb up flight after flight of stairs to where she lay propped up in bed with a whippet curled up on top of her, smoking a pipe, toothless and completely bald. We kissed her bristly cheeks and couldn't understand a word she said.

It was all strange and inexplicable – but that was fine, this was our parents' territory and not something we had to bother with. The truth for us was that most of our near relatives were either out of reach or dead. Instead, there were stories: they were the family we grew up with and, as I grew older and more curious, everywhere I looked there seemed to be more.

As far as I was concerned, this was an excellent deal. Relatives were clearly a mixed blessing, but I'd always loved stories and these, it turned out, though I wasn't much interested at the time, ranged from hundreds of years ago to the day before yesterday, and from South America to Austria–Hungary, Ireland to Germany, India to Chile and Scotland and Wales. Best of all, they were all *told* by somebody or other: my mother or my father, and later, a 92-year-old aunt with total recall and an affable stranger claiming to be a long-lost uncle.

Where to begin?

Mutti

Of all the relatives who weren't there, my mother's mother, Anny, known to all as Mutti, stood out. Buried the year before I was born, she was most definitely dead, but unlike my other three grandparents, who barely got a mention, somehow she was still there.

It wasn't that she was talked about. My mother didn't do nostalgia; she relished the present and looked forward to the future far too much for that. But she did love her mother, well beyond the grave. So, too, did my father. And somehow, on the rare occasions when Mutti was mentioned it carried a charge. Unspoken, she hovered like a ghost. It was a while before I understood just how much she permeated our lives.

Early childhood hangs like a haze. Things move in and out of focus. What's true, who knows? How things are is just the way they are – a matter of fact. I have parents, two parents, and an older sister. How could it be otherwise? This is just obvious. Normal. The objects, the pictures, the furniture too, and the people that surround us – this is just the landscape. Not neutral, not without variation, simply habitat.

For my part, I am curious. I like stories. Or perhaps, in the quiet guesswork that is childhood, they seep in uninvited. At times, it is as if somewhere in all this lie the keys to a puzzle – though I'd have been hard-pressed to say what that puzzle was.

London, 1953

I was 3 years old when we moved from Hertfordshire to London and went to live in a house that looked like a church. It was tall and I was small. It had thick walls, steep roofs, pointed windows, dark panelling and stained glass that cast gloomy clouds of purple, blue and red down its grand staircase like ghosts. The doors inside were big and heavy; they closed with a clunk and were governed by cold, brass handles I could scarcely turn, but outside – outside was the garden.

My mother was a singer. My father was an architect. She came from Austria, he from a Scottish family in Chile. He would probably have preferred a terraced house with elegant proportions somewhere in Central

The house that looked like a church. My father's Christmas card, 1954.

London. Instead, they took on Victorian Gothic: a grand house built for a retiring missionary in that crumbling, ecclesiastical Kentish ragstone that drops flakes everywhere, up on the hills of North London. My mother had taken one look at the duck-shooting punt propped on trestles across the front door, the beehives in the bedrooms, the guns at the upstairs window for shooting the wood pigeons that plundered the vegetable beds, the cavernous rooms, the half an acre of garden and Hampstead Heath at the end of the road, and fallen for it.

Big and dilapidated, the house stood in a street of other once-grand houses down on their luck, their gates melted down for munitions, servants gone, lawns dug up to grow wartime vegetables, impossible to heat. Most of them were multi-occupied, the fences between the huge gardens listing or rotted away, with thickets of rampant laurel, tangled trees, overgrown tennis courts and, in ours, a rectangular concreted hole, 24ft by 12ft, with a bath plug at the bottom – a swimming pool made from the crater of a First World War bomb.

Daffodils. London, Easter 1953.

It was a great place to be a child.

My parents took the tail end of a lease, and on the weekend they moved in they invited all their friends round and, between them, used up 73 gallons of white paint subduing the dark brown varnish that covered the whole inside like malignant treacle.

The Second World War was over and done, and so was the age of servants that once kept houses like these going; cheap consumer goods and affordable central heating were still a long way off. That first winter, I was held up to the window to see the lamplighter come with his ladder to light the gas lamp in the street outside – was it for the last time? And out in the city, bomb damage was round every corner: half-houses, wallpaper flapping in mid-air and piles of rubble overgrown with buddleia and willow herb. But change was on its way.

Not long after we'd arrived, there was a public excitement called 'The Coronation'. A princess called Elizabeth was going to be crowned queen in Westminster Abbey. For my sister, at school and knowledgeable, it was a big event. I wandered the garden, oblivious.

Until one day, she and my mother went away very early in the morning to seats in Pall Mall to watch the procession of the queen-to-be in her solid gold carriage pulled by white horses. And I was left at home with my father, near strangers to each other, and with some lunch, chopped up small, in my special bowl with the rabbits running round the rim.

We went down the road, my father, the rabbit bowl and I, to the house of some neighbours from America, a land of riches compared to battered, post-war Britain. These neighbours had, wonder of wonders, not only thick carpet on the floor and shop-made cake on the table, but something called a television set enthroned in their living room. It was the only one in the neighbourhood and the first I'd ever seen.

Set in a tall mahogany cabinet, its bulging glass screen looked down from above like a great fly's eye with two black knobs underneath. The thing had to be constantly tended and adjusted as crazy white lines zigged and zagged through snowstorms of white on the screen, but, at last, as I sat miserably on my father's knee pushing bits of chopped up food round and round my rabbit bowl, the screen cleared and showed us ... what? I wasn't sure.

'Look!' they said, 'It's ...'

... a hazy grey blob ... in a hazy grey carriage ... with grey soldiers on grey horses flanked by crowds of watching grey specks ... or ...? Which bit of this was a princess, which bit was a queen? The room was full of excited people crowding round the set. I rubbed my finger round and round the running rabbits and wished I could go home.

The rabbit bowl.

Possessions

There, things were settling. After the white paint, the house was gradually cleared and simplified by my father's mid-century modernist touch: plain walls, stripped lines, simple furniture. Chintz was not allowed. Money was short but invention abounded: a flush-panelled door propped on two low cupboards and painted white became the elegant desk my mother wrote letters at after supper; a rusty iron drain cover framed an etching by my father's painter cousin, Hans Tisdall, to perfection. Nothing was wasted; everything had the potential to become something else, as if the world was made of metaphors. Things were found, things were made, things were transformed. Anything else was 'expensive' and that word rang with fear.

Among the clear spaces there were also certain old pieces that had come from somewhere else, stories clinging silently to them like cobwebs. There were ponchos from my father's childhood in Chile for rugs; a Peruvian terracotta bull with a candle on its back that seemed to be the key to his heart; a huge carved wooden chest; a cupboard full of fragile fluted glasses, frosted at the rims; books; paintings; and the big, black Steinway grand piano. Some lurked, some loomed and others just jumped out at you. All were freighted with meaning. They throbbed in the house like a pulse beat. I eyed them warily and headed for the garden.

My parents' bedroom was no exception. It looked out from the first floor through a double-arched window, the walls plain white, the floor polished hardboard and, apart from a painting of a young woman sleeping, everything else was plain too – the curtains, chest of drawers, the bed (later, two beds), a small rug. But then there was my mother's dressing table.

It was simple enough: a small rectangular table made of dark, polished wood, with slender, fluted legs. But on it, like a burst of laughter, stood a mirror set in a mass of tiny flowers and leaves all made out of the most delicate painted porcelain. On either side there was a matching candlestick and a round pot for powder (which my mother didn't wear), with more leaves and rosebuds sprouting from the lids. This was unlike anything else in the house – hairbrush and lipstick, earrings and scent – and when ('Careful!') I lifted the lid of one of the porcelain pots, the silk-backed powder puff inside released a cloud of glittering dust and the scent of someone and somewhere else.

Beside the mirror my mother kept a photograph in a cream plaster frame rather chipped by travel. It looked old. Grey and white and hazy at the edges, the picture showed a beautiful young woman with a beauty spot on her chin and a mountain of white ringlets piled high on top of her head and tumbling down around her shoulders. There were pearls round her neck and in her hair, and she was wearing a dress with a tightly laced bodice, trimmed with more pearls and lace, from which flounced mounds of muslin skirt and sleeve. 'That's Mutti,' said my mother. 'These were her things.'

Mutti.

The young woman in the picture didn't look like anyone I'd ever seen. She was more like a princess than the grey blob on the television set. Maybe she was a fairy godmother (I knew the stories). Of course, that was because she was dead, I reasoned, standing chest-high to the table, as I watched my mother put on her lipstick and dab scent behind her ears ready to go out to a concert and wished that she wouldn't leave. And when Mutti had been alive, it had to have been a very long time ago because it was before I was even *born*. The past collapsed into a single lump – mysterious, beyond understanding, out of reach.

It was many years before it finally dawned on me that this was not a photo of my grandmother in her own time. That she was wearing eighteenth-century costume. And that it was a photograph from the production of a play. But the original impression refused to go away: maybe it wasn't so far from the truth.

'Your grandmother? She was marvellous! So beautiful! So charming.'

Whenever anyone spoke of her, it was with extraordinary warmth and affection. My father adored her. So did everyone else. And yet to my sister and I she remained elusive, hard to pin down, a phantom. Her charm and character always seemed to evoke a particular tone: hazy round the edges like that photograph, sometimes so sweet as to be almost cloying.

Here's a neighbour writing about the cottage Mutti lived in in Dorset, Myrtle Cottage:

> No other house in the village had such charm and singularity. Moreover, Baroness von Schey harnessed her village neighbours to her purposes: the bushy-eared old builder-carpenter and coffin-maker, the local farmer with the milk-round, the gardening prize-winners of the local flower shows. As she said: 'I just flirt with them a little, and, you see, they come!' Certainly she bewitched them with her charm and gaiety, her humour and her quaintness. She had them unknowing, in the hollow of her hand. RG, 1967.[1]

'What was she really like?'

'She made us wonderful feast days,' said my mother, who did the same for us, our one defiant piece of Austrian-ness in an otherwise English life, carrying on the tradition of Austria's Catholic Christmas Eve. The hidden tree suddenly revealed, alive with candles in the dark, the carols and the special feast of fish on the night of 24 December – as well as English Christmas the following day, stockings rustling on the end of our beds at dawn, turkey, plum pudding, brandy butter, mince pies.

'What else?'

'She used to teach our boyfriends how to dance, on the kitchen table at the flat in Holland Villas Road,' my mother said. 'And when we'd been out for the evening and they'd brought us home and we'd said goodnight and gone to our rooms, they would stay and sit on the end of Mutti's bed and talk long into the night.'

She was certainly a woman who made a deep impression.

This was the fairy godmother of grandmothers then, a source of love so strong it warmed my mother still and could even soften the furrow between my father's eyes. Faint as cobwebs, she trailed gaiety, independence, charm, mystery – and none of the ordinariness that seemed to surround real people.

But what about the substance? Who was she?

In childhood, the stories, the feelings, the mist were enough. Compared to them, facts were irrelevant. But as I grew up I became curious. Wasn't there more to the story here?

Facts were hard to come by and I was an adult before I began to seek them out or piece them together. There were clues, of course. Her maiden name and date of birth – Anna Caecilia Schindler – 17 June 1887 – appeared on the side of a jug that stood on one of the windowsills, and somewhere among the old books on the shelves there was a poet – her grandfather – and occasional mentions of a high-profile cousin called Alma. But when it came to understanding this as an adult I needed more. Where had she come from? What about her family?

I gathered together some background.

Origins

Four generations before Anny Schindler (Mutti), the family came from Steiermark in Lower Austria, it seems. There was a scythe smith, then a cotton mill owner in Fischamend, and then his son who saw the mill burn down and the family left destitute.* Then, in the early nineteenth century came Mutti's grandfather, Julius Alexander Schindler, and with him, official history, bucket-loads of it.

Born in 1818, he became a lawyer, liberal thinker, politician, poet and novelist in the age of revolutions. A relative and contemporary

Julius Alexander Schindler, the poet 'Julius von der Traun'.

---

* One of them married a Wedel, with a coat of arms granted by the Archduke Ferdinand of Austria in 1613. She became Julius Alexander's grandmother.

of Prince Metternich, then Austria's Foreign Minister and State Chancellor, said: 'He was one of the Austrian delegates to the famous conference in Frankfurt on Main in 1848 when the fate of the German–Austrian Federation was sealed and Prussia, under Bismarck, hived off to become, in time, the Hohenzollern Empire'. Though Julius Alexander was dismissed from his post as one of the empire's public prosecutors for his critical, published views, he was later elected to Austria's first Parliament in the Liberal victory of 1861, where he's credited with a satirical turn of phrase and with ending capital punishment in the army. Among the other jobs he held was that of Secretary General of the state railways and notary public in Vienna, but as well as all that he was a writer.

Under the pen name Julius von der Traun, Julius Alexander Schindler became known for the poems he wrote about his walks through the Austrian countryside between Steyr and Kremsmünster (*Excursionen einen Österreichers*). He was also known for his political poetry, his epic verse and novels, and in 1869 he bought the glorious palace of Leopoldskron, on the lake outside Salzburg (made famous a century

Schloss Leopoldskron, Salzburg.

Goldschmiedskinder, by Julius von der Traun.

later by the film *The Sound of Music*) and, on losing his parliamentary seat in the elections of 1870, retired there to live by his writing.

Julius Alexander's nephew was the Austrian impressionist painter, Emil Jakob Schindler, famous for his landscapes. Emil Jakob's daughter, Alma (Mutti's cousin), remembered her great-uncle's grandeur as precarious. She describes him in her autobiography as a spendthrift with heavy debts and a theatrical style, and tells how, forced to flee Leopoldskron one night to avoid his creditors, he turned humiliation into a grand performance by having his many servants dress in rococo livery and light the way with torches.[2]

When Julius Alexander died in 1885, his son and daughter divided the inheritance. Alexander Leopold, Mutti's father, held onto Leopoldskron for five years and Mutti spent some of her childhood there, living in three rooms with her cousin Alma to play with.

Then it was gone. So was Mutti's father. There's no further mention of him.

Her mother, 'Grandmother Schindler', born Anna Minich, did the rest. Before her death in 1921, she makes a fleeting appearance in the photographs of my mother as a baby,[3] and so does Mutti's brother Georg, a shadowy figure who played tennis and taught skiing. But of my great-grandfather there's not a trace. He died in 1895 when his daughter was 8.

Vienna, 1900

Anny Schindler's childhood, on the other hand, reappeared – through a similar haze of mist and mirrors – in a memoir she pencilled in German in a small, brown exercise book at the end of her life in England. Here we are in the 1890s, in the top storey of an old palace in a street in the 1st District, the centre of Vienna. She writes:

> We had to go up a broad stone staircase to get to our flat. It had large rooms with big French windows. Almost all the rooms were connected by doors so that we children could run through five large rooms without having to go out into the dark corridor. The house belonged to an old aristocrat lady who wouldn't allow any kind of modernisation, so that we had no electric light or gas: we had candles or oil lamps. And when I think of those early childhood years in that flat, everything seems dreamlike, spun round with soft light, darkness lurking in the corners.

Anna 'Anny' Caecilia Schindler, aged 7, 1893.

Burgtheater programme 1905.   Anny Schindler, actress.

Like the world of E.T.A. Hoffman and *The Nutcracker*, this is bour-
geois, Catholic life, at home in the heart of the 1st District of Vienna.
Another fairy story.

My father was the person who seemed to know more than anyone
else about Mutti and he was happy to tell us. Mutti became an actress, he
said, joining Vienna's Imperial Court theatre, the famous Burgtheater,
when she was only 17. She was a beauty. The juvenile lead. The girl
without a father. She was, he told us with admiration in his voice, her
family's breadwinner, earning the money to support her mother and
brother. Such was the legend.

The records have her first appearance as a page in *Romeo and Juliet*.
This was followed by a succession of other, slowly growing roles,
through to 1908 and, given that the productions ran for a long time, she
may have been working for several years after that. In today's sense of
the word, she was less a star, more a supporting actress. Nevertheless,
the influence of the Burgtheater at the heart of the cultural life of
Vienna, itself the capital of a huge empire, is not to be underestimated.
The author Stefan Zweig writes:

... the Imperial theatre, the Burgtheater, was for the Viennese and for the Austrian more than a stage upon which actors enacted parts; it was the microcosm that mirrored the macrocosm, the brightly coloured reflection in which the city saw itself, the only true *corigiano* of good taste. In the court actor the spectator saw an excellent example of how one ought to dress, how to walk into a room, how to converse, which words one might employ as a man of good taste and which to avoid. The stage, instead of being merely a place of entertainment, was a spoken and plastic guide of good behaviour and correct pronunciations, and a nimbus of respect encircled like a halo everything that had even the faintest connection with the Imperial theatre. The Minister-President or the richest magnate could walk the streets of Vienna without anyone turning round, but a court actor or an opera singer was recognized by every shopgirl and cabdriver.[4]

And this was a special time. As the historian Schorske puts it, 'Theatre was the Queen of Austria's arts ... By the 1890s the heroes of the upper middle class were no longer political leaders but actors, artists and critics'.[5]

The celebrities of their day knew how to enjoy themselves. As the Christmas season turned into Carnival, Anny writes:

The Imperial Court Theatre, the Burgtheater.

Now Vienna began to dance. There were Court Balls, Opera Balls, Koncordia Balls – these were the most formal, in finest evening dress, with the best orchestras and in the presence of a representative of the Emperor. To them came Archdukes, Ministers, the Press, artists, writers, painters and anyone else who was celebrated and loved, or young and attractive and full of promise for the future.

These balls were held in great halls. In most cases there was a large platform where the distinguished guests waited. In the entrance hall the general public formed a sort of corridor leaving just enough room for those people who were to be presented to pass; and through this passageway, the 'interesting people', the artists, actors and so on made their entrance – new members of the Burgtheater, the Opera or the Ballet. Each lady came in on the arm of the gentleman who was to present her.

And here, as the pronouns start to shift from 'they' to 'you' to 'we', the shadow of herself appears:

There was the young 17-year-old actress, a new member of the Imperial and Royal Court Theatre, young and timid and all in white chiffon without jewels; with her mother behind her in a silver-grey dress on the arm of a journalist. Their names were whispered. Then a young dancer, on the arm of a well-known actor. A singer, who had recently made a brilliant début came escorted by the very handsome Baron So-and-So; and then came Niese, a very celebrated actress ... and immediately there was whispering and greeting.

There. The music had started, with a Polonaise. Up on the platform the ladies could be seen curtseying or bowing depending on who was being introduced. People began to talk formally again, and then the signal was given to the orchestra. The first waltz. Who would open the dancing?

The smooth, shining parquet floor was inviting enough. The introduction to a popular Strauss waltz was playing with irresistible breadth. Everyone was ready and at the first beat of the waltz itself thousands of couples whirled out through the hall. The white chiffon dress unfolded itself around the young actress and her partner ... Many couples followed. They danced from the outermost circle into smaller and smaller circles until they got to the centre which was called 'the Island'. There you danced in double-time, turning on the spot until the waltz came to an end.

Applause broke out spontaneously. People bowed to one another. The gentlemen offered the ladies their arms and accompanied them back to their seats, in the case of young girls to their mothers, who were sitting on gilt chairs or on benches upholstered in red velvet, and in most cases talking to their daughter's escorts or to other friends.

The dancing began at 10.30. An hour later there was a dinner for the chosen at long tables, among the 'celebrated and distinguished people' with speeches and wonderful wines. Each table had a master of ceremonies appointed by the organising committee, and if you were lucky it would be amusing or even interesting. If not, if the speeches were too numerous and too long, you could steal out into the half-empty hall and dance for about a mile – and still get back in time for dessert and champagne and the closing speech.

And so they dance all night, even after the orchestra has packed up and gone, until they emerge in their ball gowns with their yawning mothers into the morning and the snow where the working people are going about the city's business.

This was the world of old Vienna, much the same as it had been for the previous fifty years. One of the great cosmopolitan cities of the world, at the turn of the twentieth century Vienna was the seat of Franz Joseph, Emperor of Austria and King of Hungary, and the capital of an empire that stretched north as far as what is now Ukraine, east across today's Czech and Slovak Republics, and south-east through Hungary, Slovenia, Croatia and Bosnia. It included eighteen countries and more than 55 million people. The city teemed with people of different nationalities, languages, races and religions and with political, financial and artistic activity.

At its centre, the emperor, who never read a book, was surrounded by the old aristocracy with their titles and their land and their horses;

then there was the new aristocracy, the '*Zweiten Gesellschaft*', among them many Jews raised to the nobility for their services to industry and the imperial finances, and then the surrounding bourgeoisie, who, unlike their fellows in other European countries, were still loyal to and dependent on the emperor. And out beyond the palaces of the Ringstrasse and the elegant suburbs were the ordinary people: labourers, artisans, more and always more people of different nationalities and languages pouring in from all over the empire to the ever-growing capital, which prided itself on being a model of international harmony.

The culture radiating from the imperial court was hedonistic, glittering, superficial. The city had a whole vocabulary of its own. There's '*Schlamperei*' – a characteristic slapdash, or '*Wiener Schmäh*' – described as an attractive form of telling lies, 'the verbal equivalent of the kind of baroque architecture where what looked like marble was in fact painted wood'.[6] It was a '*Gefühlskultur*', a culture of feeling. My grandmother's account is touched by all of that.

Writing forty years later and worlds away, she looks back on it as 'a chapter of security and contentment'. Given what followed, it must have seemed all those things. She tells the old story of 'the good Emperor' putting on disguises to mix with his people and find out their views, and how:

> The Viennese, up till the 1914 War had such an amiable humour and such pleasant manners, that the people of the outer city, the workers, the craftsmen, could mix at such celebrations with the so-called 'fine' people from the inner city or the elegant districts, without any distinctions needing to be made.

Superficial or not, this was a society still firm in its self-belief, where everyone could be relied upon to know their place.

Or could they? As the nineteenth century turned into the twentieth, the whole edifice was crumbling. The emperor was old. The establishment of the Ringstrasse was pompous, conservative and rigid with tradition – like Victorians everywhere. The empire itself was riven by the nationalisms, disputes and factions that would eventually lead to the First World War. The market crash of 1873 had shaken the economy to

The grand staircase of the Burgtheater, ceilings painted
by Gustav and Ernst Klimt and Franz Matsch

its roots. The predicament of the poor was relentless. And from the ever-growing proletariat came the demand for political participation.

In the 1880s the vote was extended and mass parties sprang up: the *Sozis* or Social Democrats, Slav nationalists, pan-Germans, antisemites. The Liberal establishment was out of its depth. In the municipal elections of 1895, they were resoundingly defeated by the antisemitic Christian Socialist Party led by Karl Lueger. No matter that the emperor, supported by the Catholic Church, refused to approve Lueger's appointment for the next two years: eventually he gave way. Vienna became the first city in Europe with an elected, explicitly antisemitic government.

Yet what Vienna at the start of the twentieth century is remembered for is not this but the remarkable outburst of avant-garde ideas that now rose up to challenge the conservative culture of the Ringstrasse from a different quarter. Passionate about poetry, art, music, theatre, a new generation of educated Viennese, my grandmother's generation, poured themselves into the arts, ignoring the 'grubby' arena of the city's politics, or oblivious to it.

'The life of art became a substitute for a life of action. Indeed, as civic action proved increasingly futile, art became almost a religion, the source of meaning and the food of the soul.'[7]

These were certainly the ideas we were brought up with fifty years later.

In music, art, architecture, literature, theatre, opera, philosophy and science, innovation and creativity abounded. There was the radical arts and crafts movement known as *Jugendstil*. There were breakthroughs in architecture and in 1897 a group of artists, including Gustav Klimt and Koloman Moser, tired of the narrow-mindedness of the art

Anny Schindler in her dressing room

establishment, founded the breakaway Vienna Secession and were soon showing the revolutionary new work of the French impressionists.

In the same year, the Vienna Opera appointed as its director Gustav Mahler – not only a radical composer but, until his compulsory conversion to Catholicism, a Jew – and gave a platform to the controversial music of Richard Strauss. And writers like the playwright Arthur Schnitzler and the young poet Hugo von Hofmannsthal, founder of the Jung-Wien movement, were also intent on breaking the mould.

Even schoolchildren were crazy about art, poetry, theatre. Stefan Zweig in his autobiography describes himself and his fellow students at the gymnasium rushing out of school to get the latest volume of poetry or see the latest play.[8] Ideas and the arts represented, for them, a value that could transcend the ugliness of politics, the crude divisions of nationality, race or the old religions, something that could transform the world and make it at last a better place. An ideal.

As for the Burgtheater, it was physically, culturally, socially at the heart of it all.

Anny Schindler was not just young, beautiful and cultivated herself, but an accomplished musician as well as an actress. Her cousin Alma married Gustav Mahler and famously went on after his death to marry the architect Walter Gropius, the poet and playwright Franz Werfel and would, so one story goes, have married the painter Oskar Kokoschka too, had his mother not taken his trousers away to iron them on the morning of the nuptials and refused to give them back in time.[9]

Anny's friends included Klimt, Hugo von Hofmannsthal and his widow Gerti von Hofmannsthal, and the famous dancer Grete Wiesenthal. They remained her closest friends for the rest of her life. She was also a gifted hostess, a talent she brought with her when she came to England; that and the furniture, the piano, the dressing table mirror bursting with porcelain flowers and the battered photo, circa 1910, of the young woman in eighteenth-century costume, the grey and white ghost that was the only grandmother I knew when I was a child.

2

Austria

But there was more. Our grandmother made a fresh appearance when it came to our first big journey. It was the winter of 1954, I was nearly 5 and we flew, which was still unusual in those days. Propeller driven, the plane roared and shook. My sister wailed, I was sick into a brown paper bag and my father said he was never going travelling with us again. Never!

At last, engines screaming, the plane headed for the ground, circling down into what seemed to be a great, dark hole. When we finally got out into the ice-cold air, legs shaking, ears aching, stomachs heaving, we were surrounded. Huge mountains reared up all around. We had arrived. Innsbruck.

The place we were going to, the Hügelhof, was an old wooden farmhouse with a steeply pitched roof set high above the medieval town of Schwaz in Tyrol. There were double wooden windows to keep the heat in and the cold out, one set opening inwards and the other out, and a carved wooden balcony that ran round three sides of the upper floor under the shelter of the eaves.

My sister and I ran from one end of it to the other, staring past the icicles that hung from the edge of the roof at the pine forest rising up behind the house, and, falling away in front, first fields, then the toy roofs of the town and the valley where the river twisted like a silver snake. On the far side, the great wall of the Karwendel Mountains rose up against the sky in shapes that seemed to etch themselves on my eyes. And everything was covered with thick, white, rounded blankets of snow.

Magic.

'First things first,' said my mother, as we walked through the narrow medieval streets of Schwaz the next day and stopped at a shop which smelt of wood and wax. Hanging from the ceiling, in every shape and size, with brightly coloured seats of woven webbing and swooping wooden runners, were toboggans, toboggans and still more toboggans. My mother laughed and talked with the shopkeeper like an old friend. We couldn't understand what they said. My father was silent.

'These are called *Rodels*,' said my mother, crouching down to show us. 'They're *Rodels* and they're special. You wait!'

My mother Inge, Schwaz, 1954.

Myself, my sister and the *Rodels*.

Our parents conferred: money was not for wasting, this was a major purchase. And then, miraculously, we found ourselves with not one but two small *Rodels*, one each for my sister and myself.

From then on they went everywhere with us. We sat on them like chariots and were pulled back up through the town. 'After this you can walk!' We rode them like racers, with me wedged firmly in my mother's lap, hurtling down the mountainside over lumps and bumps so fast I couldn't see for the ice dust in my eyes. And on the little slope below the house, my sister and I climbed up and slid down, fell off and landed face first in the mounded snowdrifts at the bottom, again and again, until we were exhausted, our clothes soaked, our home-knitted mittens caked with snow.

At bedtime my mother showed us how to put peeled tangerine segments in between the two layers of windows. The air was so dry that our hair stood on end and crackled as she brushed it, making little flashes in the dark. She shook out the red-and-white-checked feather bolsters that took the place of blankets (in England then no one had heard of duvets) and laid them on top of us, strangely light and limp.

'This is where I was born,' she said.

'What?! Here?!'

'Tell us!'

The Hügelhof in the 1920s.

So she did.

This was where they had lived when she was born, my mother told us: Mutti, her beautiful mother – there she was again – her sister Beate, who was 3 at the time, and their father, Fritz. Now our grandfather appears.

It was early March 1920 and snowing hard on the day Mutti went into labour. (Looking up from our pillows now we could see the snow ourselves, catching in the lamplight as it fell past the windows.) In those days there wasn't a road or cars that could get up there in weather like that.

But that wasn't a problem. Mutti packed up the few things she needed, got out her *Rodel* and tobogganed down the mountain. 'Just like you,' said my mother, 'bumping over the hummocks and lumps all the way down to the main street of Schwaz beside the River Inn. Then she walked across the bridge to the railway station and took the train to Innsbruck to the nursing home run by nuns called the Sisters of the Cross, at Sackengasse 12.

'The nuns were very devout. They lived by the strict rules of their religious order and they weren't allowed to see naked bodies and certainly not the private parts of the women they cared for. Even when they bathed the children in their care, the children had to wear long shirts and be washed underneath them. So, whenever someone was having a baby, there came a point when the nuns had to leave the room.

"Don't worry, Frau Baronin," they told Mutti as they went out. "We'll be able to tell from the baby's cry whether it's a boy or a girl. We always know." And they shut the door and went on with their prayers in the hall outside.

'So then I was born,' my mother went on, 'and, sure enough, I yelled long and loud.

'As soon as Mutti and I had been washed and dressed, the nuns came smiling back into the room: "Congratulations, Frau Baronin!" they cried. "Congratulations on the birth of a fine strong son!" And sitting there on the edge of my bed, my mother laughed her big, strong laugh.'

'Then they brought me home to the Hügelhof here. Apparently, I was a very good baby. I scarcely ever cried. They'd put me out on the balcony in my crib to sleep in the fresh air – everyone did that then – and because I didn't cry, they forgot about me and my cheeks got pink and frozen. My father said I looked like a thousand-year-old trumpeter.

1920. Mutti, now Baroness Schey von Koromla, with Inge.

'And then?'

'My sister Beate says we were both christened with a golden jug and a golden bowl. But she was only 3. "Of course," Mutti told us. "The only decision was what faith to choose." Neither of our parents practised any religion though he came from a Jewish family and she from a Catholic one. So, they had us christened into the Protestant Church.'

'And then?'

'Then we lived here, for a while anyway, and slept in this room like you're going to now.'

I looked at my mother with new eyes. Lucky her! Imagine being born here with all this around you. She drew the curtains and kissed us goodnight and we fell asleep in the scent of clean sheets and pine forest and scrubbed wooden floors. We woke next morning to find that our red-and-white-checked bolsters had grown into mounds of warm air so big we couldn't see over them (cue much jumping); and between the double windows etched with frost-flowers, the tangerine pieces had frozen hard as ice lollies.

So there it was, one of the first – maybe *the* first – of the special stories. A nativity all mixed up with the sparkle of the snow and the scent and sounds of the house and the mountains and the hug of my mother's arms. A fact of life, it hung like a bead on a necklace from then on, special, complete in itself and ours. It was enough.

And so I began to tell it. 'When my mum was born, my grandmother tobogganed down the mountainside to have her!' it began, and listeners in flat England widened their eyes and thought that was amazing.

Only later, much later, when I was an adult, did I think to link it with the history of its time and place, or to ask for more than I already knew under the skin. What were they doing there? What was the thread of history this bead was hanging on?

Anny and Fritz

Here was Mutti, the same Anny Schindler of the faded photo, the girl who had grown up in the flat in Vienna, danced the nights away and made a career at the Burgtheater, but now she was a married woman, living in the mountains, tobogganing through the snow, giving birth. There was a gap. Time had passed. She had a new name. The nuns were calling her 'Frau Baronin', 'Baroness' or 'My Lady', and now she had become a '*Mutti*'* too. Much had happened.

First, she was married – and that, we understood as children, was how the story was supposed to go. Her husband was Fritz, our grandfather of the sonorous name, Baron Friedrich Schey von Koromla, the second of five children from a distinguished Jewish family and the eldest son. His father, Josef, was Professor of Law at Vienna University, an eminent jurist and co-author of the law books of Austria – the General Civil Code for the Austro-Hungarian Empire – whose own father, also called Friedrich, had been a rich and influential man who had acquired the title. Both Anny and Fritz were from Vienna, born and brought up in its culture and Viennese to the core. But they were not living there anymore. Why?

---

* Mutti = 'Mummy'.

Anny and Fritz, 1915.

The two of them were, by all accounts, a most attractive couple. He was tall and handsome and made everyone laugh, a collector of books and an aspiring writer. She, the beautiful, charismatic actress, was a woman people found it hard not to love and having succumbed, never forgot. They were well connected, well educated, passionate about the arts and they had grown up in a world of stability, tolerance and peace. They had everything going for them. Except the times.

In a handful of years, the world young Anny Schindler had thought stable and secure had fallen apart and vanished. Everything had changed. Because here – 1914 to 1918 – was the First World War.

Fritz, in the army on active service on the Eastern Front, wooed Anny in cramped, pencilled letters throughout 1915 – a whole silk-covered box of them. In 1916 they were married, when he came home on leave, exactly halfway through the war, and the same year the old emperor, Franz Joseph, died and a new one, Karl, took his place.

Their first child, Beate, was born in Vienna the following June.

50

Courtship, 1915: the box of love letters.

Fritz with Beate, 1917.

But by the time my mother arrived three years later they had left the capital behind and moved more than 400km west to the small alpine town of Schwaz in Tyrol and the farmhouse called the Hügelhof, with the woods and the mountains soaring up behind and the Inn Valley stretching away below towards Innsbruck.

Was it the romantic legacy – the beauty of the landscape and the natural world that drew them to Tyrol? The kind of thing that inspired Anny's grandfather to his 'Julius von der Traun' writings and her uncle, Emil Jacob Schindler, to his landscape paintings? It would not have been unusual. Throughout the late nineteenth century and into the twentieth, Austrian writers and artists, like their contemporaries across Europe, drew solace and inspiration from the natural world and used it as a place to work. The better-off went backwards and forwards between the country and the capital as a matter of course. To have a holiday house in the mountains was not unusual in their circle. But this was different. Harsh winds were blowing, political and economic realities driving.

From the moment in 1914 when the assassination of Archduke Franz Ferdinand in Sarajevo provided the pretext for the Austro-Hungarian

The Austro-Hungarian Empire, 1914.

military action that was to draw all Europe into the First World War, conditions in Vienna began to deteriorate. The empire was a juggernaut; its military and diplomatic procedures notorious for their slowness and inefficiency. The Hungarian and Austrian governments found it hard to agree on anything, the army was poorly organised, coordination was bad. But once the wheels had begun to grind ...

It took a month, under pressure from Germany, for Austria–Hungary to issue an ultimatum to Serbia following the assassination, and forty-eight hours more to declare war. When Russia mobilised in support of Serbia, on 1 August 1914, Austria–Hungary in turn announced a general mobilisation. The order was given in twenty different languages.

Now France and England came in on the side of Russia, and Germany mobilised in support of Austria–Hungary. The stage was set. Nothing could stop the military machine now.

Strange though it seems today, the atmosphere was one of euphoria. Stefan Zweig described the mood in Vienna:

A city of two million, a country of nearly fifty million, in that hour felt that they were participating in world history, in a moment which would never recur, and that each one was called upon to cast his infinitesimal self into the glowing mass, there to be purified of all selfishness. All differences of class, rank and language were swamped at that moment by the rushing feeling of fraternity. Strangers spoke to one another in the streets, people who had avoided each other for years shook hands, everywhere one saw excited faces. Each individual experienced an exaltation of his ego, he was not longer the isolated person of former times, he had been incorporated into the mass, he was part of the people, and his person, his hitherto unnoticed person, had been given meaning.[1]

The mobilisation took on a carnival atmosphere. Soldiers marched away to war with flowers in the muzzles of their rifles, their helmets decorated with oak leaves. This was a heroic adventure not to be missed, the chance of a lifetime. 'We'll be home for Christmas,' they shouted as they went. And after forty years of peace, who was there to say otherwise? Besides, urged the philosophers, war would bring spiritual cleansing. Renewal, promised the captains of industry, eager at the thought of new markets and unprecedented profits.

Fritz, who was 25, and his twin brothers Herbert and Witold, 23, were nearing the end of their university studies when the war broke out. They had all done a year of military service on leaving school and qualified as officers of the reserve. Now they too hurried to enlist.

Fritz joined a smart regiment of dragoons, a dashing figure in the photographs in his high-necked uniform, mounted on the back of a sleek, black horse.

All three brothers were sent to different parts of the Eastern Front over the next four years – Galicia (today Poland), Bukovina (Ukraine/ Romania), Russia or northern Romania – and later to the Italian front. Amazingly, they all survived. But no one could imagine just how devastating this war would turn out to be.

The cracks in the fabric began to show almost immediately. Leaving aside the many different peoples and languages of the Austro-Hungarian Empire, the logistics were extraordinary. There were huge quantities of troops, supplies and weapons to be moved around. Then

Fritz the cavalry officer, 1914.

Fritz with his brother Herbert (on the left).

there were the horses: the Austrians alone had 600,000 (the Germans 715,000 and the Russians over a million).[2] Within months, the Imperial Army's food supplies were running short; in October 1914, 10,000 horses had to be shot to feed the troops. By December, almost a million Austro-Hungarian soldiers had been killed, wounded or taken prisoner. Things were not going according to plan.

Inside the silk-covered box, Fritz's letters start in May 1915. The relationship is new, uncertain, passionate. They have exchanged rings. But it's a secret still. The Russians are in retreat on the Eastern Front. On 11 May 2015, he writes to Anny:

My love, (today I already dare address you as my love) today I haven't ridden far. All in all we're now 50 to 60 kilometres forward from the place where I was before my leave. Here in D-- everything is pitifully burnt out. Not a soul in the town, the station completely empty, systematically destroyed, out of action, 'as planned'. It's strange to return to this place which we left seven months ago. This war has already lasted nine and a half months, my love, but the seeds are coming up here where the Russians already felt so at home that they sowed them for their own troops and hopefully we'll be the ones to harvest what others planted for themselves. Your lovely letters are a great joy to me. One of the 7th, one of 8th is with me but we are getting ever further and further away from each other.

And on 12 May:

I had to ride my Kommando [cavalry troop] a couple of kilometres towards Tarnow. I was at Prince Sanguszko's Schloss Gurniska there – in Pilzno the next day and 2 days later in Dębica, which was completely burnt out. Of the previous 10 – 20,000 inhabitants only about 100 in the place!! Railway station destroyed. On the way the Jewish temple was stripped, strewn with paper, the books stolen etc.

Then on 14 May:

Yesterday was dusty and hot, one bit, through the wood near Prz ... was very lovely. The Russians have not been in evidence any more in these last days – they're far away and so everything here seems fine as we ride over the moss. One of my grooms is with me. The other groom is leading my third horse by hand so he's a bit protected – but since 7th May the horses have marched 110 kilometres and had scarcely anything to eat.

Photographs from the Eastern Front from among Fritz's letters. The Russians occupied Eastern Galicia from September 1914 until May 1915.

If the cumbersome machinery of the empire was poor at organising its military operations, it was equally inadequate on the home front. The war had begun in August before the harvest could be brought in and Vienna quickly found itself cut off by the fighting from its principal source of grain in the Ukraine. Food supplies became erratic, rationed, scarce. As the war went on, the Allies imposed a harsh blockade on the city and the situation became steadily worse until Vienna's predicament was graver even than that of the German capital, Berlin. People began to die of hunger. Between 7 and 11 per cent of all deaths in the city during the war were a direct result of starvation, and it was a contributor to 20–30 per cent more.[3]

Despite propaganda efforts to blame everything on the blockade and the enemy's 'War of Starvation' and to urge the Viennese to stand together and endure, as time went on the people of the starving city began to turn against each other. Group against group, by nationality and language, race and religion, the great capital unravelled from within. With supplies shrinking, the people of the city even turned against their fellow Austrians in the surrounding countryside.

In late June of 1918, when the authorities proposed a further reduction in rations and the city was running out of potatoes despite a new crop in the fields outside, furious Viennese women and children, supported by soldiers home on leave, headed out into the countryside by train and on foot and threatened to burn down the homes of farmers who refused to sell their potato crops.

Then came disease.

The first waves of the Spanish flu pandemic that was to kill 30 million people across the world reached Vienna in the spring and summer of 1918. The illness was sudden and severe, with large numbers of people infected and many dying, among them the painter Gustav Klimt on 6 February.

But worse was to come. The weather that autumn turned suddenly unseasonably cold, and with no coal for heating and the food shortage weakening the population, a new wave of flu tore through the city with even greater virulence. It swept people away in a matter of days and with every week that passed, the death toll went up. By the height of the epidemic in mid-October, it stood at 58.6 million. Rich and poor alike, nobody was safe, not even the young and fit. Especially not the young and fit.

'Edith fell ill with the Spanish flu yesterday and then developed pneumonia on top of it,' the Viennese painter Egon Schiele wrote to his mother on 27 October of his wife who was six months' pregnant. 'Her condition is extremely serious and dangerous. I am preparing myself for the worst, since she is constantly struggling for breath.'[4] She died the next day. And before she was cold, Schiele, who had looked after her, fell ill himself and died three days later. He was 28.

As for the war, by this time it had gone from bad to worse for Austria and Germany. In the first days of October 1918, the two countries sent notes to Woodrow Wilson, the president of the United States, suing for peace. But it wasn't until 11 November 1918 that the Armistice was finally signed and the fighting came to an end.

For the Austrians the consequences of defeat were devastating. The Emperor Karl fled. After 700 years of Hapsburg rule, the empire fell apart overnight. What was left was a mere stump of a country cut off, not only from its previous sources of food, but also from its power supplies, coal mines, oil fields, many factories and much of its previous population: this was the Democratic Republic of Austria.

And for the old capital, Vienna, it wasn't over yet. With the terms of the peace still to be hammered out, the Allies kept up the pressure by continuing to blockade the city, while the new nations of the former

The Republic of Austria, 1919.

empire – the Croats, Czechs, Serbs, Slovaks, Magyars and others – whose borders were still being decided, withheld supplies as a bargaining tool. As the soldiers of the defeated army returned to the city, ragged and exhausted, and with them thousands of other dispossessed and destitute people, the flow of raw materials to Vienna's factories and food to its markets fell away to nothing, until the winter of 1918 made the hungry years of the war look like a time of plenty.

And when, the following summer, the peace settlement known as the Treaty of Saint-Germain-en-Laye was signed, its terms were punitive. The vast Austro-Hungarian Empire of 53 million people was divided into separate successor states – Hungary, Poland, Yugoslavia and Czechoslovakia, while Eastern Galicia, Trento, South Tyrol, Trieste and Istria were ceded to the surrounding states – leaving the new Republic of Austria, reluctantly independent, as a small, landlocked state on the lands of the former Ostmark, its capital on the brink of starvation. With a population of little more than 5 million, it was now held to account for the whole imperial military fiasco.

In the chaos that followed not only was there hunger, cold and starvation, but the old Austrian currency – the krone – collapsed. Every

Notgeld – emergency money – from Erla near St Valentin, Lower Austria.

day, money was worth less. In desperation, towns and villages printed their own emergency notes only to find that others wouldn't accept them in exchange. Those who had savings found them suddenly worth nothing, but speculators flourished – anyone who had foreign currency could buy whatever they pleased for little or nothing and the black market went from strength to strength. If you wanted food you had to have something to barter for it.

Inside the Hügelhof in Schwaz.

Fritz the book collector's *ex libris*.

The aristocrats of the old regime, many of whom had been stripped of their fortunes and estates, found themselves washed up in Vienna with little more than their outdated titles to their name.[5]

Whatever the ties of family and upbringing, the privileges of education and wealth, Vienna was not the best place to be. The war was over, the old world at an end. Anny and Fritz, with one small child and another to come, went to live in the mountains, where the air was clean and the life was quiet and the big-eyed Alpine cows with bells round their necks munched hay in their stables under the farmhouses in the winter, when everything was covered in snow, and emerged blinking in the spring to graze the lush mountain grass, higher and higher up the mountains every day.

And if the life of the peasants who worked the steep land was harsh and they drove a hard bargain, there was at least fresh milk and cheese and eggs and salami and vegetables to be had and the air was good. And so, they came to Schwaz.

They were not the only ones.

The family, Schwaz, 1920. Left to right: Inge with Grandmother Schindler, Anny's mother,[6] Anny, Beate and Fritz.

The Rotenturm Schlössl

I have in my mind, like a hazy video clip, a very early memory that has to come from that first visit to the mountains in 1954. I am standing in a whitewashed kitchen on wide, scrubbed, wooden floorboards. This is not the Hügelhof. In front of me, at exactly my eye height, is the top of a table and a wide curtain of transparent dough is hanging over it and slowly moving down and down towards the floor. The dough is so thin that I can see straight through it to the legs of the table and the feet and skirt of the large woman with the floury arms who is plying her rolling pin backwards and forwards across the table top by my head, each stroke lengthening the curtain hanging in front of me.

On that first childhood visit in the 1950s, my mother showed us from the balcony of the Hügelhof, over the fields and down the steep slope,

The Rotenturm Schlössl, Pirkhanger, Schwaz.

another house standing on its own little hill. It was poised like a sentinel above the old town and looked like something from a fairy tale. The walls were yellow, with shutters painted red, white and red flanking the windows that ran along its two-storey length, and, at the far end, a round tower rose up to a conical red roof. 'That's the Rotenturm Schlössl,' she said. 'The little castle with the red tower.' And she took us down to visit. These were Mutti's friends. And they were real.

We were greeted with cries of delight by two old ladies with hooked noses and stooped shoulders, themselves straight out of a fairy tale, who took it in turns to fold my mother in their arms as if she were their own child, with kisses and smiles, and tears standing in their eyes. Then they bent to welcome us. 'This is Sissi and Pussi.'

Of the two sisters, Pussi was the older by a year or two. She wore her dark hair piled on top of her head in an elegant chignon, the pearls at her ears matching those around her neck, her face powdered – at 5, you notice these things – eyebrows drawn with pencil and her lips painted in a sharp cupid's bow with plum-red lipstick. Sissi, like a softer echo,

Pussi (on the left) and Sissi.

played second fiddle to her sister's lead: hair coiled in a low bun, no paint, a crucifix around her neck and a look of gentle surprise around her eyes. She hurried off to bring us treats – cakes and coffee poured in delicate, decorated cups – while Pussi presided over the gathering from her seat beside the upright piano with the curly silver candlesticks mounted on the front.

To me, Sissi and Pussi were inconceivably old, an impression only confirmed by their beautiful old house and the objects in it: a carved baroque angel, Meissen shepherdesses, plates and ornaments set into the panelled walls, paintings, furniture, another carving of a naked man surrounded by flames, and the fluted porcelain *Kachel* stoves standing in the corner of the room. It was another world.

But time has ways of standing still. If Sissi and Pussi were already ancient the first time I met them, for another fifty years, all the way to Sissi's death in 2006 at the age of 108, nothing really changed. Like the house, she seemed to stay the same. Only we grew up, grew on, grew older. The world outside changed too: a motorway in the valley, electric lights spreading to compete with the stars at night and the sprawl of new houses creeping up the mountainside from the town till they jostled outside the gates and carried on beyond. Still, something about the warmth, mutual affection and the link with the past (all five generations of my mother's family) meant they settled effortlessly into the place in our hearts reserved for family, grandparents, Austria and love.

Pussi died in the 1980s, my mother in 1992. But as the twentieth century turned into the twenty-first, Sissi was still there to tell us tales of their childhood in Vienna, 100 years before. She described walking through the crowded streets of the imperial city as a small child, her sister and herself each firmly holding on to the hand of their English governess, Miss Cooper – who had developed an unfortunate taste for strong drink and a tendency to be unsteady on her feet – and trying to steer her along the snowy pavements and through the press of horses and carriages without mishap. 'And one day,' said Sissi, 'a fine carriage stopped and out stepped the old Emperor, Franz Joseph himself, and patted Pussi and me on the head and complimented my mother, who was with us that day, on her little daughters. I remember him clearly.'

Thanks to Miss Cooper, and – once their parents had realised her weakness and written to her father to suggest it might be prudent for her to be taken home – to the governesses who succeeded her, Miss Edith Silk and Miss Freda Peck, Sissi spoke perfect Edwardian English and still enjoyed beating us at Scrabble in our own language well after her 100th birthday, though she'd never been out of Austria. She spoke French too, of course, and Italian, naturally, and knew not just the languages but their music and poetry, art and literature, and the words of their songs, which she sang under her breath as she shuffled around the house.

'Austria was one country with fifteen languages,' she said. And the comment slipped by, something it was hard for us in our late-twentieth-century ignorance to imagine, with our shrunken map formed by the Treaty of Saint-Germain-en-Laye, the Second World War and the Cold War that followed. Down in Schwaz, as Sissi reached her centenary, the walls were plastered with posters arguing for and against Austria's entry into the European Union project as if such an idea were without precedent. At home in the UK, anti-EU xenophobia dominated the red-top press.

Sissi talked about the mountains, lakes and walks. 'Have you ever been to the seaside?' I asked her.

'Only once,' she answered.

'Where did you go?'

'To the Austrian seaside.'

'But Austria doesn't have any coast ...'

'Trieste!'

Sissi and Pussi's father had moved his wife and daughters out of their beloved Vienna in 1919. He found and bought the little castle on the hill, built in the sixteenth century for the manager of one of the silver mines whose tunnels deep under the mountains had made Schwaz, now little more than a small provincial town, one of the most important centres of medieval Europe. And, with great plans for developing the adjoining farm and founding a centre for the arts, he set about renovating it.

He was an art historian and collector, involved in the Austrian equivalent of the Arts and Crafts movement. The family was well-to-do, his brother a composer, known for his ballet music. The name was von Minkus.

'Oh yes we knew Klimt,' said Sissi. 'I liked him a lot, we used to talk for hours. He wanted to paint me but my parents wouldn't let me pose for him.'

Sissi playing Mozart in the Rotenturm Schlössl, 1996, Tessa Henderson.

The girls were 22 and 24 when they moved. They became fast friends with Mutti. 'She was so beauuuutiful,' Pussi would lament, waving her cigarette in its ebony holder, 'And so chaaarming.'

'Anny's mother too, *Grossmama* Schindler,' said Sissi. 'And then Inge, your mother, was born. When she was a girl she used to round up the children of the farmers on the mountain and take them home for a bath!'

Peals of laughter.

A lantern hung over the dining table in the Schlössl, between the two windows that looked out over the Inn Valley to the mountains beyond. 'That came from our flat in Vienna,' said Sissi. 'It hung over the top-floor landing outside our door and when we left my father asked the landlady if he could buy it.' He redecorated the Schlössl, lined the parlour walls with fabric and hung the artefacts and paintings he had collected on the walls. And then the clock stopped.

Pussi, the talented pianist and musician, never married. And Sissi, whose short marriage to Dr Pockels ended with his death from tuberculosis, survived a breakdown and drew consolation from her Catholic faith. Their mother died. Their father took a young boy called Franzi as his lover and, selling much of the land, disappeared from his daughters' lives. The two sisters and the house remained.

A second world war, another defeat: occupation by French, Russian, American soldiers, and after that, post-war recovery: prosperity, technology, the EU. All these came and went. And people too – billeted, visiting, paying guests, cats and, in her very last years, the local nurses of the Red Cross, who enabled Sissi to stay in her little castle, drifting through time, until she died in her own bed.

Back on that first visit when I came back from the kitchen where the pastry curtain, now rolled with apple and raisins and chopped nuts and crumbs browned in butter, was tucked into the oven, my mother had been transformed into a singer and Pussi was accompanying her on the piano in Schubert Lieder. Beside them and the piles of scores and manuscripts stood a middle-aged man. 'This is Pepi, my singing teacher,' my mother introduced him when the song came to an end. 'He lives further up the mountain.'

As he walked us back up to the Hügelhof a little later, with the sound of singing fading behind us, my father looked dark. 'The man was a bloody Nazi,' he muttered and his voice was full of anger. At 5, I knew it was bad, but how could all this be bad? It was confusing.

My father skied and we *rodelled* and did a lot of walking with my mother – mostly uphill, it seemed to me. She strode ahead always seeming just about to disappear around the next bend till the panic rose in my throat. 'Wait Mummy! Wait!' And I with my stubby little legs, distracted by snowflakes, pine seedlings, animal tracks in the snow or streams running under it, always trailing last.

When we got to the top – a top, anyway – there would be my father tugging and tightening the laces of his leather boots till his feet were firmly fixed and then strapping on the heavy wooden skis. We sat on a wooden terrace drinking raspberry juice in the sun and watched him fly past, laughing, transformed – a dancer, a bird – turning one curve into the next by dropping first to one knee and then the other, until he disappeared from sight. We learned to answer, '*Grüss Gott*' to the greetings of everyone we passed and '*Danke Vielmals*' for the many kindnesses that came our way. 'It's easy,' my father said, 'Great Scot. Donkey Fieldmouse.'

The Rotenturm Schlössl, from Sissi's death notice, 2006.

At a farmhouse door creased faces broke into smiles. For my mother, there were fond greetings – 'Where have you been?!' – and for us, entry to the warm, half-dark of the byre underneath the house where the big cows with the kind eyes and pale noses turned their heads to look at us and their bells clinked as they chewed the scented hay.

After two weeks, my father took my sister and me back to London while my mother stayed behind a bit longer to sing. We went in another bumpy aeroplane. It roared and circled and screamed up into the sky, struggling to climb high enough to get over the magnificent mountains. I was sick into another paper bag. My father sighed and winced as he bumped the shoulder he'd broken in a skiing fall.

Why would anyone ever want to leave all this?

3

A London Childhood

We never went back to the Hügelhof. It was sold apparently (I hadn't even realised it belonged to my mother) and not talked about. There were problems: an uncle of my mother's 'being difficult', a farmer who had grazed the land, claiming rights of ownership. A strip of forest was sold to make way for a ski lift. Then it was gone – my mother sad, my father relieved – a subject, or perhaps a country, best not discussed.

This was 1950s England and 'we' had won the Second World War. It was a time for going on, for building a new and better life to replace the one that had been ruptured by the events of the previous decade. No one wanted to think about that. My mother, with her musician's ear, spoke English without a trace of a foreign accent. My sister and I grew up without learning a word of German. My father and everyone else seemed happier not hearing it, though sometimes, when my mother's friends arrived from Europe, it broke out, and with it music, laughter and much waving of hands. At weekends, when we went for walks on Hampstead Heath, we would hear people sitting on the benches in front of Kenwood House in the sun, chatting and talking in German and Yiddish. '*Prittish Vest Hempstett*,' my father would joke with a heavy Peter Ustinov 'Cherman' accent.

And though my mother travelled backwards and forwards to Austria, studying as a singer, my sister and I stayed put on the North London hills.

The house and the family, London, late 1950s.

Roots

We put down roots. We acquired a dog. Then came a litter of puppies that chewed up everything in sight. My mother's sister, Beetle, drove up from Dorset one day with a box of day-old chicks. They lived in the old chicken house at the bottom of the garden and when they were grown I'd collect eggs or watch my mother turn a chicken into Sunday lunch, wringing its neck or chopping its head off with an axe and stripping it in a shower of feathers in the back yard. Until one night, the fox burrowed his way into the chicken run and ate them all and my sister got the hen house to play in.

In summer we ran around with no clothes on and swam in the green water of the swimming pool until our lips turned blue with the cold. The rest of the time we climbed trees or made camps in the stems of the undergrowth, sometimes joined by other children from the houses next door, our hands black, our faces streaked with the soot that covered everything. In autumn we looked forward to the choking yellow smog that silenced the city for days and brought normal life to a standstill. And in winter, when guests came to visit, instead of taking their coats, we'd offer them another one to wear, for no matter how much coke my parents shovelled into the boiler or coal they piled on the living room fire, the stone walls and high ceilings swallowed the warmth.

It was a time for ingenuity. Our parents improvised with verve. My mother made the clothes she couldn't buy, my father salvaged old furniture and made it good and everyone tackled our monster house. The scary stained glass was removed to storage, light poured in.

One morning we came downstairs to find an ivy plant dancing its way up the wall by the back stairs, carved out of the peeling wallpaper by my father while we slept. And for days after we'd race down as soon

as we woke to see what new leaves it had grown in the night and where it had got to now.

His sister, our painter-aunt Eliza, painted murals on the walls of what had once been the billiard room, weaving the patina of the mildewed plaster into her images: between two of the windows, a sailor in a landscape with the sea in the distance and a ship; along the wall, a child in long grass and a dog – was it ours? And, near the corner, a man and woman dancing in each other's arms.

Eliza's sculptor lover[*] – a pupil of Jacob Epstein's – did a portrait head of me in long sessions in a draughty studio. It was exhibited at the Royal Academy and sold to a bank – a great success. My sister and I sat for Eliza to paint our portraits: and there we are, two little girls, solemn on a red chaise longue, one wistful and the other bland.

The grand piano inherited from Mutti scarcely dented the space. Musicians came in a variety of languages – the legendary pianist Edwin Fischer and his students, Paul Badura-Skoda, Jörg Demus, Alfred Brendel, with Jean and Pierre Fournier and others – to rehearse there.

There was chamber music, singing, quartets and, when the room filled with an orchestra, still a place for me, on the floor under the piano to listen to piano concertos: Mozart, Beethoven, arrangements of Bach – with Fischer as the soloist.

At the end of one performance, when the discussion was over and everyone was packing up their instruments, his grizzled head peered down under the keyboard. 'And what did you think?'

'It was very loud,' I said and everybody laughed.

I understood. I could feel how important this was, how it reached somewhere deeper than anything else. I loved the sound, longed to play like Fischer myself. I began piano lessons with another Austrian friend of my mother's, alone in the big music room, but gave up after three months when I still couldn't play a concerto. Or maybe because of his eager, straying hands.

People came and stayed and went away again. Painters, musicians, photographers, architects.

We lived comfortably, though architecture pulled in little enough and money always seemed to be a huge worry to my father. Or was

---

[*] David McFall RA.

Eliza Henderson's murals on the sitting room walls.

Two sisters. Eliza's portrait of Tessa and Kathy.

With Paul Badura-Skoda.

it something else? Night after night he brooded over his drawing board, the ashtray filling steadily, as if he yearned for something that eluded him.

Occasionally, a big brown parcel tied with string would arrive from his other sister, our Aunt Joan, respectable in Scotland. Inside were our cousins' cast-off clothes. There were tweed coats with velvet collars, shot-silk party dresses that changed colour with the angle of the light, full skirts, petticoats and sashes. There were shiny shoes, tartan kilts with leather fastenings, kilt pins and sporrans. It was like a glimpse of another world. Was this what he missed? For we wore dungarees and lived in trees and I, at least, much preferred running barefoot to dressing up in 'best'.

It was as if, among all the invention and creativity that surrounded us, and came from him too, there was another current, a desire for respectability, for convention, pulling at my father the other way. He wanted the best for us. But what was it supposed to be?

My sister was sent to a private day school for girls – brown shoes, Harris tweed school uniform and all. And when one of the *Tias*, his well-found maiden aunts from South America, died and left him a small legacy, it was used to pay for a nanny. Now my mother could continue

Inge singing.

to travel abroad and pursue her studies as a singer and we would be 'properly' brought up. To me, her absences were long, unbearable, as if the lights had gone out, each one more painful than the last.

Nanny

Nanny was middle-aged and stout with a capacious handbag and tight orange curls permed to her bare pink scalp. Her scent smelt ugly. She wore a housecoat. She dressed us in skirts. My sister was old enough and brave enough to be indignant. Dark haired and turbulent, she went to war with Nanny, with the result that I, the little one with the fair hair and the dimples, was automatically cast as the 'good' child, a role that involved little more than keeping my terror to myself and having my hair brushed 100 times before bed every night while she listened to *The Archers* on the big valve wireless, a cigarette hanging off her lip.

And when our parents were away, my sister was at school and Nanny had finished reading my parents' post and drinking their gin of a morning, she would sometimes take me up the road to the local pub for her lunchtime drink. There, she'd lift me onto the counter of the public bar – smoke and beer and sawdust on the floor – and encourage me to lift my skirt, show my knickers and sing the song she'd taught me like a nursery rhyme, 'Mademoiselle from Arma-tears, Paaaarlay voooo?' to the old men who stood around and leered up at me through broken, yellow teeth. It was years before I understood the subtleties of this First World War hit, but it permanently inoculated me against any thoughts of a future on the stage.

Eventually Nanny went. We felt not a wisp of regret.

My mother held me close as if I were some kind of consolation. With her there, life was always interesting.

As younger siblings do, I had grown up in the shadow of my sister. There were advantages. As she went charging out ahead, I sat grafted to my mother's hip and watched: no pressure. When she kicked up a storm, I became invisible, assumed good. And if I wondered why the things that my sister did were so much more interesting than what I did, there was always the answer, 'When you're older'.

Now, though school brought my sister an apparently endless supply of friends and birthday parties, I had the advantage of still being at home, and one of the perks was that every now and then my mother would take me on an adventure in the city.

In Search of Oranges

Very early in the morning, before it was even light, she and I would creep out of the house, crank up the old black car and drive down the hill into the city. Sooty buildings, an early trolley bus, empty streets, pigeons stirring by the street lamps, until, turning a corner, we were suddenly in a warren of alleyways full of men and crates and noise, half-blocked by big lorries unloading food from the countryside. Covent Garden Market – the wholesale heart of London.

Here were porters, tall as giants, weaving through the crowds with towers of boxes balanced on their heads, and others rattling trolleys stacked with more crates of fruit and vegetables across the cobbled streets. There were men hurrying and shouting, and small vans loading up and roaring off in clouds of black exhaust to stock the shops. There were flocks of sparrows flying inside a great glass roof. And here was every fruit and vegetable you could imagine: a whole hall full of boxes of flowers and another piled with sacks of onions, cabbages and potatoes.

My mother was in her element. Among the shouting and talking, backchat and whistling, there would be haggling about price and gales of laughter and sometimes one of the giants would bend all the way down to where I hid behind her legs and hand me an apple like a benediction.

By the time it was light, the deal was done, our crate of oranges was loaded into the car (with lots of help) and we went for breakfast in a steamed-up café full of giants with mugs of tea and hot bacon sandwiches. And then came more. My mother took my hand and walked me along the emptying street to a big white building with a grand entrance lined with pillars and guarded by another huge man.

This giant was different. Could he be a king? I stared. He was splendid, from the shiny black shoes on the pavement, up the red trousers lined with braid and the long, red tailcoat studded with golden buttons that curved up over his enormous stomach, to where, miles away, above the smile on his face when he saw my mother, a tall, silk top hat crowned his head.

I don't know what my mother said but the king stood aside for us. We slipped in through the great glass doors, tiptoed through a silent entrance hall, across a huge red carpet – 'Sssssssssssssh!' – and into a great, dark vault of a place with rows of empty red plush seats and naked golden angels holding up the balconies around the walls. And there, in the Royal Opera House, we'd sit through rehearsals long into the morning, half-hidden in the dark, while people sang to us from the stage and the orchestra played for us, and us alone, until it was time to go home.

School

Eventually, I followed my sister to the girls' school in 'the village' up the road, wearing, at 5, not only a starched shirt and tie but a tailored jacket and skirt of thick, brown Harris tweed that scratched my chapped legs raw in winter.

In breaktime we played horses, turned somersaults round the branch of the old pine tree and ran away giggling when the occasional flasher pressed up against the railings that separated the school grounds from the park next door. And in the Kindergarten, sitting in the circle round Miss Illsley, we drank in her special game with the flash cards and soon learned eagerly to read and write.

I made new friends. There was Christina, recently arrived from China, who lived with her mother and older sister a Sunday walk away across the Heath. And Amanda, whose mother was Austrian too, except that she spoke German with her daughter from the start and only spoke English with a pronounced accent. There was my sister's friend, Sara, whose Spanish parents collected her from school in an old taxi cab with a kitchen chair lashed to the luggage space for her mother to sit on.

We all had one foot in and one foot out. Not so the rest. And now the questions began.

What Are You?
The first time it happened was in the school playground. North London. Nineteen fifty-something. And if I wasn't 5 years old, I wasn't much more. 'Where do you come from?' said one of the girls standing around me. 'What are you?'

'I live up the road.'

'No! Where do your parents come from? Are you English or what?'

Tricky this one. I had to check at home to make sure I'd got it right.

The next time I was ready. But my sister's friend Sara was quicker than me. 'My parents come from Spain. I'm three-quarters Spanish,' she said, as if it was better than English anyway.

'And I'm half-Austrian, a quarter Scots and a quarter Irish,' I said carefully, trying to sound just as convincing. 'And my dad was born in South America.' (For good measure.)

The two of us stood a bit closer together. Different and proud of it.

'Austrian?' said the big girl. 'Hitler was Austrian.'

This was more than ten years after the Second World War but everyone knew that Hitler was the ENEMY and Austrians were the same as Germans and they were all baddies and WE (that is, the English) were the goodies and had WON. I knew my mother wasn't a baddy and that both she and my father had taken part in the war against Hitler, but the big girls in the playground weren't interested. From now on, as far as they were concerned it was easy: I was half a baddy.

My friend Sara tossed her head. 'That's just silly. What do you expect? They're only English. You come to my house.'

So we did.

Sara's house was a bit like our house, except at our house the people who weren't English had Austrian accents or spoke French or Italian. At Sara's house, most people spoke Spanish; exiles from the Spanish Civil War, they waved their hands around a lot and sat over the meal table for ages. They were the same kind of people though: musicians, dancers, painters, writers, doctors, architects. It wasn't long before not only we children but my parents and her parents all became friends, a bond that has lasted ever since.

So I learnt to enjoy being different. But this called for backup. What kind of different was I? I needed evidence. Where had my parents come from? What was the story? And how had we ended up here in ordinary old England?

News

By the time I reached the Second Form we had graduated to sitting in rows of scarred wooden desks with inkwells and were learning to use dip pens, with scratchy nibs that splattered fine splashes of ink in all directions. First lesson on Tuesday mornings was 'News'. I didn't often have any. Besides, the thought of speaking out in front of the class made me want to dive under the lid of my desk and bury myself in paper and pencil sharpenings.

I listened in admiration, though. There were the rescues of injured birds, tales of lost teeth – we were all starting to shed them – the visits of uncles, aunts, and cousins, deaths of guinea pigs, excursions with grandparents, being bridesmaids at weddings. It was like a template of what a 1950s childhood was supposed to be.

But we didn't seem to have any relatives. Sometimes 'News' included a smattering of current events: elections, Khrushchev, Eisenhower. And Miss Crawford, lovely Miss Crawford, with her long shining hair

School and summer.

plaited round her head, and her gym skirt, and the silver whistle hanging round her neck, Miss Crawford presided over it all. She was the teacher everyone wanted to please.

One day I did have news. Big news. The pope had had hiccups. The pope was dead. And on the same day, my mother reading an airmail letter with an odd expression on her face. Unusually silent, until, 'It's from my father. Your grandfather,' she said.

This was news. We had a grandfather? Alive? Since when?

'He's had a baby. A boy. My half-brother. You have a baby Uncle.' And she went off to write back.

This was multiple news. Where had this living grandfather come from? Who was he? It turned out later, of course, that he was the one from the being-born-in-Schwaz story, the one with the big forehead and the arched nose in the photographs, the one on the horse in the officer's uniform, a long time ago before world wars began: faded, sepia, brown, Mutti's husband, Fritz.[1]

And here he was suddenly. Alive. Now. In South America – and not my father's Chile South America either, but a different one called

Argentina – sprung from a blue airmail envelope with a row of coloured stamps. (Though where exactly Argentina was or how it differed from being dead, from our point of view, wasn't clear.)

It was news too that he wrote to his daughter (my mother, a daughter?!) if only to tell her that he'd married for a third time, a woman who was younger than she was and who only spoke Serbo-Croat. He was 71 now and they'd had this baby and the baby was my uncle, though I was nearly 7 years old.

Well, it didn't exactly fit the usual template but it was definitely news. And besides, the pope was dead, so that was all right. I put my hand up.

Miss Crawford scanned the rows of waving arms with an approving smile. Then she saw me: this was a first. 'Kathy,' she said, beaming.

'Please Miss Crawford, the pop's dead and I have a baby uncle.'

There was a fractional pause.

'The *Pope's* dead. Good. That's right,' she nodded approvingly, 'But babies can't be uncles dear. Don't be silly.'

It was all a bit puzzling. How could you have a father and not see him? And how had Austria become South America? How had he got there? And why was he there if we were here? The thoughts flitted and disappeared. In childhood, like so many other family puzzles, that's just how things were. It was many years before I filled in the pieces.

4

From Munich to Vienna

The evidence came later. It had been a long journey. Fritz and Mutti hadn't stayed in Schwaz for long after my mother was born, it seemed. By the time their third child, her younger brother Clemens, was born in 1923 they were living in Munich, capital of the south German state of Bavaria. 'We used to boast that we had a capital city each!' my mother said. 'Vienna for Beate, Innsbruck, capital of Tyrol, for me and Munich for Clemens.' So now there were three children: the cast was complete.

Our Aunt Beate we knew a bit about, the beautiful, temperamental, artistic Beetle, and we knew about Clemens from the stories: he was funny, he was in the photos. That was all. We'd never met him. Did we think it odd? No. He was just another one of the relatives who wasn't there.

Munich was shadowy too. It never got a mention in the stories when we were children, but when I asked later, my mother recalled bits and pieces – first, a rambling house just outside the city at Geiselgasteig and, later, a flat in the centre, near where her father worked – and how her parents had recreated the 'salon' life they'd known in Vienna, with the composers Orff and Eck, the pianist Edwin Fischer and writer Sinclair Lewis among their regular visitors.

Then, in 1931, they moved back to Vienna. I asked my mother why.

'I don't know,' said my mother. 'It was a complete *disaster* anyway. But I think it was to do with something my father saw from his office window.' And passed over it.

Beate, Inge and Clemens, 1927.

There didn't seem to be a story here; just a scatter, a hurry, skips of recollection. Obviously not interesting. I let it go. But when it came to writing the stories down, I wondered again: why did they go to Munich? What was going on around them and how far did it affect them? And, incidentally, how does it get decided what is or isn't a story?

I looked it up; events followed on from what had gone before like a bad dream. In the years after the First World War (1919–21), while the new state of Austria was in the throes of hunger, inflation and economic collapse, Germany, its boundaries more or less intact, seemed at first to be doing slightly better. Despite the flood of soldiers returning from the war damaged in mind and body, despite the threat of revolution, a mutiny in the navy and Berlin's Spartacist Revolt of 1919, the country was somehow still functioning. Compared with Austria, inflation was moving slowly and Germans could take advantage of crossing the Austrian border to buy valuable goods for next to nothing or, when that was stopped, to drink themselves paralytic for a fraction of the price it cost at home. Relatively speaking, Germany was doing all right.

Maybe this was what turned Fritz and Mutti's eyes towards Munich: there was the prospect of a steady job for Fritz, the economy looked relatively stable, and it was a capital city with a rich cultural life (even if it wasn't Vienna). Best of all, it wasn't far from Schwaz — just the other side of the Karwendel Mountains — the house there would still be within easy reach for holidays and weekends.

Frying pans and fires come to mind. Their timing couldn't have been worse.

In the peace treaties that followed the First World War, Britain and France and their victorious allies demanded that Germany, Austria and Hungary should pay them compensation for the costs and damage of the war they'd started. In 1921 — the year Austrian inflation was finally brought under control, and just when Mutti and Fritz decided to move — the Allies claimed from Germany the enormous sum of 269 billion gold marks (£23.6 billion). This was three times the value of all the property in the country. And though later that year the sum was reduced to a mere 132 billion marks, the payments, 1.7 billion marks a year for the next fifty-nine years, remained crippling.

These were not the promised terms of the peace. To the nationalists in the country, smarting under the humiliation of defeat, their government's agreement to pay reparations was a betrayal, an insult to national dignity. They looked around for someone to blame: the Jews and Social Democrats who had lobbied for the peace fitted the bill. They were sure to be lining their own pockets in the process.

With an economy already damaged by war and further threatened by disease and the possibility of revolution, the German Government resorted to printing money. There were thirty paper mills and 132 printers doing nothing else until a staggering 10 billion notes were in circulation.

Before 1921, four German marks would buy one US dollar. But when the announcement of reparations came, the value of the mark began to fall. In June 1922, the Foreign Minister, an eminent Jewish industrialist and founder of the German Democratic Party called Walther Rathenau, was assassinated by ultra-nationalist army officers who were furious at the government's consent to reparations, and the fall of the mark accelerated. What followed made the Austrian inflation seem like a picnic.

On the day of Rathenau's murder, the exchange rate was 350 marks to the dollar. By the end of July, it was 670; in August it was 2,000 marks. The German Government asked for a pause in the repayments. The French wouldn't hear of it and, when the Germans stopped paying anyway, sent their army to occupy the Ruhr, the heartland of German industry. The mark continued to fall.

By January 1923 it took 18,000 marks to buy one dollar, by July it was 160,000 and by August 1 million marks. As people realised their money was losing value, they queued at the banks to withdraw their life savings and spend them before they disappeared. The banks were on the brink of collapse; the Treasury printed even more banknotes.

With prices doubling every forty-eight hours, wages were paid in money that was worthless. Food cost billions of marks. It took a wheelbarrow full of notes to buy a loaf of bread, Mutti told my mother, 100 million marks for an egg. It was, they said, cheaper to keep warm by burning banknotes than by trying to buy firewood with them. There were hunger riots.

Going up. Stamps from the German inflation.

Forty years later, after I had stuck the flowering Argentina stamps from the baby uncle letter and my invisible grandfather into my brand-new stamp album, one day when I was ill and bored, my mother took down an old, brown, leather-bound book from the old, brown, leather-bound book shelf that we never looked at. We blew off the dust and opened it up and there was her father's, that same grandfather Fritz's, stamp collection. In the pages headed 'Deutschland', were some ugly looking stamps with numbers on them, rows of noughts, some of them overprinted, 1,000, 100,000, 1 million marks just to post a letter.

Life went on anyway, but my mother didn't remember anything interesting about it. There were no stories. When I asked her again at the end of her life, she dredged up from her memory Senta, the maid, and Käthe, the cook, who was so short that tall Fritz would lift her up to stand on a chest so they could talk eye to eye. She remembered starting school at Fraulein Deuringer's, who taught seven classes in one room – brilliantly. 'She taught me to read and to write and to sing, we sang all the time. And she taught me how to concentrate in a room where everything was going on around me.'

But of the inflation and the hunger – nothing.

Her cousin Jean, who was six years older and lived in Austria, likewise only remembered how angry his mother was on her birthday around this time when he and his brother and sister proudly presented her with the sugar lumps they had saved up from the one a day they were given to keep up their strength. He told me about it at the age of 93.

But memory lurks in strange places.

Tins

All through my childhood in 1950s and 1960s London, among the kitchen cupboards of our house, my mother had a wall cupboard where she kept tins. There were cans of beans, tomatoes, sweet corn, tuna fish and peaches with shiny coloured labels all stacked on top of each other: these were luxuries at the time. And, as if by magic, the tins cupboard was always, *always* full. Whenever, as a special treat, a tin was actually used, it had to be replaced immediately, and later in the 1970s, when the house filled up with lodgers and students, my generous mother, most untypically, installed a hidden lock, a bolt that dropped down through a hole drilled from above.

When I set up home for myself I assumed that all kitchens had a cupboard like this, just as they had a sink, taps, a fridge or a cooker: a tins cupboard. Full. I never even thought about it, just established one of my own, and was shocked, indignant even, when challenged by my partner as to why such a thing was necessary and why it had to be always bulging at the seams when the shelf-full supermarket was only a short way up the road. I couldn't answer. Because. Just because.

Then one day, my father told me about the time when he came back to England at the end of the Second World War, and how, newly reunited with my mother after a five-year separation, they went to visit Mutti, who was by this time living in a small village in Dorset called Fontmell Magna. She lived not far from the church in a cottage called Myrtle Cottage, with a thatched roof and roses round the door and a garden and beyond it a field with an old, dilapidated stable building camouflaged with weeds.

Mutti took my father aside one afternoon and confided that she had a problem. Could he help? Of course. She made sure nobody

Myrtle Cottage, Fontmell Magna, Dorset.

was watching, led him up the field to the old stable, through the net-
tles, past the listing door and into the shadows at the back, where she
pushed aside the straw with her foot and pointed at the ground. There,
in a hole, lay a great heap of tins, the labels peeling off or gone, rusting,
bulging, many of them burst.

This was 1945, the days following the Second World War, more than
twenty years after the great inflation in Germany and nearer thirty
from the Austrian starvation – and though this time Mutti was living in
the country of the victors and there was no starvation, conditions were
austere. Britain was battered and exhausted, hoarding was against the
law and food was, if not short, strictly rationed then and for a number
of years to come. The contents of these tins would have been unspeak-
able luxuries.

Who knows what memories, what images of empty shops and
worthless paper money in Vienna or barter in Munich the build-up
to this Second World War had triggered when, five or six years earlier, Mutti had gathered up these tins and hidden them away. But
when war was declared and rationing was introduced and hoarding
became a criminal offence, she had been too ashamed ever to use
her emergency supplies. Or was it that the starvation she feared or
remembered never came? All through the five years of the war, while
the rain rained and the stable roof leaked, the tins lay there in their
hiding place, rusting undisturbed.

That night, my father celebrated his return by creeping outside in the
small hours like a thief and, without a light, digging a huge pit in the
field, burying the lot and covering it all up as if nothing had ever been.

In Munich in the 1920s Mutti and Fritz had managed. They were relatively well off. Fritz, after all, had a job in a bank. His office in the
centre of the city was in a fine location overlooking the Odeonsplatz
and at the end of it, the Feldherrnhalle, a nineteenth-century monument to the victorious generals of the Bavarian Army, with its three
round arches in the style of the Italian Renaissance.

There were plenty of others in Munich who'd come from Vienna too.
Among them was a failed artist called Adolf Hitler, who had left a life

The Feldherrnhalle, Munich, 1930s.

selling postcards in the street there and moved to the Bavarian capital in 1913. Seven years later, and just ten days before Mutti tobogganed down the mountain to give birth to my mother in 1920, he too had given birth, founding at Munich's Sterneckerbräu brewery his National Socialist Party, the NSDAP, the Nazis for short. By the time Clemens was born in Munich in 1923, the capital the children claimed as 'his' was in fact already spoken for: it was the '*Haupstadt der Bewegung*', the capital of the National Socialist movement, and 1923 was a critical year.

In the inflationary chaos that was now unfolding in Germany, extremist groups like Hitler's thrived. 'Nothing ever embittered the German people so much – it is important to remember this – nothing made them so furious with hate and so ripe for Hitler as the inflation.'[1] With 55,000 members, the National Socialists were the largest of these groups and notorious for their 'monitor troops', bands of thugs who specialised in harassing Jews and political opponents in swift and brutal attacks on the street.

In 1923 when, in a deeply unpopular move, the German Government decided to resume paying war reparations, there were widespread protests. And as the mark plummeted to a new low of 4 trillion marks to the dollar, Hitler decided it was time to overthrow the German democratic government in Berlin.

The plan was to kidnap the leaders of the Bavarian Government at a dinner in a beer hall on 8 November and persuade them, at gunpoint, to accept Hitler as their leader. Where the Bavarian Government led, the army would surely follow, and with it would come the glorious 'National Revolution'.

On the morning of 9 November, the people of Munich woke to find their city in disarray. Though the Beer Hall Putsch, as it became known, had not gone quite according to plan the previous evening, and the National Socialists had failed to take over the army barracks or turn the police, undeterred, Hitler and 3,000 followers were marching on the centre of the city to seize power.

When the march reached the Feldherrnhalle, its way was blocked by a line of armed police. Hitler called on them to surrender. Instead, they fired. Beneath my grandfather's office window, twenty people died, sixteen demonstrators and four policemen. Hitler, unharmed, hid out for a few days before he was caught, tried and sent to jail, where he spent the next nine months comfortably writing his toxic manifesto, *Mein Kampf*.

So, this was what my grandfather saw from his window. Shocking certainly, and violent, a sign of what was in the wind, but could this really be the 'disaster'? My mother, 3 years old at the time, didn't even know what had happened. And if the Putsch was the reason the family moved to Vienna, there was certainly a long delay. My grandparents and the children went on living in Munich, with trips to Schwaz for weekends and holidays, for another eight years. It was a time of relative calm.

In 1924 German inflation was finally brought under control. A new currency was created: each billion old marks replaced with just one of the new – though the rage of nationalism was not so easily tamed. The 'Golden Era' that followed was one of relative stability in Germany. Under the leadership of Gustav Stresemann, reparations were geared to what the country could pay. Germany was admitted to the League of Nations. There was reconciliation with France and French troops withdrew from the Ruhr. But the improvement was fragile: the overseas loans that paid for the reforms were stacking up the debt, trade was in decline and by 1928 prices were falling and unemployment rising. The year 1929 brought not only the sudden death of Stresemann but the great Wall Street Crash that reverberated around the world.

It was not long after – was there a connection? – that my grandparents left the big house on the outskirts of Munich and moved to a flat in the Widenmayrstrasse, in the centre of town. When I pressed her, my mother, who was 9 at the time, came up with all the 9-year-old essentials: the big building with the courtyard in the centre, the River Isar running nearby, the wide balcony outside the kitchen and, of course, their animals. 'We had a complete zoo! There was a snake, and a cockerel that sat on the balcony and crowed the rest of the Widenmayrstrasse to distraction. We had a dog and birds and, one school holiday, two guinea pigs at the beginning and twelve by the end.'

She remembered rehearsing for a new microtonal opera called *Die Mutter*[*] – singing quarter tones by ear with ease to the frustration of the professionals who were having trouble with the strange new intervals – until, racing a friend round the courtyard one day, she put her arm through a window and the gash turned septic and put her out of the show. Childhood mishaps.

It was all disappointingly dull: scraps, bits and pieces that came to the surface like flotsam. They lacked zest and colour somehow. My mother didn't seem very interested either, she hurried past as if they weren't worth lingering on. So, there was no Munich story then.

And yet. It was an illness that changed that – my illness, and the memory of theirs.

Tonsillitis

If there was one thing I was good at as a child it was getting ill. Tonsillitis was my speciality. The signs were familiar – the shiver in the spine, the prickling head, the heavy weariness at night and waking in the morning with raw pain flaring in my throat, my tonsils huge and spotted with pus, neck stiff with swollen glands.

My sister had had her tonsils out when she was only 2. It was common practice then, but by the 1950s it had fallen out of favour: the age of antibiotics had arrived. And so, at least four times a year,

---

[*] *Die Mutter* by Alois Hába was first performed in 1931 in Munich.

I would spend the best part of a week tucked up in bed with my teddy bears and my books, drifting in and out of sleep with, beside me on the shelf, the glass with the thermometer and the measuring spoon standing in Dettol, the bottle of sticky, pink penicillin and the drink for taking away the taste.

From time to time, my mother would appear with ice cubes or blackcurrant pastilles to soothe my throat, and, as I got better, things to keep me occupied. And every four hours she'd dish up another spoonful of penicillin.

'It's horrible!'

'I know. But it works,' she'd say and sometimes tell me again about the mould that grew by accident in Alexander Fleming's Petri dish and how, for a while during the war, she had worked as a laboratory assistant in the lab at St Mary's Hospital where he had discovered penicillin.

Swallowing hurt. The tears ran down my cheeks.

'I know,' she said. 'I had tonsillitis too when I was a child … in Munich.' And here was another story.

'That was long before antibiotics were discovered and tonsillitis was a bad illness. It took a long time to recover from. That's why they took people's tonsils out,' said my mother. 'When I got ill, Beate and Clem had already had theirs out, so they didn't get it. But then they both got something even worse: a terrible infection of the kidneys and they had to go into hospital. This was in Munich, and they were very ill indeed. The doctors told my parents that they had found the same streptococcus bug that I had in my tonsils infecting my brother and sister but because they had no tonsils to protect them it had gone to their kidneys.'

'So then,' my mother said, 'they decided I had better have my tonsils out too. And all three of us were in the same hospital. I was a strong child, I bounced back from the operation really fast and was soon home and fine again. But Beate and Clemens were still ill. They were really weak. Beate had always been fragile and highly strung, and now she'd stopped eating. She was getting thinner and thinner every day. My parents were beside themselves. And this was when, one day after new snow had fallen, Mutti had had enough and she wrapped Beate up in blankets, put her in a wheelchair and wheeled her out into the snow. "Look," she said, "are you sure you never want to go back to Schwaz again?" And that did it. Beate started eating again. And eventually she and Clemens started to get better. But it was slow.'

All this was around 1930–31. Outside the walls of their sick room the situation was growing more serious: the Depression was deepening around the world, and in Germany rising unemployment brought growing political instability, antisemitism, violence. In September 1930, Germany's general election brought a sobering result: five times more people voted for the Nazi Party than at the previous elections two years before. They now had 18.3 per cent of the vote: the Parliament had lost its moderate majority and the Social Democratic Government fell. The violence and terror in the streets grew.

How do people know when it's time to leave? I used to dream about this as a child, scenario after scenario, though why, when I had known only security and peace in 1950s London, I should be dreaming the dreams of two generations earlier is an interesting question.

Looking at the sequence of events, it seems quite possible that the 1930 election or the trouble in the banks were the last straw for Fritz and Mutti. Maybe he lost his job, for they moved back to Vienna within a matter of months.

'It was just to try it out for a year,' my mother said, and when I asked her, 'Why?' again, she answered, 'Mutti didn't like the violence, the goings-on of those khaki people. Hindenburg, the President, he was more or less all right, but Hitler was a very bad word in a childish ear … They left Munich to see if Vienna was any better …'

A pause.

'It was a *disaster*!' There was that phrase again.

'Why?'

She thought for a bit.

'… We had to leave all the animals behind!'

There was a certain logic to the move. Austria was not Germany. Vienna was not the 'capital of the Nazi movement'. Most of Fritz's family were there: his parents, Josef Schey, the law professor, and his formidable wife Hansi, and all his Schey brothers and sisters. It might be further from Schwaz but Fritz's eldest sister, Gerda, and her husband, Herman Goldschmidt, had a country house at Erla, near Linz, where the family gathered in the summer and at weekends, and for Inge and Beate there was a new school, the *Frauenerwerbverein*

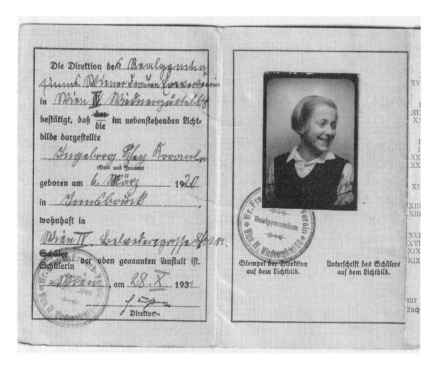

Inge's school ID card, Vienna, 1931.

(Establishment for the Improvement of Women), swiftly nicknamed the *Frauenverderbverein* (Establishment for the Damaging of Women). But the move was not a success. Things were starting to unravel.

The city they came back to was not the Vienna of Fritz and Anny's youth – and anything but stable. The empire had gone, titles had been abolished, Austria was now a republic. Vienna itself, run since the end of the war by the left-wing Social Democrats, had embarked on progressive social and economic policies, earning the name 'Red Vienna' for its eight-hour working day, unemployment benefit, tax on luxuries, an overhauled school system and a famous venture in public housing – 60,000 workers' flats in super-blocks that were virtually independent cities within the city. But it was out of step with the rest of the country – resentment was brewing.

After 650 years of imperial rule, the new democracy was fragile. As in Germany, violence and militarism had come back from the First World War with the returning soldiers. There were political militias here too – uniformed and armed paramilitary groups, including the right-wing *Heimwehr*, formed from local guards in 1918, and the Social Democrats *Schutzbund*, formed in 1923–24. The situation was polarised, unstable.

Violent demonstrations in 1927 saw the Palace of Justice set on fire and militias fighting in the streets for control of the city. Antisemitism was rife. The Depression only made things worse. In May 1931 Vienna's biggest bank, the Creditanstalt, went bust. There were plenty of unemployed – was Fritz one of them?

Some people clung to the wreckage. As George Clare writes:

It was an unhappy country, the remnant of the huge Monarchy with a capital, Vienna, suitable for the Empire that had been, but far too big for the dwarf state that it became. Neither the country nor the city had come to terms with their dismal present. Most Austrians dreamed of their splendid past, disliked the world as it was and feared the future – quite rightly as it turned out. Theirs was now a country which one Austrian historian aptly called 'The state nobody wanted'.[2]

As I tried to pull the scraps together and pondered over what exactly constituted the 'disaster' my mother spoke about, it took a while to connect the last piece. Although adventures would be turned into stories and illnesses could be anecdotes, there were certain things it seemed – money, sex, grief, betrayal and the darker side of private lives – which weren't for the telling. (Or was it just that I was hearing it through a double layer of childhood shelter?) These silences had their own power.

When my mother was coming to the end of her life and I was in my forties, I ran back through it with her wanting, if nothing else, a few more scraps, a chronology, and to be sure. That's how I heard the coda.

'What happened to Beate and Clemens after the hospital bit? Were they ok?' I was asking.

'Not really.' She sounded matter of fact. 'They were still very weak when they came out and the doctors said that another infection would almost certainly kill them unless they could build up their strength and that they had to go away to somewhere healthy to convalesce. So Mutti took them off to the sea or the mountains or somewhere. And I was left behind with my father in the flat.'

Boring. Boring.

'What was he like?'

'He was very glamorous, extremely good looking, he sent us post-cards with poems he'd written for us, he played the violin and he could play anything on the piano by ear. He was writing a novel* and would read it out to us.[3] He was a real butterfly. And I was his favourite because I could always make him laugh.'

She was not his only favourite. Fritz had never been short of admirers and now, in a world where, after the slaughter of the First World War, women greatly outnumbered men, there were plenty of them.

I was hardly listening. My mother only said it once – a passing mention, drab fact. It sounded slight compared to the colour and energy of the rest.

'And while Mutti was away with Beate and Clem, getting them better, my father moved his girlfriend, May, and her daughter [also, confusingly, called May] into the flat to live with us.'

There were consequences. When Mutti returned: enough. Not only was her husband publicly humiliating her with his girlfriend, but Vienna, with its political instability on the one hand and its snobbery and hierarchies, its backbiting and forelock-tugging to the three little baron and baronesses von Schey, was not a place she wanted her children to grow up in. There was tittle-tattle about her too, possibly scandal, though I've never found it. Besides, Germany had followed them to Austria: the Nazi influence was growing, the swastikas were spreading.

My mother was 11 years old. She recalled almost nothing about that Vienna year except for one small scene. A moment. A feeling.

She is standing with her best friend from school in the playground, or maybe the street, chatting, giggling, laughing together as children do. The ground is littered with election leaflets. 'Who are your parents going to vote for?'

The friend drops her eyes and doesn't answer. She just stares at the ground and putting the toe of her shoe on a piece of paper printed with a fat, black swastika, she pushes it round and round in circles.

---

* 'Nobody read it!' said my mother.

Mutti decided it was time to go. Leaving her husband, her marriage and her homeland, she took the children and set out for Italy. It was 1931.

5

Long Division

Twenty-five years later it was our turn. In 1956, when my sister was 10 and I was 7, my mother also decided it was time to take us away.

How far the past works as a blueprint is an open question. Maybe what your parents do is just 'how it's done'. But sometimes the parallels are striking. And whether it was a conscious or unconscious echo, my mother had her reasons. After all, it was more than time for us to have another language. There was an urgency about this – any educated person should know *at least* three, you had to start early if you were going to speak without an accent – very important – and here in England people were *so* bad at languages.

What followed was an adventure of our own – and the making of a new story, this time ours.

Snapshot

1956: London, and there's something happening at our house.

'One, two, three o'clock, four o'clock rock!'

Unless I'm up the tree by the front wall, I'm pretty small. Mick the builder's boy is pretty tall. He looks like no one else we've ever seen. His hair is lacquer black, slicked up into a shiny question mark at the front and a sticking-out bit at the back, with long sideburns running down the side of his cheeks. He wears a long jacket, drainpipe trousers moulded to his skinny legs and long, black, pointed, fascinating, winkle-picker shoes with silver buckles.

'Five, six, seven o'clock, eight o'clock rock!'

Mick's nice. He smiles. He can whistle with trills and frilly bits like nobody else. He dances around with his shovel and he sings.

'Nine, ten, eleven o'clock, twelve o'clock rock!
'We're going to rock around the clock tonight!'

And what's he doing? He's mixing sand and cement in a big pile in the front drive and wheeling it by the barrow-load into our house.

'So put your glad rags on and we'll have some fun!
'We're gonna rock around till the day is done.'

When Mick gets a break he takes us by the hand and shows us how to jive round the sand pile. We love it. My father says Mick is a 'Teddy Boy' and he doesn't seem to mean it as a compliment.

'We're gonna rock around the clock tonight.
'We're gonna rock, rock, rock till the broad daylight,
'We're gonna rock, we're gonna rock around the clock tonight!'

Change is in the air.

In a daring move, my parents had finally bought the freehold of the house-that-looked-like-a-church from their landlords, the Church Commissioners. At £900 it was a bargain, even for those days, but then the place was a liability. My father decided that the only way to manage was to divide it into two houses: one at the front, which could be sold to cover the cost and, at the back, in what used to be the servants' quarters, a smaller house for us, keeping the lion's share of the garden and, of course, our beloved, slimy-green swimming pool.

It was going to be a whole winter of messy building work, the house uninhabitable. Rather than wrestle on with the rubble and dust, my mother saw it as the perfect opportunity to take us off on an adventure.

The British economy was overheating at the time and under special rules introduced to sort out the 'balance of payments' crisis, nobody was allowed to take more than £50 out of the country in any one year. Was this going to stop my mother? Of course not. Leaving the dog in kennels and the builders and the house to my father, she loaded my sister and myself into the car that had replaced the old Austin and, taking a total of £150 with her, set off for Paris.

Of course I *knew* that there were other countries in the world, but it was only on the road to Dover as I listened to my sister and my mother talking about France and French that I suddenly understood for the first time that we were really going to *live* in a place where everything was different and where I wouldn't be able to understand or speak a word. As soon as we had crossed the Channel in a ferry belching smoke, my mother switched to speaking French so effortlessly it seemed quite natural. It couldn't be impossible then.

France was certainly different. The food, the water (don't drink from the taps!), the hole with two footplates lavatories, and strange foods like yoghurt, which didn't exist at the time in battered Britain where rationing was only just coming to an end.

Arriving in Paris we went to stay in a *pension*, a guest house near the Bois de Boulogne that was full of strange smells and different sounds and a collection of elderly residents who seemed alarmingly interested in us. The friendly ones expected to be kissed on both cheeks at breakfast and kept bending down and chucking us under the chin as they passed in the long, dark corridors. But within a day or two, my sister and I put on our special school *tabliers** over the top of our clothes and went off to school at the Cours de la Terrasse.

I had it easy. At school in London, I had to read and write and had just got on to long division. (Somewhere in the suitcase was an exercise book full of sums I was supposed to practise on while we were away.) Here, where children started school a whole year later, I was put into the Kindergarten, where I spent the first morning drawing pictures of giraffes to much praise from Mademoiselle. This was all right.

My sister, three years older, had a harder time. She was expected to read and write in French with a curly cursive script and to switch from our pounds, shillings and pence, inches and feet to metric system maths, a move which left her muddled and confused for a long time after. Then there was the language.

At the end of the first morning, we were among the children who stayed behind for lunch. We sat at a big table with the teachers and to our amazement were offered wine to drink and at least three courses of food. Then we were sent out to play in the walled yard that was the playground.

I stood there, not knowing anyone and unable to speak a word of French. A child came up and said something to me. I hadn't a clue. Another ran past and shouted something else. Others laughed. Several children stood at a distance and stared in my direction, whispering to each other. Finally, one child picked up a stone and threw it at me in an experimental kind of way. It missed. The dust spurted and I took a step back. Then someone else tried: closer this time. I backed away again, and again, as other stones came until I found myself with my back against the schoolyard wall unable to retreat any further. And the stones were still coming. Maybe this was what you did in France? I bent down and picked up a stone too.

I was not good at throwing. Something about the holding on and the letting go always eluded me and nothing ever went in the direction I meant it to. But if this was the way things were done here, well ... I could try.

The stone flew but I couldn't see where it had gone. Then there was a thud and a silence and a cry. And suddenly there was a child on

---

* Pinafores.

102

the other side of the yard with blood on his forehead and the others all gathering round him, only turning to scowl back at me over their shoulders as they led him indoors to find the teachers. I felt sick. I'm sure it wasn't meant to be like this. I'd hurt someone. I hadn't meant to. I don't like this. I want to go home.

The adults came. The blood was staunched. The wound wasn't serious. Peace was made and class resumed for the afternoon, where I took refuge in copying double-looped fs from a handwriting sheet onto pages that looked like crazy graph paper. When lessons ended we each had to shake Mademoiselle's hand as we left the classroom, then we filed out past the kitchen where we were handed a piece of hot French bread with a lump of dark chocolate stuffed into the middle of it. Bread and what?

My mother was waiting for us outside on the pavement and my sister was already pouring out her news.

'And how about you?' my mother asked, giving me a hug.

'How do you say "Leave me alone!" in French?'

'*Laisse moi tranquille*,' said my mother. 'Why?'

'Lessmwartron ...'

'*Laisse moi tranquille.*'

'*Laisse moi tranquille, laissemoi tranquille, laissemoitranquille*,' I muttered it over and over again, tuning it, polishing it, holding onto it like a talisman, a shield, all the way back to our room at the *pension* and all the way out to school the following morning. And so I began to learn French.

Inspiration

£150 was not going to last forever. After about ten days my mother broke the news that we were going to find somewhere else to live, somewhere of our own, somewhere less expensive. We were going for a walk at the time, through the park and along some raised ground overlooking the River Seine as it ran through Le Port-Marly and on into the centre of Paris. 'Look!' said my sister, pointing down at the river, 'What about one of those?'

She was pointing at the *péniches*, the big Seine barges that were growling along the river below us. With their small cabins and huge long holds they were much wider and bigger than English canal boats and on some of them you could see bicycles, children and dogs as well as the barge men and women – whole families living on board. At the edge of the river below us there was even a kind of boatyard where rows of empty and apparently abandoned barges were moored alongside each other, three or four deep in places, quietly rotting.

'Why not!' said my mother, and down we went.

Monsieur Deumeuré, the manager of the boat yard, was sitting inside the wooden hut that served as his office, under the big sign saying '*Halle de la Marine*'. It was surrounded by hanks of rope, chunks of metal, old timbers, wrecked engines and pools of oil and he looked a bit surprised when my mother walked in with two little girls in tow. These were not perhaps his usual customers.

He and my mother began to talk. They chatted away in French, then they began to jabber. He waved his arms and shook his head. She smiled and spread her hands. He looked discouraging and wagged his finger. She batted her eyelashes and made him laugh. And in the end he shrugged his shoulders and couldn't hide a smile as he called one of his men in from outside.

Next thing, we were being taken on a tour of the boatyard, jumping from one huge barge to another and walking sideways for the first time along the narrow walkways at the edge of their decks with the scummy brown current of the river racing along below. Most of these giant working boats hadn't been used for years. There was even one that had been a floating church for the barge community. Now, like all the rest, it was empty, mouldy and damp. When we got back to the office there was more talking, laughing, and by the time we set off to walk back to the *pension*, my mother and Monsieur Deumeuré shook hands as if they were the oldest and the best of friends. That's how it was with my mother.

And that's how we came to live on a disused coal barge called *Louis* on the River Seine at Le Port-Marly all through the winter of 1956–57, my sister, my mother and I.

My sister's painting of the *Louis*, the *péniche*.

The *Halle de la Marine*, M. Demeuré's office.

A Barge Called Louis

Things moved fast once Monsieur Deumeuré had agreed. The *Louis*, out of action for many years, was towed from its place among the other hulks to a mooring right beside the riverbank with a row of trees and a petrol station above. The hatch to the galley, which had been screwed shut for twenty years, was prised open and, when the reek of damp and mould had started to disperse, we climbed down the steep ladder to scrub and clean the little space that was to be our kitchen.

A water supply was rigged up: a long, black hosepipe connected to a tap on the island about 300m away in the middle of the river. Monsieur Deumeuré and his men built a wooden shed on the main deck to serve as our living room and a place for my mother to sleep and the nearest of the coal holds was opened and we spent a day whitewashing it out for my sister and I to sleep in. Finally, a smart wooden gangplank connected us to the riverbank beside the boat. There it was: our very own home.

All through the winter and into the spring we lived on the *Louis*, my sister and I, with the hatch to our hold propped open day and night, frost and ice, and on one exciting morning, snowflakes floating past.

The *Louis*, Le Port-Marly, 1957.

And I, who had always been sickly with colds and tonsillitis and every childhood ailment going, wasn't ill once. We had plenty of clothes but no heating that I can remember. We 'adopted' as a pet the single huge goldfish that swam round and round the barge when it felt like it, and from time to time, for added excitement, the longest and most disgusting yellow slugs we had ever seen would appear in our kitchen sink, crawling up the waste-pipe from the river below.

My mother made a bedcover and curtains for the cabin out of coloured floor cloths from the local Monoprix and when one night she couldn't sleep for the cold, she simply lifted the cabin door off its hinges and put it on top of her for an extra layer of warmth. We were fine.

My sister and I carried on at school and new chunks of French soon stuck to the first ones like loose snow sticking to a snowball. Gradually, it gathered momentum and started to roll and when, one weekend, our father came to visit, bringing us messages and homework from our English school (long division again) and news of the dog and the builders, it was odd to hear how awkwardly he spoke French and how strangely out of place he seemed in our new world, and we were faintly relieved when the time came for him to go home.

When the money ran out, my mother, who spoke four languages, put on her one set of smart clothes and took a job as a multilingual secretary to a Russian count who lived in a smart part of Paris and was convinced she lived on a luxury yacht. When things were tight we would sing the two- and three-part songs we knew for our suppers – it was fun. And all the time the River Seine flowed past, brown and swirling, and on it an endless succession of working barges carrying goods – coal, flour, bicycles, grain – into Paris, and rubbish out. And the bargees would wave at us and probably wonder why we never did any work or went anywhere.

Because, whatever the Russian count thought, this was not a place or a time for yachts, pleasure craft or houseboats. At Le Port-Marly, the boats were either working or abandoned. Except for *Louis*. And yet, we weren't alone. Although there weren't any officially occupied boats around us, there were always the young men who came stepping past from one empty barge to another as if strolling on a pavement. They waved at us, greeted my mother, smiled and even played with us. They had dark eyes, brown skin, beautiful Arabic names and they spoke French with strange, strong, throaty accents. My mother would make them tea and sit and talk.

They came from North Africa, from Algeria, she said, and they hadn't got the right papers, so they couldn't get jobs in France, or money, or a proper place to live, and they weren't keen on the police, or *gendarmes*, knowing they were there. 'Sssh.'

This was at the height of the Algerian War of Independence. Still officially a colony of France, the Algerians had been fighting for many years to win their independence. The Battle of Algiers had been going on since the previous September and 400,000 French troops were trying by the bloodiest means to hold onto their former colony while the Algerian rebels were trying with equally bloody means to get rid of them. For whatever reasons, these young men had fled from the war in their country and were now living rough on the *péniches* in Paris, homesick, unofficial, on the run.

And when one morning, after days of heavy rain, we woke to find the Seine had burst its banks, leaving us floating high above the flooded towpath and closer to the tops of the trees than their trunks standing in the swirl, while the gangplank, which had always taken us straight onto dry land, now pointed steeply down into a wide stretch of swirling filthy water inexplicably awash with wine-bottle corks, as we stood and wondered how we were going to get ashore, it was one of the young Algerians who appeared – as if by magic – in a battered red canoe to ferry us onto dry land in time for school and work.

Eventually, our time in Paris came to an end. Then it was back to London, home and my father. I don't remember much about the changes to the house. Seeing our dog again and climbing my favourite trees were much more important, as was squeezing through the gap in the fence to catch up with my friend Weezy, who lived in the bottom part of the house next door. Her family had a television now and, by special dispensation, we could go and watch *Lassie* and *The Lone Ranger* and live out their adventures for the rest of the week on imaginary horses in the back garden. Then there were the builders who were still finishing off. They were much more interesting.

French

Soon we had to go back to real school, back to scratchy, tweed uniform, brown knickers, rows of little girls and the dreaded long division I'd never quite mastered in Paris. The teacher greeted our class with important news. 'This term,' she announced solemnly, 'we're going to start learning French.' Pause. 'I expect some of you know a few words already.'

I put my hand up. 'Please, Miss,' I said. 'I know some French.'

'Oh?' she said, raising an eyebrow, not exactly pleased, 'Well, if you stay behind at the end of the lesson we'll see what you can do.'

When everyone else had gone, she gave me a pencil and a piece of paper and walked up and down the empty classroom dictating a long passage in French for me to write down. I understood every word. I could also hear that she had a strong English accent and that the notes of the tune were in the wrong place. But writing it down was something else.

I had spent a lot of time in my French Kindergarten drawing horses and giraffes, perfecting crossed 7s and the swirling, loopy letters that made up French handwriting – and for this I had earned smiles and kisses and '*bons points*' from *Mademoiselle*. As children do, I'd also quickly learned to understand and speak French with ease and fluency and an almost perfect accent. But disentangling one word from another was another matter. As far as I knew, phrases like '*je ne sais pas*' and '*il y'a*' were as much single chunks of language as my original '*laissemoi-tranquille*'. Where one word ended and another began was not at all clear. I did what I could.

When I'd finished, the teacher read over what I had written with satisfaction. 'I thought so,' she said, smiling restored. 'You'll just have to start at the beginning like everybody else.'

We were back.

But not quite the same.

As for our time in Paris, it took up a place of its own, just a bit outside normal life (and not necessarily welcome there). The experience, vital and fun to us, settled, encapsulated. Ignored by everyday, it sat there – normal for us, not normal for others, our friends, teachers, even our father. If somebody wanted to know or wondered how we came to speak fluent French, it could, of course, be told. And slowly the telling turned into an entertainment, an explanation, a story of our own. If it was other, then so were we.

The under-theme, the growing strain in our parents' marriage, was invisible, untold and as hard to see or extract as the roots of a tooth – just like my mother's memories of 1931 Vienna, a generation before. What was the point of remembering that?

6

Journeys

After Paris we were fledged. Old enough now, and fluent at least in one language other than English, our travelling days began in earnest. My mother took us roaming whenever the opportunity could be found. It was as if something had given way, she had reverted to being herself.

My father was travelling too, but in a different direction. Born and brought up in Chile till the age of 7, then schooled in Britain, he had spent the five years of the Second World War in the Middle East, mainly Turkey, and now more and more of his architectural work was coming from that part of the world. He went to the Lebanon, Kuwait, Yemen for weeks and sometimes months at a time, during which he sent us wonderful letters just as he had to our mother through their long wartime separation, illustrated with ink-and-wash drawings of interesting things: big men on small donkeys, children flying kites, people at the market, villagers and views. 'I'm so sorry to miss your holidays but you must just be your clever and nice selves and don't *WORRY* ... I will be back all right.' And we replied with letters and pictures of our own.

When he wasn't away, he was working long hours at the office, or sitting over his drawing board at home late into the night, shrouded in smoke, exhausted in the morning. Preoccupied. 'Ssh! Daddy's working.'

A second bed appeared in their bedroom. He was too busy for holidays.

We hardly saw him or the two of them together. It didn't seem strange. That was just how it was.

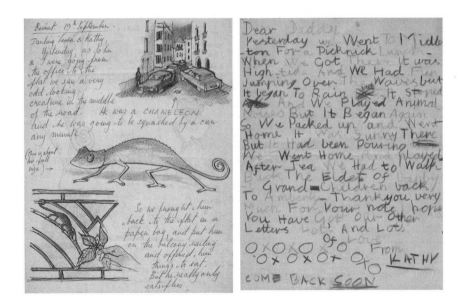

Letter from my father, 1957, and from me to him, 1958.

Cars

In 1959 my mother got a new car – a whole new kind of car – a match-box on wheels called a Mini. One of the first. It was squat, cherry red, with windows that slid sideways and doors that you opened by pulling a string.

As soon as school was over, on the first or second day of the summer holidays, she would get out the roof rack and fix it onto the car. On top went an enormous waterproof canvas bag she'd had made for the purpose and into that went the tent, the camping stove, saucepans, plates and cutlery, a bag of clothes and a bedding roll each, and more, until the sack bulged to half the height of the car again and every pocket and space inside was stuffed to capacity too. Then the three of us would squeeze into what little room was left and set off for Dover.

Where were we going? I wasn't always sure. South. And there'd be camping and sunshine and talking other languages, and beaches and strangers who became friends; time stretched out forever and the world, this world of my mother's that she gave to us, was a Europe without boundaries (except, of course, for the Iron Curtain blocking the way to the East).

This was not so usual at the time. In the early 1960s cheap package holidays and bargain flights had not yet arrived. Most people at school spent their summer holidays in the English countryside or at the seaside with their families. We had done something similar until then, huddling on windswept English beaches, where my mother made fires out of driftwood and cooked risotto in a blackened pan with the shrimps we caught in our shrimping nets. Now we crossed the Channel. It wasn't about money but horizons: my mother's world was wide.

The car was small, noisy and hot with a lingering smell of petrol, no seat belts, no car radio, no sound system. Lying curled up on the back seat, I'd watch the poplar trees flick past huge fields of bright yellow mustard as we drove down the long, straight roads of northern France, and get sick on hairpin bends as we climbed up onto the Massif Central or over the Alps. Sometimes we played games to pass the time or sang: rounds and canons – '*Frère Jacques*', 'London's Burning' – three-part songs which my sister knew from school choir – 'The Ash Grove' or 'Linden Lea'— or the Tyrolean folksongs – '*Ein Tiroler*' or '*Alle Vöglein*'

Tessa, Kathy and Inge with the Mini, 1960.

– a rare snatch of German, which my mother had taught us when we were small, squabbling about who would do the top part.

Then there were stories. 'Tell us the one about how you came to England!' This was our favourite – the one about her childhood journey with her mother and her brother and sister when they left Vienna and set out across Europe in the early 1930s as the political situation grew darker. And as we stifled and yawned in the hot little car thirty years later, they became part of us and we part of all that too. This travelling thing was something that our kind of people did: women on adventures, mothers and children. Here was precedent.

When Mutti decided in 1932 to take her three children and leave not only her husband and Vienna but Austria itself, it was a bold move. Unlike my mother's adventure with us in Paris, for them this was a one-way trip.

There were certain practical difficulties. She was short-sighted, spoke other languages badly, if at all, and couldn't drive. Beate and Clemens were still very frail after their illness and, having missed months of school, they needed to catch up on their education. But what Mutti lacked in practical skills she made up for in charm and ingenuity.

The previous year she had taken on a young Harvard graduate called Ettl Renouf* to act as both tutor and driver to Beate and Clemens. Now she loaded them all into the family car – a Studebaker and something of a prize in those days when only very few people had cars – and, with Ettl at the wheel, set off over the mountains to Italy and the seaside town of Alassio.

There they lived by the beach with bare feet and boats and swimming. New friends were made – painters, musicians, writers. American, English, the bohemians of the Mediterranean coast, they flocked to Mutti as people always flocked and visitors came and went. Fritz came to visit from time to time and the three blonde children grew even blonder in the sun and became stronger and healthier by the day.

---

* This was the American Painter Edward Renouf (1906-99) who at the time was planning to be a writer. Nineteen years younger than Mutti, his feelings were intense. His letters and love poems to her are now in the archive of Tate Britain

The Studebaker, 1931.

Another snapshot. There in Alassio, so the story goes, Benito Mussolini, Fascist dictator of Italy, ally of Adolf Hitler and, like him, preoccupied with racial purity and the perfection of the Aryan race, saw the three blonde, blue-eyed children playing on the beach one day.

'If only I could see the father of three such perfect Aryan children!' he exclaimed to his aides.

If only. Fritz was tall, dark haired, brown eyed and born Jewish.

For Mutti, that was close enough. At the end of the summer, when Ettl went back to America, she moved them on again. In September they crossed into France where she rented the house of an English couple – friends of friends of painter friends in Alassio – further along the Mediterranean coast at Cagnes-sur-Mer. The Villa St Anne was high on the hill with a palm tree outside the door, a big carved marble hippopotamus that the children slid around on and a terrace that looked out over the sea.

With Ettl gone, it was time for them to go to school. One morning, my mother said, Mutti called them together, handed them some

Inge on the wall at Villa St Anne, Haut-de-Cagnes, 1932.

Clemens with the rabbits.

money for the bus fare, told them where the bus stop was and sent them off to find a school called the Cours Moulin.

There was the small matter of another language to deal with. 'When we got to school that day,' my mother said, 'I was given a wind-up gramophone and a box of Linguaphone Teach-Yourself-French records and shut in a bathroom to listen to them until I'd learnt it.' She enjoyed it, thought it was fun. And it wasn't long before she was starting to speak French, and, once out of the bathroom, improved it rapidly, found a new best friend, joined the *Eclaireuses de France*, the French Girl Guides, and went on a camping trip where the Mistral wind blew the tents away in the night and she came home with an adopted dog hidden under her coat.

Fritz still came to visit them from time to time and on one of these occasions, he and Mutti announced that they were going away for a day or two. 'They left Beate and Clem and me in Cagnes and went off to Innsbruck to be divorced. So Fritz could marry May. The judge wasn't at all pleased when they walked out of the courtroom arm in arm.'

The year flew past.

Beate, turning 16, was tall and delicate and prone to emotional outbursts. Given rich food and cream to build her up, she slipped it under the table to where Roland the dog grew fat as butter. In Cagnes, she went through her 'Greek dancing' phase, to the raucous amusement of her younger brother and sister. She 'listened to the music with her soul' and wafted around in long, white dresses and drifting scarves, wearing shoes made by the shoemaker to the legendary dancer, Isadora Duncan, who had famously died five years earlier, strangled, just down the road in Nice, when one of her scarves caught in the wheel of her Bugatti sports car.

My mother, who was now nearly 13, was fat and funny as ever. When painting became the next craze, she was co-opted as a nude model for her sister, only to writhe in embarrassment when Beate held an exhibition. And Clemens, at 9 years old, was athletic, full of jokes, a mimic, with a passion for animals and his father's delight in practical jokes.

This period seemed light years away from the tensions of Munich or the amnesia of Vienna. The story had zest and energy and the ease of something told many times. But maybe it was not far away enough.

They had a radio in the house at Cagnes. One afternoon, the big valve set poured out the unmistakeable, high-pitched rant of Adolf Hitler addressing a rally of the party faithful and my mother watched her brother, caught up in the mania of the sound, march round and

Beate, 1932.

round the room. The faster the Führer spoke, the faster Clemens marched, pulling his clothes off piece by piece until he was quite naked.

For Mutti, it was time to move on again; time the children had a proper settled education. England at this time was not only the most politically stable country in Europe but had a reputation for its progressive schools and efforts to create a new kind of education that moved on from the hidebound pomposity of the past. This appealed to her. And so, on 21 September 1933, Mutti, Beate, Inge and Clemens arrived in England and a few days later the children went off to boarding school.

My mother always finished the story the same way. 'When I woke up on that first morning at school in England,' she said, 'I looked out of the dormitory window and there were the maths master and the gym mistress rolling naked in the dew. "Aha!" I thought to myself. "So *this* is how they do things in England".'

And we would laugh and laugh. We loved this story. It was full of energy and humour and sunlight. What a life! What an adventure! My mother was special. It made us special by association. And, sitting in the back of the Mini, newly released from our scratchy tweed uniforms and, knowing only too well the dire penalties that awaited any girl over 10 who dared even to turn a somersault and show her (regulation brown) knickers at *our* English school, we fell about laughing at my mother's unfounded optimism.

As time went on, I began to tell this story myself, by way of explanation. This is where my mother comes from. This is who she is, we are, I am. It went with the tobogganing down the mountain to have a baby story – intrepid mothers, joyful adventures, lots of languages, a world without borders.

The reaction of listeners was gratifying. Gradually, it took on a life of its own as stories do. It stretched and expanded, underlining the important bits – my grandmother and her children were on the road *for ages* or, '*at least three*' years; they lived '*all over*' Europe; how daring, how multilingual, how carefree they were! And the quieter bits that slowed the telling – the details of sibling character or place – those could be put in or smoothed out as necessary to hold the audience's attention.

So complete in itself had the tale become that, when I ran through the chronology with my mother in the last weeks of her life, it was a surprise to find the events were actually so swift, and almost slight. But then this was a story that shone with the intensity of childhood.

When, much later, I tried to fit it into its context, the backdrop grew darker with every page I read. It tugged and pulled and chilled the heart. This stuff could swallow a lifetime.

In July 1932, while the children played on the beach in Alassio, the Nazi Party increased its presence in the German Parliament. In January 1933, when the children had been in Cagnes for three months, Hitler became Chancellor of Germany. The first concentration camps opened almost immediately. On 27 February, the Reichstag, the Parliament building itself, was burnt to the ground, and the following day all civil liberties were suspended. Persecution of Jews became routine. The Gestapo started work in April. By May, books were being burnt in the street, trade unions shut down, strikes banned.

In Austria too, Chancellor Dollfuss, alarmed by the Nazi threat to Austria's independence, himself assumed dictatorial powers in March 1933, and banning both the Nazi and the Communist parties, suspended the freedom of the press and proposed, 'a Christian German state on Fascist lines'. No wonder England seemed an attractive alternative.

How did the two narratives fit together?

The temptation to make 'our' story conform to the familiar (if slightly later) model of innocent victims fleeing the Nazis was intense. This was the hero tale of our post-war generation – and the one which bestowed instant immunity from that playground crime of originating in Austria. It was so much easier to tell it that way. As the 1960s went on, it became the shorthand that overlaid and replaced the actual flux and confusion of the run-up to the Second World War, the fight against territorial ambition, invasion and dictatorship. Surely what was happening must have been obvious?

Not so. With every year that went by it was more tempting to tell it that way, with my grandmother and her children as victims. So much easier. But it was not the story we were given.

Why did she leave Vienna? I asked my mother.

'She didn't like the backbiting, the dishonesty, the tittle-tattle,' said my mother. 'The way people would say one thing to your face and another behind your back: "Yes, Frau Baronin, no, Frau Baronin." And the deference, the tugging of forelocks, she didn't want that for us either.'

Perhaps she was just travelling? At the time she set off, this was highly popular. 'Never did people travel as much as in those years,' wrote Stephan Zweig. 'Was it the impatience of the young to absorb quickly what they had missed during their forced separation from each other? Or was it, perhaps, some dark premonition that one had to escape in time before the barriers closed down anew?'[1]

But Mutti was not 'travelling'. She was leaving. And this was not so usual. Not yet.

It wasn't a forced flight. She abhorred the Nazis, but these were still early days of the regime in Germany and what was to follow was not self-evident. For children of the Enlightenment like my grandparents, religion was a private matter. The toxic racism of the Nazis was still revealing itself. Besides, Mutti herself had been brought up Catholic, the children were baptised Protestant and her soon-to-be ex-husband, though from an eminent Jewish family, described himself as *Konfessionslos* – 'non-denominational' or 'non-religious' – on any official forms. To enter into the discussion at all was to give it credence, to collaborate with antisemitism – better to ignore.

The laws which were to deprive Jews of their citizenship of the Reich in 1935 and later make even a sixteenth part of inherited Jewish blood grounds for annihilation were not yet on the statute books. As for infidelity, this was a common story in their class and time and many marriages persisted with serial affairs on both sides. No, in 1932, when Mutti took off across Europe with her children as a determined free spirit, a single mother – and soon, a divorceehe at a time when divorce was still a stigma, socially uncomfortable – she was drawing a line, setting out in search of a better life.

The ideas that she was steering by had their roots in the old world, too. Having grown up in Vienna, at the heart of the empire – 'one country with fifteen languages', as her contemporary, Sissi, put it – hers was a world larger than national boundaries, one with an international outlook. Mutti herself spoke other languages badly, but she wanted better for her children. Any educated person would, of course, speak at least three European languages and know the literature and music and art of these countries too, as Fritz would have been the first to agree. Liberal Austrians like her grandfather, Alexander Schindler, had turned their back on Germany after the rupture of the mid-nineteenth century. They idealised France as the centre of European culture and admired England for its positivist tradition and its parliamentary system. To this, in the 1920s, was added a high regard for its educational innovation. Above all, there was the belief that art, music and culture were the highest values.

One century leaked into another. A generation – indeed, two – later, these ideas were still active. 'I'm *not* German, I'm Austrian!' my mother would insist indignantly to anyone who made that mistake and my sister and I proudly made the same distinction – with no real understanding of why.

When she decided to widen our horizons, it was Paris she took us to: it was important we learn French properly and speak it without a foreign accent. On holiday, Europe was our domain – Austria, Switzerland, Italy, France, anywhere this side of the Iron Curtain except Fascist Spain. And though when we were young she would take us to church on Sundays and expect us to say our prayers at bedtime every night, it was quite clear that music, literature and the arts were the highest form of spiritual and intellectual aspiration and the soul food that really kept us alive. On this, they agreed. Without these things, life was not worth living.

We went to rehearsals, concerts, the opera – and when I began to learn the violin, my mother opened up the big chest and got out an instrument that had come from my great-great-grandfather Schey. All this came with Mutti, and more.

And Fritz? Well, he had pretty much disappeared from his children's lives. Where Mutti was a presence, he was an absence. Fathers, it seemed, were an optional extra, not part of adventures like these.

My mother sounded cool when I asked; not much to tell. 'He and May got married in Rome. They lived there for a while and then they went to Argentina. 1930s sometime, before the Second World War anyway. He had a friend who'd gone there and made a lot of money and he thought he'd do the same.' The less said the better.

A very long time later, when it was too late to ask, I found Fritz among the few letters my mother had kept, writing to her from Argentina in the 1960s when we were children. The tone is demanding, petulant, full of blame; he's asking her for money. What happened to the books he left behind in Austria in 1932 (when she was 11)? Why has she sold the house in Schwaz? Her agent must be a crook. Letters arriving through our growing up. It was scarcely surprising we didn't hear about him.

In among them is a copy of just one reply from her, spelling it out: the Second World War, the aftermath, unpleasantness in Schwaz, the impossibility of keeping the house. 'I didn't know where the money to live was going to come from', and at the end, 'My marriage is a dismal mess …'

7

Growing Up

The big stories seemed to stop once they'd settled in England. There was information; bits and pieces available on request, and I thought, if I gave it any thought at all, that it must be because things were less colourful here, ordinary – like our lives really – and we knew about those already. Compared with what had gone before it was just plain dull.

We knew the basics. The children had gone to school. Learnt English. Beate was too old at 16 to lose her Austrian accent but not Inge or Clemens, who soon spoke the language flawlessly. Mutti made homes for them: in London, Dorset and later Oxford. She sent Clemens to school at Bryanston. This was a school known for its progressive approach at the time – an independent organisation of study under the Dalton Plan, no compulsory games, lots of performing arts – and it attracted the children of parents with liberal ideas, or of clergymen 'intense about mankind'. She took a cottage nearby – and, as one of the school friends who used to cycle over with Clemens on Sundays to visit described it, she continued to hold court – the Baroness von Schey with her lightness of touch, her Viennese ways and her unlimited capacity for fun and enjoyment:

> Your grandmother had the kind of luminosity that the French mean when they boast of their country's 'rayonnement'. At the age of 85 one has to beware of False Memory Syndrome, but I still have a mental picture of her addressing her schoolboy guests on subjects like Dorset cottage gardens, or eating pickled onions to disguise

en-route pub-crawling. Clemens was I think the only one who was not totally in awe of her. We thought all Baronesses were like that, but of course we were wrong![1]

We got the basic plot: Mutti was special, they grew up, all was well. Now it was our turn to do the same.

The same cycling school friend, who was to become a distinguished diplomat himself, added that Mutti was well aware of the storm clouds gathering over Europe. She saw only too well what was coming and commented on the naiveté of their teachers' complacent views.

The political backdrop was certainly grim and getting grimmer. In 1935 the Nazis' annual gathering in Nuremberg passed new laws defining a Jew not as someone with a particular religious belief but as a member of an inferior race. Under the 'Law for the Protection of German Blood and German Honour', whatever a person's actual religion, Protestant, Catholic or anything else, anyone who had Jewish grandparents was now excluded from citizenship and forbidden to marry or have sex with those of 'German or related blood'. All such marriages were now invalid, their offspring 'racially suspect'.[2] And by implication, persecution of members of this sub-class was now legitimate.

And there was so much more; library shelves more. The poison lapped all around. That was Germany. Maybe Austria was different?

In the neatly typed 'Directory of Houses in Schwaz' for 1935, entry number 437 is 'Schey-Koromla Friedrich'. Next to it, handwritten in blue ink, is the word '*Jude*' – Jew.[*] There weren't many Jews in Tyrol but there was more than enough antisemitism to go round. Here were the perfect scapegoats for the collapse that had followed the end of the First Word War.

So what about Fritz? Information is a scatter, hard to find. Now married to shipping heiress May,[**] he seemed to go to and fro. Until 1937, he visited Schwaz from time to time but meanwhile moved between Vienna, Munich, Hamburg and back to Vienna, settling in

---

[*] By 1939, Anny's name is listed as the sole owner of the Hügelhof. Safely 'Aryan', it was not expropriated like other Jewish property in Tyrol.

[**] May Reincke was the daughter of a Hamburg shipowner and, on her mother's side, heiress to a banker and a shipowner.

Rome from 1937 on. Then, off he went to Argentina, as my mother said. But the reason? Not quite as it was told perhaps.

The year Fritz left was 1938. This was the year the Nazis marched into Austria to annex it in the *Anschluss* of March. It was also the year in which Mussolini enacted the racial laws that dispossessed Jews in Italy – and that was where Fritz was living. Far from being the entrepreneurial adventure that my mother suggested, his departure sounds more like a run for his life.

All four of Fritz's brothers and sisters left Austria in the same year too, some to America, many to England. Gerda, the eldest, went from Belgium to London, of the twins, Herbert, with his wife Hanny, went to New York and Witold, with Gretl and their children, via Brussels to London, while their younger sister Irma went with her husband Heinrich Simon to Washington DC via Tel Aviv and London. Whatever else it was, this was not voluntary emigration.

How far did this affect Mutti? She welcomed the Scheys and other friends who came to England and stayed in contact with them but it's still hard to know. Such things were separate, not talked about. We (or was it they?) were to be protected from those years. It was as if any connection with persecution, or discussion of Jewish origins, was a form of collaboration with the ideology they rejected, and as distasteful as antisemitism itself. Or some kind of shame.

It was almost as if my mother didn't know.

'Did you ever go back?' I asked her as we sorted out the dates at the end of her life. It had never occurred to me to ask before.

'Oh yes. All the time! We went back every school holiday: 1934, '35, '36. Until we discovered Cornwall. We went to Schwaz in the winter, to Vienna, Salzburg, France, Italy. We always went by train.'

And I was surprised by her answer, reminded again of how little I understood. Who knows? Was it Cornwall and luck or the Nuremberg Laws and judgement at work here? Young memory was not interested.

Instead, here were new anecdotes: how on one of these holidays Clemens was trying to breed a blue mouse and the three children sat on the train and watched with gleeful horror as the shoebox in which the mice were travelling slowly began to drip from the luggage rack opposite onto the hat of an unknown lady sitting underneath. Or Mutti, with her shaky grasp of languages, instructing the French

Summer holidays, 1936. Inge, Beate and Clemens.

railway porter as to her three children and fifteen suitcases, '*Nous sommes quatre et nous avons quinze soutiens gorges.*★'

Sometimes, Mutti stayed behind in Austria and the children travelled back to school on their own. On one of these occasions, when it was just Inge and Clemens, they discovered while changing trains somewhere in Switzerland that Mutti had forgotten to give them the second part of their tickets. Unable to continue the journey without tickets or money, they went and sat on a bench in a park. An hour or two later, a friend of Mutti's just happened to walk by and notice them. 'What are you doing here?'

'And he took us home and gave us something to eat and then gave us the money for the rest of our tickets back.'

As my mother spoke, I realised how little we actually knew, how little she had ever talked about it. It was as if the story of their journey

---

★ 'We are four and we have fifteen bras.'

across Europe had come to represent all the rest, as stories do, and was enough in itself, a way of telling and not-telling at the same time.

'Weren't you worried?' I had been a permanently fearful child and the fear still lingered. She laughed her big laugh.

'No! What was there to be worried about? Something always turned up.'

'And what about when you came to England, all these strange places? Weren't you homesick?'

I myself couldn't bear to spend a night away from her. More laughter.

'No! It was fine!' and then a pause. 'You see, for us, *wherever Mutti was,* was home.'

This, then, was the nub of it. For if my mother was larger than life for us children, behind the wheel of the little red Mini in her shorts and T-shirt, her hair tied back with a cotton scarf, her skin sun-brown, changing languages with the same ease she drove us across borders and ready for anything, behind her was the presence of another. And if ours was glory by association with my mother's childhood story, that in turn glowed with the myth of Mutti.

The 1960s

That was how it was meant to be for us anyway. But this is where raw evidence intrudes upon the tale, another layer so raw it was almost inaccessible and so out of keeping with anything worth retelling that it was only after I'd written all this that I realised that I hadn't included it at all – and that, in a real sense, it would be unallowable. This was sorrow, sadness, loss. Like my mother with the Munich and Vienna years (and probably her mother before her) I had simply excluded it.

There had been suicide as we grew up – of my father's painter sister, Eliza, the one who did our portraits and the murals on the walls of the house-that-looked-like-a-church, and the one who had anchored him after their mother died in their childhood. One Saturday morning, when he was on his way to visit her and stopped for a haircut, she lay down, put her head on a cushion in the oven and turned on the gas without lighting it. Old gas, the kind that killed.

This was a hurt so deep it couldn't be spoken. It was dangerous for us children even to mention her name by accident. Absentmindedly singing 'There's a hole in my bucket, dear Liza, dear Liza' brought my mother running to clutch my arm, 'Don't sing that song! *Ever again!*'

Not so many years later, our parents' marriage finally came to an end. Infidelity. Grief. Divorce. They made heroic efforts not to disturb us. We knew no details. Saw no anger. Heard no rows. He had always been away a lot. She had often shouted.

One summer day, he made a special visit to tell first my sister and then myself that he was moving out. But he was always going to be there for us; we would see him often. My mother, my sister and I stayed in the house. He moved to a flat further into town and sank into depression so deep you could smell it, his new relationship lurching towards failure. We were almost exactly the same age as my mother and her sister had been when Mutti and Fritz had parted.

Nothing changed and everything did.

We moved schools from the one for young ladies up the road to a more 'progressive' girls school, forty minutes away – progressive apparently meaning long school days, the Dalton System (again) and a herd of horses and goats on the grounds. I liked horses.

Within weeks of starting, my sister bruised her ankle falling out of a tree and not long after became seriously ill. In a horrible echo of my mother's childhood and her siblings' illness, she lay in bed at the top of the house, her fever mounting, as doctor after doctor came to see her. The bone marrow had become infected, amputation was discussed. The house swilled with anxiety. I stayed out of the way: I was 'fine'.

At last came a pioneering surgeon and an operation to save her leg at a hospital the other side of London, then post-operative infection on a grim Victorian ward. She recovered painfully slowly. My mother shuttled to and fro, worried sick.

I carried on at the new school and started to make friends in my new class until educational fashion intervened. This took the form of the IQ Test – benchmark of modernity at the time. It seemed to consist of some papers, puzzles and an interview with 'the expert' in an empty classroom. He drew a circle on a piece of paper and handed me the pencil, 'If you lost your purse in a field this shape how would you set about finding it?'

When it came to her turn – for Sara, gloriously expelled from the previous one, had moved schools with us – Sara's response that she would go and get another purse got her rated borderline 'subnormal'. I on the other hand, walking my pencil round and round the hypothetical field in ever smaller spirals, was duly labelled with an IQ of 140 and moved up two years into the class my sister had been in for the few weeks before she became ill. The girls there were a lot bigger, three years older than me and they were my sister's friends.

Over the four years that followed I stopped growing, refused to eat school dinners and did my best to disappear. I hung my head and looked at the ground. In break times I hid behind the coats in the underground cloakroom. The deputy head, a formidable Irish woman with spectacles dangling on a chain around her neck, pulled me out. 'You're a troglodyte,' she said. 'Look it up.'

And for months I cried. Uncontrollably, inconsolably, for at least an hour every morning when I got to school, I cried. A kind teacher would sit with me offering handkerchiefs, 'What's the matter? How can we help?'

I couldn't say. I had absolutely no idea.

My sister, when she finally came home and out of plaster, had it far worse. Before she could go to bed at night she had to line up every bottle and object in the bathroom exactly so, tapping each three times on the shelf in its precise position. Any mistake or interruption meant she had to start all over again. The heavy Bakelite light switch on the wall between her room and mine also had to be clicked on and off three times and her door handle tapped the same before she could go to bed. I would drift off to sleep to the sound of this crazed percussion, half-braced for her next explosion at my mother.

The tougher the confrontations, the more I hid. It wasn't difficult at one level – being 'good' and 'fine' was by far the easier role: don't make waves, go to bed at 7.00 p.m., don't want, don't need, don't cost money.

There was plenty left to enjoy in the garden. I took refuge in music, playing the violin for hours at a time or riding in the wake of my mother's adventures, and with my sister in possession of things artistic, I had been handed 'academic' as my terrain.

But it was also full of anxious effort. There were worries about money. I had already asked to sit the Eleven Plus exam and won a scholarship that paid my school fees. If I could just do everything right and not make difficulties we might just make it. I did my school assignments as soon as they were set, couldn't rest until they were finished, even if they didn't have to be in for another two weeks.

That I'd be able to finish school years before normal was the consolation. 'It'll all be worth it in the future,' my father comforted me. But the Cuban Missile Crisis* rather demolished that argument: who knew if there would even *be* a future? I worried about the bomb, impending nuclear war, the end of the world and, on the publication of Richard Doll's finding of the link between smoking and lung cancer, begged and begged my mother to give up her after-dinner, letter-writing cigarettes.

The world was full of dangers. If anything happened to her we'd be finished and if I wasn't careful, really, really careful, the whole edifice would crumble.

As my sister (now back at school and in the class above) became ever more challenging, and the girls in my class grew breasts and hips and spots and agonised in clusters over boyfriends and whether they were fat, I watched from the sidelines, a stunted child, and decided to give adolescence a miss.

By the time I'd done O-Levels 'Swinging London' had arrived. My sister went to parties and started at art school. Still years younger than the rest, I joined the sixth form of the local girls' grammar school and something more like 'the real world', amazed and refreshed by the sheer number and variety of people there. I watched. Somehow, mysteriously, the girls transformed the drab green uniform: shortened their school skirts, wore white knee socks, had manes of long straight hair, and painted their eyes black and their lips pale.

Some of my classmates would be met at the gates by older boyfriends with cars, some lived with their men, others fought turbulent battles at home, and a few joined the professionals and worked the streets at night. There were even other girls there whose parents had divorced and who actually *spoke* about it. This was not something I'd ever dared

---

* As the evening of 23 October 1962 drew in, I stood on the stairs listening to the radio and President Kennedy's ultimatum to Premier Khrushchev over the Soviet nuclear warheads on Cuba and understood, viscerally, that tomorrow might actually never come.

Reading in the apple tree, 1964.

to do, aware that it was in some way shameful. Here, everything was new to me, and interesting. At school I listened and watched. At home I played the violin, went to bed early, studied and sat and read in the branches of the apple tree in the garden, waiting till it was over.

Holidays

There was another strand of life, though, and that was the holidays – my mother leading the way. These were our lifeline, like another world.

She was now qualified as an Alexander Technique teacher and, as we moved through our teens, built a teaching career that later took her all over the world. But while we were still at home she made a point of stopping work for the holidays. Our travels continued and took on new characteristics as we reached adolescence. Funds were limited despite my father's loyal support, but she found ways, and the older we got, the more she added other young people to the crew – school friends of ours, the nearly grown children of her friends or colleagues – as company for us, or was it for her? Help with expenses? They loved her and she them and wherever we went she made more friends – friends for life and often long into ours.

In summer, now the drive south was sometimes in convoy with her former chemistry tutor, his wife and six children to camp beside beaches in the south of France; or we would venture to Italy and the beautiful monastery of Monte Conero, above the village of Sirolo on the Adriatic Coast, with extra friends following on Lambrettas, guitars slung over their backs.

In winter, she would fund holidays for us and a return to Austria by taking a group of other people's children skiing, thirty at a time. We

Sirolo, 1960. My mother in the centre.

travelled on the cross-Channel ferry and then the sleeper train from Calais, with its extra carriage turned into a dance car where we danced our way through the night across Europe and through the 1960s to the sounds of Chubby Checker, the Beatles and the Rolling Stones, until we found ourselves in the mountains when the sun rose. For us, these were the highlights of the year.

As for her family – I have to think hard to find any connection at all. Yes. My sister did a French exchange with some Schey cousins in

On the cross-Channel ferry, coming back from skiing.

Belgium, and if I search, a few more bits surface, but trying to retrieve those bits is like watching the scratches on the surface of a film, not the film itself.

A scene, an afternoon, end of summer: we've stopped on the long drive home from the south to stretch our legs and climb the mountain above Schwaz, my sister and I, my mother and someone else's son borrowed for the holidays. It's possibly the only time we ever went there in summer. Cocooned in silence high above the valley, we're climbing a meadow slope full of flowers and ripening berries when, out of nowhere, a man in Tyrolean costume emerges from the trees, starts with surprise, doffs his hat, long, black feather curling like a pig's tail, and reaches his hands out to my mother. '*Ja, Frau Baronin!*' he says, astonished, and they talk.

'Who's he? What's that about? Why did he call you Frau Baronin?'* We want to know.

'He's one of the woodcutters, a nice man. Take no notice of all *that* nonsense!' She's impatient, flicks her hand as if she's brushing away a fly.

Then there's a different return journey: another interminable road. Though we're getting big now, we're still squashed into yet another Mini, heading across France after weeks of camping. We have salty skin, dirty feet and we could all do with a bath. The road goes on and

---

* *Baronin* means Baroness.

on, when, passing a sign, my mother suddenly brakes, reverses back to it and swings off down a lane to the right. Watching the shrinking fingerpost through the rear windscreen, I can just make out 'Stud farm of Baron Guy de Rothschild'. Horses? Ok.

'Where are we going?'

'My cousin Alix's place. I thought we'd go and see if she's there.'

Who?

She's not there. But there are horses, beautiful racehorses, looking over their loose box doors in a yard that is wide and spotless, and not far away a gallery hung with paintings by Braque and Picasso. We are directed to the house and park in its driveway, the dusty car an overloaded speck. My mother gets out and goes off. We wait. She comes back.

'Come on. Alix isn't here, but we can use the loo.'

A butler, smiling at my mother, shows us to a cloakroom in the lobby. It has a marble floor, a proper lavatory (we've been squatting over holes in the ground) and two china basins. The taps are gold and shaped like lions and the water that comes out of their mouths is hot. We wash our hands, our feet, our faces, even our flip-flops, and as we cross the hall and say goodbye, the butler hands my sister a white box tied with a silver ribbon, containing four perfect peaches in a nest of golden tissue paper.

It was a complete disconnect.

Leaving Home

When at last I finished school in 1965, though, it was to Vienna that I went to study the violin. Quite how that decision came about I've no idea, except that Vienna was considered the best place in Western Europe to study music.* Now I began to learn German for the first time.

I had never ventured out on my own before (apart from a French exchange when I was paralysed by homesickness). It was like jumping off the top diving board into unknown water: to my surprise and relief, I discovered I could swim.

The weather was cold and I was permanently hungry and Vienna was the world capital of sticky cakes but they were behind plate-glass

---

* I was welcomed by Paul and Eva Badura-Skoda who had me to stay for the first week or two and whose 3 year old son was the best possible German teacher.

windows and out of reach. It didn't seem a very friendly place. The streets were battered and grimy, the people scowled, dirty snow piled up in the gutters and the area where I lodged in a crumbling flat with some other music students was dark and dilapidated, bullet holes still visible in the walls outside. When I ventured into wealthier parts of town, older women in fur coats would stop me in the street to tell me off angrily for the length of my skirt – too short – and my hair – too long. Why had I not put it up? – and the crime of wearing boots.

Preoccupied with music, immersed in the baroque and practising eight hours a day, I took little interest in the family connection or history here. That my grandparents had come from Vienna was just about all I knew – and so had the violin I was playing, had I thought about it. But there were some actual relatives to meet.

These were my mother's uncles and aunts, the Scheys, the very same brothers and sisters of Fritz, our absent grandfather, who had all left in 1938 and now had returned. To me they seemed ancient (I was 16). They had high foreheads and big noses and held themselves very upright. They all spoke several languages fluently. I struggled to speak any German at all. I met Onkel Herbert and his wife Hanny, who had spent some years in America during the war; and lovely Tante Gretl, widow of Onkel Witold (Herbert's twin), in whose flat I eventually lodged – they had been in England during the war.

Tante Gerda Goldschmidt, the eldest, in town on a visit from her home in Brussels, took me out to tea. She invited me to Demel, the most wonderful and expensive *Café-Konditorei* in all Vienna. It had curlicues over the doors and mirrors round the walls and glass shelves

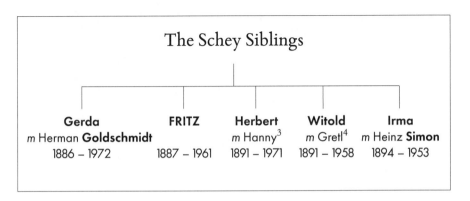

The Schey Siblings

Gerda	FRITZ	Herbert	Witold	Irma
m Herman **Goldschmidt**		m Hanny[3]	m Gretl[4]	m Heinz **Simon**
1886 – 1972	1887 – 1961	1891 – 1971	1891 – 1958	1894 – 1953

dressed in the most irresistible cakes – fantasies in chocolate, whipped cream, toffee, meringue, nuts, fruit.

Tante Gerda handed her fur coat and hat to the waitress. 'What would you like?' she asked me.

If only she'd known how hungry I was. With difficulty I chose a single slice of *Dobos torte* and tried not to lick the plate it vanished from almost instantly.

Tante Gerda took her time and talked. She was well over 80, which was several hundred years old, as far as I was concerned, and full of energy. As she finished her coffee she stretched out her hand in the air above the café table and looked at it thoughtfully. 'Do you see that?' she asked.

What? I wondered, noticing the wrinkled skin, the freckle marks, the enormous age of the steady, floating hand.

'What bothers me about getting older,' she said, 'is that if my hand starts to shake, I shall have to stop shooting wild boar.'

It was beyond me.

Hunting, by Marie-Louise von Motesiczky, Albertina, Vienna.

I went back to England with some relief, got a job to earn money for the summer and went travelling in Greece.

My mother added a few finishing touches to my education. When I marked my 16th birthday by buying an ancient Lambretta for £10 and teaching myself to ride it by roaring up and down the street, hair flying, she presented me with a crash helmet. (They were not yet compulsory.) When I met her for a night in Italy that summer on my way back from a solo trip to the Greek islands – 'How are you getting home?', 'I'm hitch hiking.' – she bought me a souvenir keyring with a tiny gun that fired real, tiny (and probably useless) bullets and waved me goodbye.

'We all live in a Yellow Submarine,' sang the Beatles.[*]

And when autumn came and it was time for me to take up the place I had been offered at Oxford, she was right behind me. I was extremely unsure about the whole thing. I had only taken the entrance exam because the school headmistress had announced the previous year that I was *far* too young to leave school after A levels and had to stay for an extra term. 'By the way,' she told me. 'You won't get in.'

But somehow I did.

My father was quietly pleased and my mother was certainly not letting this one go. When October came, she put on her best clothes and drove me there with my suitcase and a box of books.

I realised it was a mistake at once. The college, one of only five women's colleges in the university compared to the twenty-five there were for men, immediately conjured up the girls' boarding schools I'd always so dreaded being sent away to. It buzzed with excited new students with their mothers and fathers moving them into neighbouring rooms in the halls of residence.

The room I'd been allocated was hard to find. Nobody we asked seemed to know. After much searching, it turned out to be halfway along an empty, semi-basement corridor, a dirty box with mould growing up the walls and, above the bed, a high sash window that looked out onto the exhaust pipes of the college car park. It must have been a storeroom until a few hours earlier and looked as if it had only

---

[*] And I earned an evening meal and a comfortable night in a French barn for translating the words for the farmer's family.

just been cleared of boxes and had a bed and table stuffed in. There was a palpable smell of damp. While the rest of the college seemed full of people at every turn, down here there was nobody. The nearest bathroom was a long walk away. To me it was obvious: they had forgotten I was coming, the place I'd been offered was an administrative error.

'I've changed my mind.' I told my mother, 'I don't think this is a good idea. I'll just come back with you and do something else.'

'Hmmm,' she said, and disappeared, returning half an hour later with a gallon can of white paint and two large brushes. 'Woolworths!' she announced triumphantly. Stripping off her skirt and top and kicking off her shoes, she pulled the bed out, opened the tin and, dressed only in her vest, stockings and petticoat and clearly visible from the car park, she set about painting the room. She passed me the other brush, 'Here you are!'

By the time I was called to meet the principal later that afternoon, the room was repainted, the mould subdued and I had broken about five of the college's strictest rules before even starting. I was also one of the youngest students in the place.

The three years that followed brought a press of new concerns: new people, friendships, work, boyfriends, play, anxiety, essays to write and endless wonderful and terrible reading. And, predictably of course, it brought one of those sudden moments that change things – this one on a street corner, late at night talking to a young man, when there came a sudden flash of certainty: 'But I *know* you!'*

Love struck.

---

* My father worried. 'Jew and Gentile don't mix,' he warned gloomily. What?! Ever careful, I didn't say, 'What does that make me then? Haven't we been here before?'

8

Love Story

It had all happened before, of course. I wasn't the first to fall in love. And if stories are one source of subliminal guidance, the details were all there in our bedrock tales. We knew about love, or so we thought.

There had been Mutti and Fritz in the middle of the First World War (ancient history), and a generation later, thirty years before it took

War declared, Sunday, 3 September 1939. My father's drawing.

me by surprise on a dark street in Oxford, my mother and father on the eve of the Second World War. Inge and Bill.

Here was the source of the final story in our childhood set, the keystone piece that locked the arc of our parents' different worlds together and created our own.

1939

Most people have a story like this, how they came to be here – genesis – and ours was about how our parents got married. (I still don't know how they met or how long they knew each other before they did.) It was very short, though I never wondered why, a thumbnail tale, more sketch than story, and the way my mother told it, it went something like this:

- she was very young when she married (this she said with some pride – an achievement, and somehow I thought she was 18);
- she had always wanted children, *lots* of children (two was obviously a shortfall);
- the wedding was in April, and it snowed and thundered and the sun came out all in the same morning (or was it afternoon?);
- they only had a pitifully short time together before my father was sent abroad to serve in the war and they didn't see each other for five long years. Heartache.

Then the war ended and he came back and they were together at last – my sister born in 1946, myself two and a half years later.

It was Love Conquers All. A romance. And our great good fortune.

And strangely, though the text was brief and a lot more remote than the experience of its unravelling, the power of it is that it stays a romance still, despite everything.

The ghost at our parents' wedding, of course, was the Second World War, but the war was never story material. It just was, squatting there in the background like a toad. In many ways, it permeated everything about our growing up, a landscape so familiar we didn't even notice it, like the bomb sites derelict in the city, full of fireweed and buddleia,

Drawing from my father's sketchbook on the troopship *Orbita* anchored
off Port Suez, dated 6 March 1941, my mother's 21st birthday.

and on our visits to the English seaside, chunks of rusting metal still
sticking out of the beaches where we played hide-and-seek around pill-
boxes and corroded gun emplacements.

Nobody talked about the war in our childhood, easier just to push
it aside as a big inconvenience, an interruption. Was it that they didn't
want to think about it? Was it too soon, too undigested? Or was it just
that now it was finally over, our parents' generation were intent on
making a better life, catching up the stolen time, making sure it was
not going to happen again and that the many who had died had not
died for nothing. All will be well. Don't look back. Move on. Life is
now. And we were the beneficiaries, the future, *their* future as well as
our own. Above all, our lives were not to be spoiled by all that.

We gleaned some bits to bridge the missing years. My mother
wanted to be a doctor. We knew that. When war broke out, the

Troops 'at leisure' on the SS *Orbita*, March 1941. W.A. Henderson's troopship
diaries are now lodged at the Imperial War Museum, London.

letters later explained, she was studying in Edinburgh for entrance
to medical school but suspended her studies for six months the following spring to marry her Bill and spend the time with him. After
he left in January 1941, she took up her studies again at St Anne's
College, Oxford. (Was that where her insistence on my giving
Oxford a chance came from?)

When she failed a crucial exam, there were no second chances.
Wartime rules meant she had to leave and take up war work with-
out delay. She worked in a lab, trained as a dietician and served in the
American Army Venereal Disease Unit, treating infected soldiers.
There were a few jolly anecdotes here that passed the time on car jour-
neys – the gloriously named Hobart-Shot-to-Pieces from Wounded
Knee in Indiana, or the big, brave general with a chest full of medals
who fainted away at the sight of a needle.

My father kept silence – and didn't talk about 'his' war at all. But all
through our childhood, on the bookshelf in the house-that-looked-
like-a-church, there were three box files bound in blue cloth to look
like books, with 'WAH to IVH 1941–45' lettered in gold on the red
band on their spines. They contained his wartime letters to my mother

from Turkey where he was posted with the Royal Engineers – his slanting writing squeezed onto the cramped regulation letter forms – and they were wonderfully illustrated with watercolour and ink drawings. Love letters. Their relationship. The box files stood in for why we were there. Private. One day, I thought, one day I will read them, and understand what it was, but not yet.

The years of separation were formative ones for them both. Growing up from the age of 20 to 25 separated from her husband, my mother, always feisty, funny and fearless, became ever more her own person and he likewise in far-away Turkey. As for so many others, his return was not perhaps the happy reunion they had been dreaming of – but they had waited long enough. On with the plan.

Sixteen years later, the marriage foundered … The box files waited.

Then, twenty years further on, after their divorce, and well after my father had remarried, I noticed that they had disappeared from the bookshelf.

'He asked me to burn them,' my mother said.

Things Not Told

'Private. Keep out.' This was never territory I intended to explore and it was long after both parents had died before I looked any further. But when it came, the second look brought surprises. The gap between story and source was huge. No wonder it was so short. Had they ever stood a chance?

The process was strangely disturbing. I preferred the original, however oversimplified.

The letters my mother kept tell a much less comforting story than the thumbnail tale. At the time of their thundering, snowy wedding – she was, in fact, 20 and he was 25 – all the older generation were against their marriage. Still a year short of legal 'majority', Inge needed her mother's permission to marry. The letters to her in the preceding months sound a chorus of disapproval.

Bill makes his debut in London in November 1939, writing to Mutti. 'Dear Baroness,' he writes, declaring his love for Inge and their informal engagement. He is waiting to be posted by the army, doesn't have a job. On the same day, Inge writes from Edinburgh where she is studying:

how much she loves him! They want to marry and she mentions (the only time) the practical benefit of the security that becoming an English citizen would offer, compared with the disadvantages of 'Alien' status.

By 20 November, Mutti has paid a surprise visit to Bill in his room in Markham Square and – 'Dear Baroness' – he's apologising for the untidy house. Writing to Inge, Mutti is not happy with the match. By the end of the month – as Inge tries to organise her brother's education (he's begging her from Bryanston to get him out of there to somewhere he can study properly for medicine, could he come to Edinburgh too?) – she is calling her mother out about her opposition, insisting how much she loves Bill.

By midwinter the chips are down. The Schey relatives, recently arrived in the UK from Austria, are keenly aware of their aristocratic, historic family status. They are talking to Mutti, divorced or not, concerned to protect the family name. Inge accuses her mother of snobbery:

> We're living in the year 1939, in a War, in a country which has taken us in and above all offered Witold and Gretel and the children and many others like them true friendship and the chance of a new life. For centuries this country has been ahead in one thing and that is – a farmer can have a fine family tree and still be a farmer but they would still be admired if they were a great human being. With us in Austria and Vienna above all <u>a name</u> is all that matters. This has to change.

In January, Mutti writes to Bill, furious, refusing her consent – NO!

On Bill's side, too, there is trouble. His father,[*] director of the firm in Chile, is against the marriage. His wife, Bill's stepmother Tinny, in England on a visit and representing that father, is against it and joins forces with Mutti to that effect. Even the long-absent Fritz in Argentina is roped in, writing to Inge in February that he's not in favour of her marrying Bill, '*so hast du jetzt schon die ungünstige Prognose fur eine gute Ehe*',[**] and urges her to concentrate on her studies and becoming a *verdienende Frau* – a woman who can earn her way.

---

[*] John Allardice Henderson, Bill's father and director of Balfour Williamson, a Liverpool-based major trading company on the Pacific coast of both Americas, which his father, Bill's grandfather, William Ritchie Henderson, had headed up the generation before.

[**] 'This doesn't bode well for a good marriage.'

And Mutti? Above all, Mutti. Her daughter's touching declarations of love make no impression. Why does Bill have to be in such a hurry to marry? she rails to her. It's selfish, irresponsible. What about his prospects? You won't have any money. He's a dreamer not a man. You should be studying!

Here, for the first time, the mist clears and the fairy-tale grand-mother speaks with a human voice. Her letters are harsh, distraught, unrestrained. This is a woman at the limits of her jurisdiction and unable to bear it. It's also a confrontation between generations – between the old wisdom and the new.

She wants them to sign an agreement not to marry. Bill resists:

Why must Inge not love? Why, just because I must be a soldier may I not love too? How can I make contracts not to love her more than a fixed amount, as if such a love could be tied in by signed documents? That is not human.

'That's just it,' Mutti retorts. 'That's what young men have always said when the laws were inconvenient for them.'

There are deeper insecurities too. She writes to Inge:

I have to tell you now, we have <u>nothing</u> left – no money – no homeland, etc but the way we conduct our lives has to be beyond reproach; it is [*heikliger*] more challenging than for English families who are already known here.

Above all, she insists, if they have to get married they must wait until *after* the war. This is interesting, coming from someone who had herself married in the middle of the First World War, her bridegroom home on leave from the Eastern Front, the *'geliebtes Annerl'* of Fritz's 1915 letters.

Then suddenly, in April, it's over.

Inge and her Bill were not to be stopped. On 27 April 1940 they were married at Chelsea Old Church, London.

When my mother submitted her marriage certificate soon after to the Dorset Constabulary as regulations required, Inspector Foster, returning it to her, ended his letter:

The marriage between
William Anthony Henderson
and
Inge Schey-Koromla
took place quietly at Chelsea Old
Church on Saturday, April 27th.
This is to send you their best wishes

Inge and Bill, 27 April 1940.

I note that your ultimate goal was only gained after much adversity but it is very apparent that you now consider the Herculean effort well worth while. I wish you all happiness for the future.

The older generation mended fences as best they could, distant Fritz with a grudging 'since you love him he may be worth it. At least I do hope so.' Taking the opportunity to ask Inge write to him, 'so we shall slowly get accustomed to each other again. It is long time ago since I saw you last.' Mutti writes about her garden. And Bill's father takes the trouble to write a long letter to welcome this daughter in law he'd never met:

I do understand that you love each other and that in these awful times you want to be together while you can … Don't think of me as an ogre any more. I want to be friends and I will try and help you both all I can.

It was done. The happy couple went to live in a farmhouse near Derby and the camp where my father was training as a soldier. How long before he was posted and where he would be sent, they didn't know.

The important thing was to seize the moment: love and war hand in hand. Bill writes to his mother-in-law:

Royal Engineers No 3 Co-y, 141st O.C.T.U.R.E.

Dear Ingemutti,

Holland is almost done for and Belgium again invaded, so the result is that I am wandering about the woods with a bayonet tonight instead of being with our Inge. It is pretty terrible to be imprisoned like this and to see her so seldom, and it is no joke for her. But Inge as you know is a wonderful person and puts up with everything very wonderfully and I am hoping that it will be better next week and that I shall get out at night anyway.

Meanwhile Inge comes up to the camp, invades the officers mess, gives buns to my fellow prisoners and generally 'collects' everybody in that way of hers which I love ... I think we are happier together every day and every hour is precious to us beyond words ...

This is a bloody war in every sense, and it is so near now ...

My whole self is half a mile away, in a roof room with check curtains where Inge sleeps under the brown rug, and I ache to be there.

My love,
Bill

My father's picture of the roof room with check curtains.

The 'awful times' continued to unfold.

Enemy Aliens

That April 1940, the April of our parents' wedding, was significant for more than their marriage. Things had been quiet in Western Europe for the six months since war had been declared the previous September – a time so quiet, it was nicknamed the 'Phoney War'. Fevered preparations had been underway of course: conscription, munitions, fortification of the coastline, rationing and much more – and among them was the scrutiny of foreigners in Britain, especially those who came from countries with which Britain was now at war.

Well-connected though they were, my grandmother and her children certainly fell into this category. They may have been émigrés of choice rather than refugees, deeply opposed to the Nazi regime and had been here for seven years, but they had still come from Austria. They still had Austrian passports. The end of the First World War was only twenty years before and anti-German feeling, the same that lingered in our 1950s school playground, was close to the surface. It was also, to complicate matters, a sentiment they shared.

In 1933, the year they arrived, roughly 2,000 refugees came to Britain. After the *Anschluss* in 1938, the trickle became a flood. By the time war was declared in September 1939, Britain had accepted 55,000 refugees from Germany, Austria and Czechoslovakia, among them Fritz's relatives. Then there were all the other Germans and Austrians who were already here of choice, on business and more. The problem for the authorities was who was friend and who was foe? It was a sensitive issue.

The government was keen not to repeat its disastrous internment policies of the First World War. Instead, the day after this Second World War was declared, the Home Secretary announced that 120 tribunals would be set up to decide which 'enemy aliens' might pose a risk. Lawyers, judges and elderly magistrates brought out of retirement were summoned to chair them and began their secret hearings in October. Their task was to sort aliens into categories: sifting through to decide who were 'refugees', those who were fleeing Nazi persecution and were no risk to this country; 'non-refugees', who had lived here for some time and made their

Aliens Order, 1920. Mutti's registration book.

home in this country (they would need to prove their good character and connections); and those who were likely to support the enemy. The least dangerous, Category C, were to be left free; Category B would be restricted – prevented from travelling or owning cars, maps or cameras, and Category A were to be interned at once.

Marianne Schey, a cousin of Fritz's, whose father, Moritz (Fritz's father Josef's youngest brother) had been Austria's Imperial Ambassador to Britain before the First World War, gave a verbatim account of her tribunal experience in a letter of November 1939:

```
Chairman: When were you in England?
I: From 1909-1918. We went back to Austria after the
last war.
Ch: Now what exactly do you mean by back to Austria? I notice
you were born in Biarritz?
I: I say back to Austria because my father was Viennese.
Ch: I see. Now what did you do in Austria?
I: After my father's death in '21 I gave English lessons and
did translation.
Ch: What did you say?
I: (bawling) I gave English lessons and did translations.
```

```
Ch: (turning to the interpreter) What did she do?
Interpreter: She gave English lessons and did translations.
Ch: (writing in his book) Had a private governess. Was a
teacher and did translations. And what are you doing now?
... I suppose you had to leave Austria as you couldn't
have gone on working there.
I: No, I certainly couldn't. Besides my brother, who is a
British Subject...
Ch: What's that? How can he be a British Subject?
I: Because he was born in England.
Ch: But that wouldn't make him a British Subject!
Det: Oh, yes it does.
Ch: (shaking his head) There's something very wrong about
that. Now, are you Catholic or Protestant?
I: Neither, I am a Jewess.
Ch: Oh. Was your father a Jew?
I: Yes, and so is my Mother.
Ch: Both parents Jews. Well, I think that's all. (He then
handed over my papers to the detective.)
Detective: Well. Is the lady a refugee?
Ch: Eh. What?
I: (Before he had time to answer) If you mean me, very defi-
nitely I am!

Then they all laughed and I got all my papers back and was
told I was free of all restrictions except that I must
notify the police of any permanent change of address as
before the war.¹
```

That anything like that could have happened to our mother or to Mutti had never been mentioned, never crossed our minds, but a look at the public records show that Mutti, too, was called to a tribunal that October. Classed as a 'Female Enemy Alien, Non-Refugee', she was exempted from internment because she 'has formed ties of association and sympathy with this country'.

The Austrian thing was complicated though. Internationally minded Mutti was proudly Austrian as well and still had an Austrian passport.

Anna Schey Koromla's registration book and the exemption granted by
the tribunal of October 1939.

All applications for British 'naturalisation' had been stopped with the
outbreak of war.[*] For her, and other liberals like her, when the Nazis
marched into their country in the *Anschluss* of 1938 it was an invasion
and a violation of all that they believed Austria stood for, and it only
sharpened the distinction between 'Austrian' and 'German' that was so
important to them. But given the common language and the fact that so
many of their fellow countrymen were so quick to welcome the invading
Nazis and join in the persecution of Austria's Jews with gruesome
enthusiasm, this was a distinction that was lost on many in Britain.

---

[*] To apply for naturalisation, you had to have lived in Britain for five years.

On the day war was declared, Bill was instructed to drive Beate and Inge down to join Mutti in safety in Dorset. They arrived to find her with the cottage windows open, defiantly playing '*Gott Erhalte*', the old Austrian national anthem, as loudly as she could on the piano, apparently oblivious to the fact that now the Nazis had appropriated the tune for their '*Deutschland über Alles*' anthem her performance might be misinterpreted by the neighbours. There was much to learn.

'I'm looking forward to your next letter,' Mutti writes to Inge in November 1939, 'but please don't write in German on the envelope.' And soon after, she changes to writing all her letters in English.

We never heard anything about all this as we grew up. It was not to be remembered. The closest we came was a small mention by my mother of some anti-German unpleasantness from some of my father's relatives, who he had asked to look after her during his long absence. It never occurred to us that we or our mother didn't belong.

This could just be part of the general silence, troubles to be shrugged off, trivial unpleasantness in a war that was so full of real suffering. Or it could have been unease. But when the war in Western Europe went from phoney to real in April 1940, that wedding month, the mood darkened.

Norway was the turning point.

According to Peter and Leni Gillman's excellent book *Collar the Lot*,[2] which has been an invaluable source here, Winston Churchill, who was First Lord of the Admiralty at the time, had been planning a British invasion of Norway, hoping to cut the Germans off from their supply of iron ore and obstruct their access to the North Sea, when on 9 April, Germany seized the initiative with an alarmingly efficient invasion of their own. When the British landed in Norway on 26 April, what followed was humiliation. They were badly equipped, badly organised and without any air cover. By the end of May they had to withdraw. 'The Norwegian campaign had proved an ignominious shambles.'[3]

This was a serious blow to morale for a country itself expecting a German invasion at any day. What had happened to the script? To the skilful, indomitable British imperial forces, admired throughout the world and afraid of nothing? How to explain it?

There had to be another reason. Something else must have tipped the balance in favour of the Germans.

As if the British press had collectively risen to cry, 'Eureka!', a flash of inspiration illuminated the confusion and gloom. An editorial in the *Yorkshire Post* on 16 April was typical, 'There is no doubt that help from a "Fifth Column" in Norway figured in Hitler's invasion plans.'

Within a week, almost every other national newspaper had written in similar terms.[4]

Of course. There must have been enemy supporters embedded in the Norwegian population who helped the Germans to success. And Britain should learn the lessons – the real threat here surely lay with the enemy hiding within.

The frenzy that followed was not quite as bad as the stoning of dachshunds that followed the sinking of the *Lusitania* in the First World War, but there were warnings everywhere. It wasn't just men who posed a threat either, women aliens, too, were seen as dangerous, seductive and German or Austrian women who had married here were

Wedding day. Clemens, centre, with Beate and her husband Roger Ward to the left and Inge and Bill to the right.

among the suspects. As the panic grew, so did the rhetoric. By the time
the Netherlands fell to the German invasion on 14 May, the fear had
become an article of faith. 'Every German or Austrian servant, however superficially charming and devoted, is a real and grave menace',
wrote one Old Etonian after the fall.[5]

Anti-foreigner feeling was running high. By the end of April 1940,
both my mother and her sister were married to British officers, which
may have offered some shelter.

But what about Mutti? And what about Clemens, who had arrived
aged 9 and by now had spent the second half of his life becoming an
entirely British schoolboy and a fledgling member of the public-school
class? He was still a boy, studying at school. Surely he was protected
by his youth?

Perhaps, but in a letter to my mother at the beginning of May Mutti
urges her to:

> ... please write and tell Lady Sinclair that Clemens has given
> Archibald as a reference for his new tribunal questionnaire it is <u>so</u>
> [four times underlined] important. He could have problems if they
> ask about it and please tell her that his name is Schey-Koromla just in
> case the Edinburgh police inquire about a Mr Koromla.

Lady Sinclair's husband, the Liberal politician Sir Archibald Sinclair,
was the leader of the Liberal Party at the time and the Secretary of
State for Air in the all-party coalition government. They were lucky
and well connected. This storm would pass over, like the others. Or
would it?

And that's another story.

9

My Disappearing Uncle

I first heard this one from my father in his flat, wreathed in cigarette smoke, sometime in my teens. I can't remember my mother ever telling it. It seemed strange enough then and rich in undercurrents of anger, indignation and the sadness that was my father's hallmark. But it was also remote. Uncle? What uncle?

Of course I knew my mother had a brother, the one born in Munich, the boy who could walk on his hands with his knees over his shoulders, the one who tried to breed a blue mouse. His name was Clemens. He

lived in South America somewhere and my mother wrote him letters, met his wife when she came over on business and once made a difficult and expensive long-distance phone call on his birthday when he refused to come on the line. But for us, he was just another of those relatives who weren't there, our parents' business, not ours.

It was all the more surprising, then, when he suddenly appeared in London in 1990, arms outstretched, 'Hail fellow well met!', 'How looovely!'

Clemens, 1991.

The agile boy of the childhood stories was now 67 years old, grey haired and balding and I, in my forties, with children of my own. His wife Lida had died (as had his sister Beate by now) and he arrived on a visit as if it was the most natural thing in the world, stayed with my mother and set about looking up all his friends from school fifty years before: affable, charming, friendly. He felt instantly familiar. He said nothing about the half a century of complete silence. So, then we asked.

The story, as he told it, was a ripping yarn, an adventure – fun, exciting and, in the family tradition, with barely a cloud in the sky.

156

1940, Edinburgh

It began in Edinburgh in the same spring of 1940 and, looking at the dates now, less than two weeks after our parents' wedding. Moved from Bryanston by his sister's efforts, Clemens had now followed her to Edinburgh and was staying in the same boarding house that Inge had been living in before pausing her studies to marry Bill: Miss Turcan's boarding house in Manor Place. Like my mother, he wanted to be a doctor and though she had taken a six-month break, he was carrying on. Money was scarce, food rationed and Clemens, 16 years old and skinny, was permanently hungry.

During the week, he said, he studied, and at weekends he rode the trams to the end of the line for a penny a time, went for long walks and rode back again. He visited the zoo, when he could afford it, and more often after he discovered a way in over the fence at the back. Sometimes he climbed the big hill at the back of the railway lines to watch the trains. So far, wartime life in Britain was uneventful. People went on with their plans, jittery but much as usual.

A look at the background was not reassuring. As April turned into May, the war news worsened. Britain was expecting a German invasion any day and Edinburgh was among the 'coastal counties' considered most at risk. On 9 May, a parliamentary vote of no confidence forced Prime Minister Neville Chamberlain to resign over the Norway disaster. With striking irony, Winston Churchill, himself the architect of that fiasco, succeeded him as prime minister. On 10 May, German forces invaded the Netherlands, Belgium and Luxembourg. Churchill wasted no time: on the evening of Saturday, 11 May, the Home Office sent a telegram to all the chief constables of the coastal counties.

One Sunday morning, Clemens continued (12 May and no coincidence), he was chatting to one of the other lodgers at Miss Turcan's, a boy from Brazil, about beaches and rainforests, about exotic birds and animals and the glories of South America – oh, to be able to see such things! – when there was a knock at the door of the room. There was their landlady.

'There's a man downstairs to see you,' she said to Clemens. 'He's a policeman.' And she was trembling.

The policeman was in plain clothes. He was very polite. 'I'm sorry,' he said, 'I've come to pick you up. We're picking up all aliens and taking them in.' He accompanied Clemens up to his room.

'What should I take? What shall I pack?'

'Pack enough for the weekend,' said the policeman.

So, Clemens filled a small bag, just enough for the weekend, and followed the policeman down the stairs to the car, leaving everything else just where it was.

The police station was crowded. The waiting areas were jammed. As fast as the police reloaded the people they'd detained into big black vans and drove them off, more were brought in. Soon it was Clemens' turn. When the doors of the Black Maria van opened again, he found himself staring at a great, grey Scottish castle, which he recognised as one of the places at the end of the penny tramline.

For hours he and the other detainees waited in a big stone room – and waited. When Clemens needed a pee he had to pee in public, 'a hard and uncivilised sort of a lesson'. Eventually, they were given something to eat and, when night came, taken upstairs. The great stone rooms were empty: no mattresses, no blankets, nothing. The authorities were clearly unprepared. That night they slept on the bare floors. And the next and the next.

Internment

The telegram the Home Office sent to all the chief constables of the thirty-one coastal counties on the evening of 11 May instructed them to intern all male enemy aliens between 16 and 60 years old, starting at 8 a.m. the following morning. Clemens was among the first to be swept up. In this opening round of arrests 2,000 people were interned, but in the chaos of the moment nobody knew how many or who they were. He too disappeared from the record.

In the next few days, as first the Netherlands and then Belgium fell to the German advance and the British began the retreat that ended in Dunkirk, anti-enemy rhetoric intensified, and with it, panic. The Home Office with their careful procedures were overruled by Churchill and the Cabinet and the internment process was handed over to a secret committee. The thing took on a momentum of its own – unstoppable.

After several uncomfortable days in the castle, my uncle said, they were loaded onto a train and taken south. It took all day to get as far as London and then they were unloaded again and taken to Scotland Yard. The legendary Scotland Yard! What an adventure! It turned out to be a horrible place with tiled walls and a bad smell, the threatening smell of police station.

The next day, another train. This one took them to Surrey and what had previously been Lingfield Racecourse. It was heavily guarded and surrounded by high fences of coiled barbed wire: it had been an internment camp since the previous November. Clemens and his companions were marched through the gates to the racecourse grandstand. Under it were rows of mattresses. 'That's where you sleep,' said the guard.

Time passed and life settled into the surreal routine of internment: nights under the grandstand, life behind barbed wire. Clemens talked to people, made friends. With German as well as perfect English and, thanks to the family's wanderings on their way from Austria to England all those years before, French and Italian too, he was useful. The camp information officer gave him things to do. The way he told it, here was a camp full of older men with lots of exciting stories. It was fascinating.

Really? I wondered, listening. Was that all? He had lived in Britain for nearly half his life. How must it have been for a patriotic and fiercely anti-Nazi British schoolboy to find himself rebranded as an enemy alien? The answers didn't make it into the story.

Most of the internees at Lingfield were merchant seamen captured from German ships. They weren't necessarily German, but because they worked on German ships they had been rounded up anyway. One of these was a big man who used to walk up and down, always smoking his pipe. He was an Estonian by the name of Helmut Witt. One day he ran out of tobacco and Clemens, noticing, gave him his own cigarettes. Witt was so touched that he kept an eye on the boy from then on. He saw to it that he got the best food, the best place to sleep; he made sure that no one gave him trouble. Helmut Witt became his friend and guardian.

Clemens was surprised to be summoned to the camp office one day. 'You have a visitor,' he was told. It was Mutti. That was the first time he had been able to speak to her since he was taken in Edinburgh. Somehow, she had found out where he was. Somehow, she had made her way through the difficulties and been given permission to visit.

'Don't worry,' she told him. 'We're working on it.'

'After that I went on more happily, expecting to be released at any moment,' he said.

It didn't happen. One day in late June the prisoners were all told to pack their bags and report to the gate immediately. They were marched out, loaded onto a train again and off it steamed. Where to? Nobody knew. What for? Nobody said.

The stations they passed were unmarked, their signs removed to confuse invaders, but eventually Clemens recognised the outskirts of London, and a while later, the train came to a halt on the sidings at the back of Earl's Court. From his seat in the carriage of the prison train, Clemens could see the kitchen window of his mother's flat in Holland Villas Road. It was too far to shout. Impossible to get out.

At this point in the story my mind conjures shadows, figures moving against the light of the kitchen window, and the heartache of the boy in the carriage. The story admitted nothing. The train sat there for what seemed like hours. Eventually, it started moving again, left Earl's Court behind and headed on north out of London. The next time it stopped they were in Liverpool. At the docks.

Waiting for them at the quayside was a big ship called the *Empress of Canada*,[*] said Clemens, 23,000 tons. (The memory is particular.) As armed guards herded them off the train, Helmut Witt appeared at Clemens' side. 'Stick with me,' he said. 'Just do exactly what I say.'

And so my disappearing uncle followed him up the gangplank.

---

[*] While Clemens is specific, it seems that the *Empress of Canada*, though definitely used for these deportation journeys, had been renamed the *Duchess of Richmond* from 1928 to 1947, when she recovered her original name on returning to service. On 21 June 1940 she carried 500 German prisoners of war, 1700 German seamen and 400 internees towards Canada.

Deported

The *Empress of Canada* was full by the time the Lingfield train arrived. She was packed with German military prisoners, navy and army officers and men – and now refugees and internees were added to the Nazi prisoners of war. Every cabin was full to bursting.

Helmut was undeterred. He found Clemens a table in the dining room to sleep on. Clemens told this bit in the same way as all the rest. 'It was fun,' he said. 'Oh, it was a big adventure!'

Shock? Loss? Uncertainty? Fear? All this in the listener, but none apparently in the teller. To be seen as any kind of victim would be unthinkable.

Instead, here was Helmut Witt again:

He'd seen how hungry I was. 'I'm going to see if you can work in the kitchen,' he told me. 'Then you'll get good food.' And somehow he arranged it, he talked to one of the cooks and I went and washed dishes for the rest of the voyage and got very well fed.

The ship left Liverpool by night, its lights blacked out against enemy air attack and its prisoners locked below decks. When they were eventually allowed out, all they could see was sea and no hint of where they were going.

Helmut the sailor looked up at the stars. 'We're heading north,' he said. 'The next stop in this direction is Iceland.' He looked around, 'And we're sailing alone.'

The year 1940 was known by German submarine commanders as 'the happy time' when the power of their U-boats on the oceans was virtually unchallenged. This was June, a month in which they succeeded in sinking fifty-eight British ships.

Most Allied ships travelled in convoys, with warships to protect them. Not the *Empress of Canada*. She was sailing alone. She was a fast ship, said Clemens, fast enough to get away if a submarine tried to attack. But that seems unlikely. Some way behind, the *Arandora Star*, another unaccompanied British merchant ship packed with many more detainees than there was lifeboat space, was travelling in the same direction. Attacked by a German U-boat, it sank with the loss of 654 lives.

Soon Helmut noticed a change of course. 'We're heading west. They must be taking us to Canada.' He was right. They made landfall at Newfoundland and steamed into the mouth of the great St Lawrence River. The tape cassette rustles, 'It was beauuutiful,' Clemens said with a sigh, doubly beautiful after the huge grey oceans, with green fields on either side and quiet water. No sign of war here. One of the internees from Lingfield decided to make a break for it and jumped overboard to swim for the banks. The guards on the ship shot him dead in the water.

When the *Empress of Canada* tied up in Quebec, there was quite a reception committee. 'I have never seen so many soldiers in my life,' said Clemens. 'The Canadians were really scared.' This was the first contact they'd had with the enemy, with prisoners of war, their first sight of German soldiers in uniform and they had mobilised literally hundreds of armed soldiers to meet them.

The fact was that Canada hadn't wanted to accept Britain's detainees but, still part of the British Empire at the time, it had little choice. The British Government twisted their arm. If he had had his way, Churchill would have had every 'enemy alien' in Britain deported; instead, it was argued that it was essential that the most desperate, dangerous and vicious of the internees be removed before they had a chance to help the Germans invade. Reluctantly, the Canadians agreed, but, when the order was given to select the internees from the camps for deportation, the British authorities were quite unable to find the promised number of desperate cases. Instead, they took whoever was at hand – a round-up in which Clemens, like so many others, was swept up at random.[*]

The main result was that those Canadian officers and soldiers who had been led to expect a dangerous consignment of spies and saboteurs found that the men they were to guard included a high proportion of doctors, lawyers, pianists and Talmudic scholars.[1]

And at least one 16-year-old schoolboy.

---

[*] Instead of the promised 2,633 Category A internees, 1,500 Italians and 1,823 prisoners of war, by 15 July they had actually sent 1,700 merchant seamen (Category A), 2,700 Category B and C internees, 400 Italians and 1,950 prisoners of war (numbers from *Collar the Lot!*).

The Canadians were not to know. Disembarking the prisoners at gunpoint from the *Empress of Canada*, they marched them to a table piled high with large, sealed cardboard boxes 20in × 20in × 20in, sealed shut – one for each prisoner. What was inside? Nobody knew.

Then, an old train appeared, 'like something out of a cowboy movie'. The cars were made of wood and inside there were wooden bunks along the walls and a potbelly stove at each end of the carriage. Loaded aboard, the prisoners could now open their boxes. After months of wartime rationing and internment Clemens couldn't believe his eyes:

> The boxes were full of <u>food</u>, beautiful fresh food! There were great big purple onions, the kind you could eat raw, there were apples, there were pears, there was fruit and vegetables, there was white bread, there was black bread, there was cheese, there was salami. 'Watch out,' we were told, 'this has to last you for about 4 or 5 days.'

The train moved slowly away from the docks and every time it stopped at a station crowds of people would swarm round to peer into the locked box cars at 'the German prisoners'. The journey went on for days, 'we had no idea where we were heading', until eventually the train stopped and everyone was ordered out. This was it.

In time, they learned that the place was called Nipigon and was on northern Lake Superior. For now, they were marched into a large compound surrounded by barbed wire, searchlights and watch towers, containing dozens of big wooden barracks – formerly a paper mill, now a brand-new prisoner-of-war camp. Again, nothing was ready: there were no mattresses, no blankets, 'no nothing'. For the first night or two, they slept on the bare ground, but that was no great hardship – it was summer and warm. Then things started to get organised.

Nipigon*

The camp was full of sailors. The camp authorities let them divide themselves into groups. There were the German sailors, another group of younger people, cabin boys and the like, and there were the communist sailors. They were all given camp uniform to wear: blue denim overalls with a big red circle on the back for the guards to shoot at if anyone should try to escape.

Canadian internment camp shirt.

Huts were allocated, mattresses, blankets and pillows issued. Helmut Witt took Clemens by the arm as they walked into the long hut, past row after row of double-decker metal bunks. 'This way', steering him to a particular place. 'See that hole in the roof?' he pointed. 'That's for a stove-pipe. This is where the stove must be going. When winter comes this is where we need to be.'

---

* There were numerous prisoner-of-war camps in Canada during the Second World War, some only now coming to light. It's not clear exactly which one Clemens was in but Red Rock, a camp with a mixture of Nazi prisoners of war, merchant seamen and deported 'enemy aliens' would have been a similar kind of place. Created with prisoners escorted from Quebec in July 1940, it went on to experience a lot of tension and even fights between the different groups.

The lessons continued: not medical school, but certainly an education nonetheless. The sailors showed Clemens how to make lanyards and belts out of knotted yarn and sell them to the camp guards in return for cigarette money. They made beautiful model boats and taught him how to put a ship inside a bottle, with painted putty for the sea, delicate rigging made from cotton thread and sails of cigarette paper. They sold those too.

The camp authorities set the prisoners to work making camouflage nets for the war effort and building more wooden barracks to house yet more prisoners, with Clemens dizzily astride the roof tree, learning how to cross the timbers over and trying not to look down or think of what would happen if he fell. 'I learned how to drive a 6 inch nail straight into hard wood without twisting and how to make the heavy hammer sing a satisfying *doing, doing, doing* as it went.' And Helmut Witt got Clemens a job in the officers' mess where the cook sergeant, a Canadian called Spike, took a liking to the boy and fed him waffles with maple syrup and fried eggs, riches unlimited.

But summer was fading. One day all the prisoners were issued with long johns – 'We thought it was funny, so funny we did a long-john dance.' They were marched out into the forest to fell trees and chop firewood. As the autumn arrived they were issued with hats and gloves and huge, warm, heavy greatcoats. The lake froze over, smooth and flat, and the cold of northern Canada began to bite.

This was no ordinary winter cold, such as Clemens had known in the mountains of his childhood. This was the Arctic, and it was a harsh teacher:

You couldn't touch any sort of metal with your bare hands because your skin would stick to it and tear away; if you wet the end of your cigarette when you were smoking, by the time you got it back to your lips it would be frozen solid; if you were chopping wood and you weren't careful the metal head of the axe would shatter and shards of metal fly in all directions.

Lying in their bunks at night they could hear tremendous cracking noises from the forest as the great trees split in the cold. There were snowstorms and blizzards. The frozen surface of the lake became sculpted with hills and peaks of snow and ice like some strange mountain range.

Somewhere the war was raging, but the hills surrounding the camp were so rich in iron ore that radios wouldn't work. Even the camp authorities could only get news the slow way.

There was an escape attempt, a tunnel, dogs and guards. Clemens got thirty days' solitary confinement for his part in it, another 'adventure', as he put it. Others weren't so lucky, the ones who escaped were shot dead by the guards who went after them.

Lost

Sheets of letter paper flutter from the file my mother kept: pale blue ones, some small, some larger, with Mutti's handwriting swaying and stretching in distress through watery marks on the pages; a single

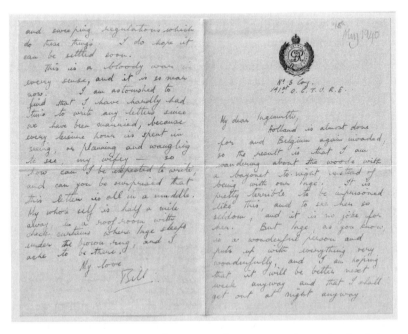

Bill to Mutti, May 1940, just as Clemens was being interned – and nobody knew.

densely typed sheet of onion-skin from Fritz in Argentina; my father's measured script, still in its pre-war form, beating across cream sheets, 'I will do anything I can'.

Mutti and all the family were thrown into a frenzy of disbelief and worry. Clemens had simply disappeared. Barely two weeks after the wedding she had fought against so hard, Mutti's anguish of the preceding months was nothing to this. If it's bad when Clemens is first interned, it only intensifies when, with the deportations of June, he vanishes again – lost without trace in the muddle while rumours tell of ships laden with internees torpedoed in the Atlantic and prisoners, hopelessly outnumbering the lifeboats, fighting to escape as the water rises.

For weeks they don't know where he is, then my father writes:

21 July 1940 from Bill to Mutti

My dear Ingemutti,

I can't tell you how revolted I was by the news which Inge brought back last night.

I would do anything I can, because I believe that England and the English are good things and fair at heart, and these incidents are an insult to us all, and worthy of the worst Nazi attitude.

He offers help through his father's firm and makes contact with a Mr Scott:

Mutti to Bill

… This is nearly again an English kindness as I always believed in it. God bless Mr Scott.

Finally, at the end of July she learns where Clemens is and with that comes new worries:

29 July, Mutti to Inge

I know now for certain Clemens has gone to Canada, and if he would be released there, what to do?

She must send him clothes at once, and a suitcase; she needs to look after him. It's a mistake. He's only a boy. He shouldn't have been deported; so now he'll be released surely? It's essential he continue his education, make something of himself.

> I am sorry I lost again my nerves after the wedding – but the two nights now, after I know Clemens well in Canada, have done already wonders on my health.

For Clemens, up in the Arctic, change came in the form of a letter. This was extraordinary. Prisoners didn't get letters. Nor were they allowed to write them. Clemens hadn't been able to let anyone know where he was and, as far as he knew, nobody else had any way of finding out. But he had reckoned without Mutti and his sisters and their husbands and their many friends and contacts.

The letter came from a certain Mr Mercer, who introduced himself as a Canadian friend of Mutti's and urged Clemens to keep his courage. 'We're on your track,' it said, 'we're making progress', and 'we hope to get you out, to get you released as soon as we can. Keep your pecker up!' And with it, Mr Mercer sent some cigarettes.

From that moment on things began to change. For the first time, Clemens was able to write to his mother and receive letters from her. 'At last. At last. I didn't know where you were!'

Behind all this was a major political row which had finally broken out in Britain about the hasty treatment of internees and the indiscriminate deportation of so many. The Fifth Column panic had subsided and, called to account in Parliament in the wake of the *Arandora Star* disaster, now the government handed the management of the debacle back from the secret committee and the War Office to the Home Office. Mr Paterson was appointed High Commissioner of Internment and charged with sorting out the mess. (His was the *Report on Civilian Internees Sent from the United Kingdom to Canada during the Unusually Fine Summer of 1940*.)

❧

Mutti did not want Clemens to risk his life again coming back across the U-boat-infested Atlantic. She began the search for people who would have him to stay or vouch for him, stand guarantor so he could go to university in Canada. Hopes were dashed and raised again:

My dear Children
So it is now – I don't think it will work with the release of Clemens in Canada. I only can have him back to England what I <u>don't</u> like to risk.

But then, written diagonally across the first page in fresh ink:

Now I heard on the telephon that it <u>can</u> work.

Taken up again on the last page:

Happy postscript: my solicitor speak with Mr P– on the telephon (don't expect an answer from him) that in the parliament it was mentioned to release the Boys and to send them to schools. Now Mr Scott should arrange for Clemens to be picket up or to be received in an English family (<u>Mercer</u>).

And at last, she hears from him:

I had today the second letter of Clemens, he is really so clever to take the situation with so high spirit as possible … The hours are important now, nothing must be postponed.

Determined to lobby influential people, get legal advice and pursue every possible lead, Mutti left the relative safety of Dorset and Myrtle Cottage for London at the height of the Blitz. The bombs were falling all around. Her handwriting deteriorates and so do the nerves:

**23 September 1940 – c/o Evans, Hill Farm, Weston on Trent,
Derby – my father to Mutti**

Dear Ingemutti,
Poor you being bombed. We were a bit worried about you, but

your account of how you lay on your mattress and gave encouragement to the people walking over your head was magnificent and we laughed to bits about it.

Well I'm glad you're in Oxford.

I had a letter today from Mr Scott enclosing a copy of a telegram from Mercer in Montreal which reads as <u>follows</u>:
'After consultation with friends, I consider it unwise for Clemens to remain here if released because probably impossible to find employment and cannot guarantee maintenance as would be required by Canadian Government.

14 October 1940, Mutti to Bill

In Oxford are now few students – I often think I see Clemens.

Did Mr Mercer cabel that he is unwilling to sign the undertaking as guarantor?? Please tell me when did this happen ... You know paper and scrap is worth more than young lifes. Satanism is spraying over the world – what do we want here any longer??

Two days later:

The most important thing is Clemens is in a very strong mood. He received all my cabels and admired my sprit – Good.

She sends more letters. Raises new hopes: if he can't stay in Canada, what about America? Bart Hayes, a friend from the Alassio days, contacted Harvard and established the possibility – remote but real – of a scholarship there for Clemens. But they had reckoned without the hostility of the US Government to the internees:

Department of State Washington, to Bart Hayes 19 April 1941

Dear Bart

I just received your letter this morning about the German boy interned in Canada and I'm afraid I only have bad news for you.

All German internees in Canada at the present moment are mandatorily excluded from entry into the United States for a period of two years after their arrival in Canada because of Section 17 of the Immigration Act of 1924, which provides exclusion for persons arriving in countries adjacent to the United States on steamship lines which do not comply with the provisions of that Act. It so happens that all the boats on which these internees were brought to Canada did not so comply.

What was left? Determined that her son should not risk his life crossing the Atlantic again, Mutti could only think of one other way. She wrote to Fritz and he wrote back, untypically in English, for official scrutiny maybe?

From Fritz in Argentina, 25 March 1941

Dear Ann

... one has to try first to get him along here as it seems the only possible solution ... it was a great chance to have the right to get him landing in the Argentine. I have his landing permit since November 27th ....

Mutti to Fritz, 11 May 1941

I had an information that Mr Paterson, the High Commissionar of Internements had 3 times interviewed Clemens; he gave a very good discreption of the Boy and his charming manners as well as his charakter and spirit, he regretet that he shall send the Boy to the Argentine instead of sending him back.

Mr Paterson

In Clemens' version, fifty years later, he tells Mr Paterson like a character in an adventure story and the choices as his own. He remembered Paterson arriving at the camp and interviewing him in the camp office to the effect of: 'Bit of a mix-up. Hope to get you out shortly. Question

171

is, then what?' There had been discussions with Mutti and the family in England. 'We can offer you three choices,' said Mr Paterson, like something out of a book.

'Yes?'

'The first is to return to England.'

'If I go back, can I join the RAF?' asked Clemens.

"Fraid not,' said Mr Paterson. 'You can join the Pioneer Corps or the Home Guard. You can help clear up rubble after the air raids.'

'Look,' said Clemens, 'I've already been across the U-boat infested Atlantic once. I'm not going to risk my neck crossing it *again* if I can't fight when I get there.'

'Very well,' said Mr Paterson. 'Then your second option is to stay in Canada and study at McGill University.' And he set about making all the arrangements.

This, of course, was a serious offer. McGill was an excellent university. Clemens could pick up where he had left off all those months ago, years ago it seemed now, as a schoolboy in Edinburgh. Back to study. On to medicine. And yet ...

After the rupture of the last fifteen months and all he had seen and learnt in that other university that was the camp Clemens-the-boy had grown up and outgrown the plan. No. The truth of it was that Clemens refused the offer. But that only emerges in his mother's poignant letters of thanks to Mr Mercer and Mr Paterson. Instead his own account gallops on here, makes no mention of his own refusal, but skips and races on to the punchline.

'What's the third choice?' he asked

'Well,' said Mr Paterson, 'The third option would be South America.'

Now that was something else.

His mind, Clemens said, went back to that sunny Sunday morning at Miss Turcan's Edinburgh boarding house and the conversation with the boy from Manaus, his last in freedom, when the knock came at the door. He didn't mention if it touched on his father, whom he hadn't seen for years, gone to Argentina to make his fortune in the New World. No, uppermost in Clemens' mind, he told us, were two books by William Henry Hudson which my father had sent him, *The Purple Land* and *Far Away and Long Ago*, each about different South American countries. 'These had so inflamed my imagination that I wanted to go to South America or die!' said my disappearing uncle, fifty years later. So that was that.

Mr Paterson left. Clemens heard no more. Life in the camp went on as usual. Until one afternoon, without warning, he and ten other men were told to pack up all their stuff and report to the gate.

There was no time for goodbyes. He never saw Helmut Witt again, despite trying desperately to find him after the war. It was winter and dark, and so cold at the railway stop that two of his toes turned black with frostbite waiting for the train that took them south to a transit camp near Montreal. In spring, he was transferred from there to another camp in an old French fortress on an island in the river. And it was summer again before he was taken, at last, to see Mr Mercer himself in his office in the centre of Montreal.

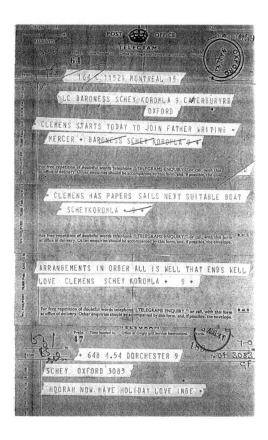

When Clemens walked into his office dressed in his prison uniform, the same blue overalls with the red circle on the back, he remembered Mr Mercer wagging his finger at his secretary. 'Watch out!' he warned, 'This is a prisoner of war. He just might shoot you,' and laughed. Mr Mercer produced $100 and a ticket for South America. 'You can go,' he said.

Clemens, 1942.

So, my disappearing uncle bought himself a linen suit, took off the overalls, cutting out a piece of the red target as a souvenir,[*] and collected the small bag he'd packed just for the weekend two years before. He took a train across Canada to Halifax, Nova Scotia and there, on 3 August, boarded a small cargo ship with about twenty passengers, *Lady Nelson*, bound for the south. He was 18.

---

[*] In Buenos Aires in 2007, Clemens' son, John, showed me the piece of cloth he'd inherited.

It was not a direct route – from Boston and Bermuda (not allowed to disembark in the America or any related territories) they sailed to the West Indies – Anguilla, Antigua, Martinique, Montserrat, St Lucia to Barbados, Trinidad and Tobago – and on with a group of fifteen American chorus girls to Rio de Janeiro; then came Santos, Montevideo and a whole night crossing the River Plate to finally arrive in Buenos Aires at the end of September, too cold for the linen suit.

Looking over the rail – his father came to meet him with the landing permit. 'There he was on the quay below, and May was with him. I'd forgotten about May!' They had him to stay for two weeks and then he was out on his own. With no money, he made animals out of pipe cleaners and sold them on the street. From there, he worked his way through.

And he never came back.

He made a life, a successful life, and a career as a research scientist, consultant and industrial chemist with a business card that read 'Baron Clemens Schey von Koromla'. Love held him there too: surviving a serious car crash on their honeymoon, his marriage to Lida McGillycuddy lasted until her death in 1991. They had three children, spoke English at home, sent them to German schools and forbade them to speak Spanish in the house. Of their seven grandchildren, four grew up in their house with Clemens as paterfamilias. He died in 2004.

In 2007, on a visit to Argentina, I went to find my unknown cousins and heard mixed accounts of both his kindness and his strange harshness.

'Well, I suppose it could be understandable in some ways,' I found myself saying to these cousins I had barely met, 'given their childhood story – you know the one?'

'No.'

'And, of course, what happened to him in the war – that's quite a story too – must have affected him. You must have heard it.'

'Only some of it.'

And so I found myself sitting on a fence in the purple land of Patagonia telling these stories like some Ancient Mariner to those they had probably affected more than anyone else without their knowing. And reflecting on the power of stories not told and what lies under stories told too – with damage told as adventure – was it to spare us or them?

As to why he never came back, even to visit for that half-century – the school friend in whom he had confided on his 1990 visit back was crystal clear: 'He was so offended by the treatment he received that he didn't want to know.'

And Mutti?

Mutti finally got to see Clemens again when she flew out to Argentina soon after his honeymoon car crash in 1946. The journey was difficult and she had problems with her health but she was welcomed by Clemens' wife, Lida, and her Irish parents and stayed with them until he finally came out of hospital and went to live with them too. With the

Eliza's portrait of Mutti – Anny Schey-Koromla.

war over and the restrictions lifted, it was now that she finally applied for British naturalisation, appropriately, for this woman of many countries, swearing her Oath of Allegiance to Britain at the British Embassy in Buenos Aires. She was still there when my parents' first child, my sister Tessa, was born in England that October.

The health troubles continued after she came back in January 1947 and in September surgery showed inoperable pancreatic cancer. From the hospital, she moved in with Inge and Bill, calmly said goodbye to all her many friends, and died in January 1948, the year before I was born.

She was buried in Dorset, in the churchyard at Fontmell Magna, under a tombstone carved by the sculptor David McFall with a relief of a village in the mountains and a garland of myrtle leaves. 'Anna Caecilia Schey-Koromla,' it reads. 'Born Weikersdorf, Vienna, 17th June 1886. Died 11th January 1948.'

So, that was the end of the story.

Or maybe not.

Part II

WHEN THE CLOCKS RUN BACKWARDS

Le mort saisit le vif

Le mort saisit le vif, French for 'the dead seizes the living' is a legal term. According to this an heir is considered as having succeeded to the deceased from the instant of his death. There can be no gap in the possession of a freehold estate in land. The legal title vests immediately in the heirs upon the death of the person through whom they claim title.

10

Of Love

Clemens and his story emerged long after I was grown up. It was a kind of postscript, the rounding out of the faintest tale in the maternal set. And Mutti's death completed it. That was enough.

For us, childhood had given way to university and as the 1960s moved towards the '70s, we strode on into our new world, the world that was going to be different. Proud optimists, we were strangely oblivious to what had happened little more than twenty years before as we reaped the benefits of new universities, student grants, the National Health Service and more, much more. Our parents didn't want to talk about the Second World War, or for us to be tainted by it, but was it really a coincidence that, quite apart from the unexplained nightmares, many of us were so fiercely, anxiously anti-war?

Not only was the Cold War icily present but the world around us was changing fast. Remarkably fast. And it wasn't just music and fashion. Just look at the law, and the dates. In the UK, racial discrimination was addressed for the first time in the Race Relations Act of 1965. In 1967, the Abortion Act made abortion legal, the Sexual Offences Act decriminalised homosexual acts for men over 21 and, after our furtive teenage scurries to brave but hidden sources of help, the Family Planning Act of the same year at last made contraception available to all, regardless of marital status. The contraceptive pill arrived and I was not the only one to grow heavy and lethargic on its large doses of hormones.

In 1967, consumerism set sail when the first credit cards appeared – but of course, a woman was not allowed to have one in her own name. In 1969, we sat up into the small hours of the morning to see the first men land on the moon, yes, but the same year saw the Divorce Reform Act make it possible for both sexes to seek divorce on the breakdown of marriage. In the background stood the Berlin Wall, the Cold War, the American war in Vietnam, CND.

At Oxford, the ancient university had barely flinched. It was firmly set in its ways. As women students we were locked into our colleges at night; male visitors were forbidden. I had never been locked in anywhere and had no intention of starting now, so it was lucky that I knew how to climb.

Then there was the curriculum. For those of us reading English, the course excluded anything written after 1898 because, we were told, the authors had not been dead for long enough to establish whether or not they were truly 'Great'. As for American or other English-language writers, Good Heavens, no! The new field of linguistics was excluded too, though the university invited its great proponent, Noam Chomsky, to visit and he lectured to us in packed halls, not only on linguistics but on the iniquity of the American war in Vietnam.

Something had to give. In March 1968, like so many others, I went to the big London demonstration against the Vietnam War. For as far as the eye could see, chanting demonstrators filled the streets – Piccadilly, Regent Street, Oxford Street – from one shop-windowed side of the road right across to the other. Turning the corner into Grosvenor Square, we found the US Embassy, all glass and steel and railings, guarded not only by US Marines armed with machine guns inside the entrance doors but our own 'boys in blue' everywhere else. The situation erupted in a bottleneck crush of police and shields, batons wielded and people kicked, arrests, injury and confusion. I avoided arrest by climbing a tree as the police horses charged across the square below but something had shifted.[*] I was up there for a while.

---

[*] 117 policemen were injured, 246 protesters arrested and charged and St John's Ambulance said it treated eighty-six people on the spot. Innocent as we were, we were shocked.

Two months later, in May 1968, came student riots in Paris, the Sorbonne occupied, workers on strike in sympathy. Student revolt followed in Britain, too. Even in Oxford, the English faculty was occupied and discussions held about how the courses could and should be in the future; this was education for real. Back at the college, a key system was introduced for students who wanted to come in late.

That summer Soviet tanks rolled into Prague to crush the Prague Spring.

When university was over I got a job, hugely relieved to be out in the 'real' world, and embarked on a career. Returning to London, I drew cartoons in my spare time, printed posters – Margaret Thatcher, Milk Snatcher – in a damp vault under the railway lines of Camden Town for others to carry off into the dark and paste on walls; and was involved in the start of the Women's Liberation Movement with its conferences and consciousness-raising groups. The world was ours to change (if we could change ourselves). I worked, I played and wrote and drew.

An adult now, I was busy with my own life and, as people do, had long since packed all the stories away on a small shelf in the mental library, the one marked 'Back Story' – an interesting but inert (or so I thought) collection – in case anyone was interested.

My parents were still there. Between them they hosted the stories, absolving us from responsibility, making the past safe. Since they knew everything, we didn't have to. (Childhood takes a long time to wear off!)

My father remarried,** was happier at last – a great relief for us all. My mother was dynamic, busy, away a lot and travelling, always travelling – for work from London to Cambridge, Munich, Vienna, Cincinnati and California, for adventures like trekking in Nepal and, with her astonishing gift for friendship, for summer breaks with friends in Italy, the south of France or Norfolk. In between times, she taught in London, people of many kinds – actors, writers, lawyers, students and especially musicians, from young singers and rock performers to

---

** To Natalie Greening (née Robertson) who he had known since childhood, on 15 February 1971, the day 'Britain went decimal'.

world-famous conductors. She also gardened, walked and cooked us wonderful meals, and every day without fail, as she had every day of my life, she took a rest after lunch, whenever possible in the garden in the sun wearing as few clothes as possible. She was forever, of course.

By the mid-1970s I had settled down with a house and partner. From what I had seen growing up, marriage was neither a safe place nor any guarantee of a stable future and the idea of being owned by anyone was offensive. I decided against. No piece of paper could hold a relationship together, I reasoned, and maybe the assumption that it could even made things worse. No, a partnership of equals, love and work was the only chance. Above all, I must not go the same road as my parents with their broken hearts.

Then we decided to have children.

This was a revelation. How was it possible to care so much about anyone? I was amazed by the fierceness of the connection. Here was the biggest certainty I'd ever felt, a fire in the mind as well as the heart. Who were these new people? Where had they come from? And how could they be so interesting?

Everything took on a new perspective: this vertical connection, ourselves as links in a chain. So, this was what it had all been about? I looked at my parents with new eyes. How do you do this thing?

By the time the 1980s unfolded I was utterly absorbed by children and work.

My father suffered over my refusal to marry. 'What if he leaves you?' he pleaded, oblivious to the irony. The fact remained that, though he was eternally kind, I had shamed him. My mother appeared to have no such scruples; untroubled, she delighted in her grandchildren and joined in enthusiastically, supporting us on holidays and more – when she wasn't away, that is.

As the children grew older, I remembered about the stories. They might enjoy them too. I needed to get them straight. I dusted them down, asked the parents a few questions and moved them to the mental shelf marked 'Entertainment (car journeys?)'. It was an unexamined, automatic thing to do – the blueprint again – telling stories is what parents do, isn't it? And these ones belonged to our children too. The adult, the parent, the storyteller: I thought I'd got it sorted.

How wrong I was.

The past didn't want to lie quiet. It seethed and bubbled and kept threatening to break through the thin surface of our lives. Not even death seemed to put an end to it. Especially not death. As we headed towards the twenty-first century, the ghosts were still on the move, though I was almost too busy to notice. I was, however, still a sucker for a story. And stories can unpick what you understand and recast it all over again.

The Wrong Initials

So it was, on one summer day, when I'd gone to visit my mother and found her clearing out her linen cupboard. There was a big pile of sheets and towels and tablecloths to be sorted and we brought them out to the table in the garden in the sun while the children ran and played.

Among the linen was a pile of damask tablecloths and napkins embroidered at the corners. These were things that Mutti had brought with her to England and which had passed to my mother after she died. They were hardly ever used: too precious, too old for every day, a nuisance to wash and iron, but despite that, it would be upsetting if anything happened to them. They had been part of my grandmother's trousseau, the things a girl collected for her married life, equipment for a home chosen to last a lifetime, and here they were, still going well into our lifetimes, two generations later. One of the characteristics of the trousseau of course was that when a girl became engaged her new initials were embroidered on everything to mark the match.

We shook the linen out and checked it as we talked. 'So, these are your mother's initials?' I said, smoothing the embroidered monogram on a napkin.

'Mmmm.'

I looked. There was something odd about it. 'I can see the "A" for Anny and that must be a "v" ... But wasn't she either Schindler or Schey? I don't see an "S" on these at all? Can that be right?'

'Well,' my mother said.

And suddenly we were back at the beginning or a bit before. Unpicking a knot in the history thread that I hadn't even known existed.

The wrong initials.

Between Mutti's life as an actress and her marriage to my grandfather there had, it seemed, been another chapter in Anny Schindler's life. It was important, not only for her but, as things turned out, for Fritz von Schey and many of his family, for their children Beate, Inge and Clemens and for all of us who came after. Without it, we might not have happened at all.

By the time I heard it on that summer's day, grown up, in my forties with a job, a house and family of my own to support, I was uncomfortably familiar with the problems of making ends meet. The past didn't get much of a look-in but if I did think about the stories now, I had new questions: ideals aside, how had Mutti managed it?

Strength of character is one thing, of hers there was no doubt, but means are another. The Schindlers' finances had always been precarious. There was no mention of Mutti working after her marriage and money apparently fled Fritz, carefree, feckless, and some said a little crazy, like water down a drain. But Mutti's journey across Europe with her children was not a penniless flight. There was the car, the tutor, the house in Alassio, the villa in Cagnes, the boarding schools in England and yet more travelling every holiday after that. How did she do it?

As the napkins unfolded, suddenly we were back to events that happened before my grandmother's journey across Europe, before the years in Italy and France, before Munich and Schwaz, before she married Fritz, before the First World War even.

1911 – click and a new screen opens.

With apologies for upsetting the sequence, here we are again: the disobedient past, history as a repeating question, a series of knots. It won't go smooth. Begin again. Begin again.

Von Lieben

It is 1908, 1909 or 1910 perhaps. Mutti, who is still Anny Schindler at this point, is in her early twenties and in new-century Vienna. The world is about to change. Across the road from the Burgtheater, above Landtmann's famous coffee house, a young man called Robert von Lieben[*] has set up a laboratory in the grand apartments belonging to his family. He is an enthusiastic follower of the theatre to which he goes with his close friend, the writer Hugo von Hofmannsthal, or with one of his many cousins, and the windows of his lab look out over the street below with a fine view of the theatre entrance.

And here's the story. Somehow, on the winds of change blowing through the new century – at a ball, a salon, at the theatre, among friends, through the window – they met, the young actress Anny Schindler and the scientist Robert von Lieben. They fell in love and, in 1911 when all the linen and the silver had been marked with the initials

---

[*] *Von Lieben* means literally 'of Love'

The Von Lieben house today, with Café Landtmann on the
ground floor. Robert's laboratory was on the first floor

'AvL', they married and set about living happily ever after in their new
villa in the Döblinger Hauptstrasse.

They didn't have much time. Soon after they were married, Robert
fell ill with leukaemia. There was little the doctors could do. Anny
wouldn't leave his side, not for a moment. Even when she developed
appendicitis, she refused to have an operation because it would have
meant being away from him for days, a decision which had consequences for her health for the rest of her life. But it was no good. Early
in 1913, little more than a year after they were married, Robert von
Lieben died, aged only 34, leaving Anny von Lieben, 27, widowed,
childless and heartbroken.

It was three years later that she married our grandfather – Baron
Fritz Schey von Koromla, one of her first husband's many cousins.

It was a sad interlude, but these things happen. So what?

I might never have looked any further, except that it wasn't only in our family that there was more to tell. As the twentieth century moved toward the twenty-first, something else was going on in the world outside, new information was surfacing. Jewish history was insisting on a hearing and a different kind of Austrian history was being exposed; an account of the past that had been silenced by the events of the previous century.

As the shadows of the Second World War gave way to the light of day,[*] Austria was being painfully forced to acknowledge its past. There were articles and books, of course, but it's almost hard to believe that it was not until the new century and January 2001 that the Washington Agreement finally committed the Austrian Republic to return or pay reparations for assets and art looted by the Nazis and, significantly, placed it under an obligation to include and preserve Jewish heritage.

It was a process that took me to Vienna in 2005, tipped off by a friend of my mother's about an exhibition that might be interesting. There, to my surprise, I met my grandmother for the first time. Face to face.

Walking into the second room of the exhibition in the Jewish Museum, there she was, standing in front of me as large as life: a cut-out figure enlarged from a black-and-white photograph from 1911, when she had been about the same age as my own daughter was now, the one named after her. And sitting nearby was another figure, that of a slight and handsome young man with dark hair and eyes.

This was not Fritz, the lanky cavalry officer of the First World War photos. This was Robert von Lieben. And here was more of the story that had brought me there, the one I had come across quite by chance, buried in the folds of cloth in my mother's linen cupboard.

The exhibition – *The Liebens, 150 Years History of a Viennese Family* – and its catalogue were rich in information; they in turn led to books and articles and websites, and from it all emerged a remarkable man. As I followed the trail, there was much to know about Robert von Lieben, and clues as to why he had possibly made such a difference to us all.

---

[*] The war had ended in 1945 but for the following ten years Austria was controlled by the Allied powers, until the 1955 Declaration of Independence re-established sovereignty.

Anny Schindler   Robert von Lieben

Largely self-taught and a brilliant scientist, Robert von Lieben had been deeply interested in the science of the early twentieth century – electricity, telephony, radiation, optics, manned flight. The Liebens – like the Scheys – were one of the Jewish families for whom the laws of toleration that followed the 1848 revolution had opened the doors. Robert's father, Leopold, had made his mark – earning not only wealth but position and influence – and, raised to the nobility, had gained the prized title 'von' to add to the family name. Now he was not only head of the Lieben family bank but the president of the Vienna Stock Exchange, vice president of the Austro-Hungarian Bank and an influential member of Vienna's new aristocracy.

Robert's mother, Anna, came from another prominent Jewish Viennese family, the Todescos, whose palace next to the Opera House in the heart of Vienna was famous for its social gatherings. She was a gifted painter and poet but like many women of her class stifling in their wealthy settings, she suffered from 'neurosis' and, unable to sleep at night and with an equal terror of the dark, was said to live on caviar and champagne and to keep a professional chess player waiting outside her room all night in case she wanted to play.

Her lasting fame was to come from her contribution to another of the new century's sciences: psychoanalysis. As 'Cäcilie M', she was one of Freud's first patients, the one he called his '*Lehrmeisterin*', or teacher, and visited at the Lieben home each day to supervise her injection with morphine.

Commemorative stamp, 1936.

These were families rich in talent: writers, philosophers, artists, scientists, musicians, as well as the men who made the money. Unlike the old aristocracy, they sought integration in Vienna's high society through their education and culture and their women earned their influence in non-Jewish society through their legendary hospitality and the 'salons' they held, gathering round themselves the great names of the day.

It was in houses such as theirs that the balls Mutti described in her brown notebook memoir were held. Robert's older brother Ernst remembered how as children in the Todesco Palace:

We ... used to gather in the evening behind these mirrored doors to watch the great balls that made my grandparents famous. Crouched here as a small boy I watched Brahms and Liszt and the great politicians of the day, and the great poets and painters. It seemed to me that the whole world came to our house.[1]

Robert, the fourth of the five von Lieben children, was not a success at school. Judged 'wanting' (*Ungenügend*) in maths and physics at Vienna's renowned Akademische Gymnasium, he moved to the less academic *Realschule*, but never finished his studies. At home, though, he conducted experiments, invented things, devised and installed an intercom system in the family house at the age of 11, and, with his cousin 'Pol', entertained the family at parties with demonstrations of the newly discovered X-ray photography. By the time his contemporaries were sitting their school-leaving exams, he had abandoned school altogether and was busy at the family estate in Hinterbrühl, 20km south of Vienna, converting a mill into a generator so that he could install the new technology of electric light that would turn night into day for his suffering mother.[2]

Then came military service. Within weeks of volunteering for a cavalry regiment, he was seriously injured in a fall from his horse. The result was a long stay in hospital in Vienna followed by convalescence at the family estates in Hungary and Bad Vöslau. He never fully recovered.

With his family's enormous wealth, Robert von Lieben was under no pressure to earn his living and was able to pursue his scientific interests unhindered. As soon as he was well enough, he went to physics lectures at Vienna University as a 'guest' listener, then sought out practical experience by working unpaid at the Siemens works in Nuremberg and in 1899, he took himself off to Göttingen to study at the Institute for Physical Chemistry with Professor Walther Nernst,* who was to become his lifelong friend and mentor. Travelling in France with Nernst that year, the two men visited the Wright brothers, who were developing their first aeroplanes. Typically, Robert von Lieben bought one of the planes and, dismissing the engineer who came with it, made a number of improvements of his own before giving it to the Austrian military.

---

* Inventor of the Nernst lamp, the first bright white light, Nernst won the Nobel Prize for Physics.

In the course of his short life, he produced and patented inventions in a wide range of fields including optics, cars and aircraft construction. But perhaps his most important contribution was in the field of telephony. In 1904, he bought a telephone factory in Olmütz. Then he bought a small telephone exchange and set about tackling a critical problem of the time, namely how to amplify weak signals so that telephone messages could travel longer distances. There followed a series of inventions and patents, among them the cathode ray relay and the Lieben amplifier thermionic valve, which not only transformed telephone communications (and made possible the long-distance communications of the First World War) but were to become the basis of a whole new technology: that of radio and television. These were inventions that were to change the world.

In March 1906, Robert von Lieben patented his cathode ray relay and six months later, an American called Deforest patented a very similar device. In 1912, the year after he married, having refined his designs, he set up the Lieben Consortium with all but one of the top electrical companies of the time, to exploit his inventions. With considerable business acumen, he not only sold his patents to the consortium for the enormous sum of 100,000 marks but ensured a royalty payment for

The Lieben-Reisz-Strauss valve, 1910.

every single valve and machine produced from his inventions. The deal was signed on 19 February 1912. A year later he was dead.

❦

Anny, as his widow, received royalties from the patents.* She was financially independent. Her second husband Fritz, on the other hand, was not. In his courtship letters of 1915, he struggles to explain – with heavy crossings out, broken sentences, embarrassment at having to talk about such things – that he's dependent on his father, Josef, the law professor, who was an academic and not rich himself. 'I started working late in life,' he tells her. He had courted another girl for four years and wanted to marry her but had to withdraw because he couldn't assure her father that he could support them.

Anny clearly wants children. He would, of course, like children, he says, but unfortunately he's not in a position to provide for them. Could he dare to hope? A few letters later and it's all settled.

It seems very likely that it was Robert von Lieben's business acumen that secured our grandparents' marriage. On 11 November 1918, the day the First World War ended and with it the old Austro-Hungarian Empire, Fritz and Anny bought the Hügelhof in Schwaz as joint owners. And there they lived, as the new Republic of Austria began, with Fritz, as his aunt Mathilde wrote in a letter to her cousin, living 'more or less on his wife's money'.[3]

They had their three children, and when, in 1931, this second marriage broke down, it was partly Lieben's legacy (reflected in the divorce settlement), that and her own courage, which gave Mutti the means to set out in search of a better life. It enabled her to support herself as a single mother in the 1920s, when it was an uncomfortable thing to be; it enabled her to educate her children, travel with them across Europe in search of a 'civilised' place to live and, as the doors swung closed on Nazi Germany and Austria, to help a number of Fritz's Jewish relatives to settle in England after he had left for South America in 1938 with his new wife, May (née Reincke), a shipping heiress from Hamburg.

My mother said she even paid Fritz alimony.

---

* In fact, the valves were only produced until 1922.

Mutti's connection with the von Lieben family did not end with Robert's death either. Not even the move to England could break it. His sister Henriette remained her close friend. Fritz was one of Robert's cousins, and like so many of the big Jewish families of Vienna's Ringstrasse, the Schey and Lieben families twined and tangled together at every turn.

The connection even followed us into our childhood life in London, though my sister and I had no idea of its source. We never heard anything about Mutti's Schindler family and the Scheys were rare birds, but at weekends my mother would often walk us from the house-that-looked-like-a-church across the Heath to Hampstead with the dog bounding alongside chasing circles in the grass. There were different destinations – our friends, her friends, but from time to time we would end up at the door of a tall, red-brick house in Chesterton Road where an elegant, silver-haired lady called 'Piz' would greet my

From Night into Day. Marie-Louise von Motesiczky's portrait of her mother Henriette, née Lieben, now in the Tate Gallery, London.

mother with outstretched arms and kisses and the language would change to Austrian.

To us children, the house seemed full of deep shadows and looming furniture and on every visit we would be taken upstairs to see Piz's mother, the poet, Henriette, unfathomably old, who lay in bed propped up on cushions with a whippet curled up on the counterpane. Yes, our mysterious old woman, the one who was bald, bearded and smoked a pipe —was Robert von Lieben's younger sister.

And Piz, the silver-haired daughter whose name was Marie-Louise von Motesiczsky, was not only Mutti's niece from that first marriage (and my mother's godmother), but an exceptional painter who, after coming to England at the start of the Second World War, quietly worked for the rest of her life in that tall, red house in Hampstead and whose series of portraits of her mother in her extreme old age are among the finest of her generation.

Mother in Bed, Marie-Louise von Motesiczky, now in the Fitzwilliam Museum Cambridge.

196

11

Death and After

Two years after Clemens reappeared, my mother saw a shadow in her eye. The optician sent her to the doctor.

'I don't want to be a grey face on a trolley in a hospital,' she said in late July as the cancer stole her breath. 'Let's go camping.'

So we did, in the field near the sea in Norfolk where she'd spent her August break for many years in a tumbledown caravan belonging to her friend Noreen Amis. She had a caravan; we were in tents. There was me and our three children, their father was away working. We had a cold tap, oxygen, morphine, rain – the fight was tough, but it was a beautiful place and a precious time.

From the diagnosis three months earlier, my mother had made it clear that no one other than the closest family was to be told. 'I don't want anybody looking at me with *those eyes!*' she said and continued to teach uninterrupted. 'If the doctors want to treat me it'll have to be early in the morning before I go to work.' To her many friends and pupils, now she was just on her usual summer holiday, she'd be back at the start of term.

Two days after we got home, on a golden day in early September, she died in her own bed with me and the children holding her hands.

My 4-year-old daughter helped me wash her body and brush her hair that evening before we sat down to supper. She drew a picture of her grandmother, big and strong and bounding with energy. 'Is she still dead?' she asked me next morning.

It was a good question.

Inge, Christmas 1991.

For me, my mother was always huge. Now, as the tributes and letters poured in, obituaries appeared in the national papers and people
from all over the world sent us anecdotes and memories of parts of my
mother's life they'd shared, far from fading away, she seemed to grow
bigger and bigger until my own loss was compounded. There was so
much I didn't know, hadn't asked, and now that she had gone so had
the possibility of knowing. There were so many questions still there.
The ache for what we'd never had was intense. And mixed into it was
the puzzle of the past and the family. Things she knew and we didn't.
Or did she?

Death does funny things. The creaks and groans of the generations
shifting are well documented, and so is the longing of the children of
parents from other countries to understand their parents' other worlds.
It's also a new licence, as if their absence gives us permission to tiptoe

INGE HENDERSON
Born 6th March 1921
Died 4th September 1992

Friday 11th September 1992   3pm

St Marylebone Crematorium

September 1992, 4-year-old Annie's drawing of her grandmother.

onto territory that previously belonged to them – and, with a vague sense of trespass, to try and fit it onto our very different lives.

It's a common experience.

Clearing the house-that-looked-like-a-church was another. We put it off as long as possible, reluctant to let it go, but it had to happen. After more than forty years the task was huge and booby-trapped with little explosions of loss. It wasn't just memories of our own childhood we were tripping over. Deep in the dark, the things we pulled from cupboards and lofts were heavy with the fingerprints of an earlier past. It too seemed to grow as we worked. What became clear was how much we'd been sheltered from the weight of all that history, whether from my father's sense of lean design or her impatience with it all.

An eighteenth-century oil portrait of a white-chested woman in a powdered wig emerged from the roof (a relative perhaps, why else

Inge's memorial stone, Cley next the Sea.

would she be there?), a framed photograph of Toscanini, a not-very-good portrait of Mutti, and more. And one day, reaching into the back of a high cupboard I found a shoebox tied with string. It was thick with dust and crumbling at the corners so I took it into the garden to open. Inside was a jumble of dull grey discs. What? A closer look showed them to be miniature pewter plates, 3 or 4cm across, with tankards and pots and pans of a similar scale, all decorated with the curlicues of nineteenth-century Europe, and with them a copper warming pan, a ham made of wax, and even a miniature iron roasting spit.

I went to see my father in his flat in Fulham Road, 'Do you know what that box of stuff is?'

'Oh yes,' he said. 'When I got back from the war, I made a trip to Schwaz to see what had happened to the house. It was a mess. There had been soldiers billeted there and they'd smashed up the furniture and everything else that would burn for firewood, including Mutti's dolls' house which she was very fond of. The little plates were lying on the floor, kicked into a corner. So, I picked them up and put them in a shoebox and brought them home.'

This would have been some years before I was born. But not even fifty years had been enough to let them out again. A friend made a wooden box with shelves and doors, we painted the inside to look like an old kitchen and gave them to my now 6-year-old daughter, named for the grandmother we'd never met. She played with them endlessly in preference to plastic and, taking them to school, was a star for a day.

Annie's Austrian Kitchen

Somewhere in the London suburbs, the Year Two children made a class book: 'Annie's Austrian Kitchen 1995'.*

Three years later, my father, too, was dead. Now there was no one left to ask.

The void was huge. Almost without realising it, I began to read and search and try not only to explain the stories that had accompanied us through our lives but to hook them onto the history of their times. And this coincided with the rising interest in Austria's tarnished history. Gradually, I pieced together the background to the stories we'd grown up with.

---

* These were known as 'Nuremberg kitchens': single room doll's kitchens that were very popular in the nineteenth century but go back to the 1500s.

Schloss Erla

Among the people who came to my mother's funeral was her first cousin, Jean Goldschmidt, from Belgium, a big man with a twinkle in his eye, who I remembered from his visits when we were growing up. His was the family my sister had gone to for her French exchange and she had kept in touch.

Tall, distinguished and funny, he would appear in London from time to time on his business trips and always make a point of visiting my mother. Now, at my sister's suggestion, he generously invited me and my family, all five of us, to visit Schloss Erla, the family house in Austria where they spent the summer. The same one my mother had told us about from her childhood.

Erla was no ordinary house. A twelfth-century Benedictine abbey, it stands on a hill above the banks of the River Danube near Linz – old stones, cool courtyards, big trees – a place that breathes quiet survival. There is a cloister, courtyards, a park, a magnificent sixteenth-century tithe barn, a bell tower and, stretching out below it, a rustling blanket of forest reaching down to the banks of the river.

Jean's parents, captivated by the view, had bought it in 1904 as a country retreat from life in Vienna, and this was where Jean had been born and spent his childhood, and his mother Gerda – yes, she of my afternoon in the cake shop in Vienna with her love of shooting wild boar – she was our grandfather's older sister, my mother's Tante Gerda.

Jean and his wife Jacqueline and their daughters could not have been kinder or more generous. They welcomed us to the house as if we belonged – where children ran about and older, young and other people, all of them apparently relatives, came and went in a pattern of summer life unchanged for the best part of a century. Here, for the first time, the Scheys came into focus.

The household was free flow. There were bicycles and walks and places to read, there was a library to explore, the park, the tennis court, a ping-pong tournament in which Jean beat us all soundly. At every turn, on every wall, there was a fascination of things to look at, and down across flowering fields of hay there was a tree-lined lake with waterlilies and a wooden landing stage – the *Sperberteig* in German or *l'Étang* in French – to swim in. In the background was

Schloss Erla from the park.

the sound of bees and children's voices, or the chapel bell marking the hours.

When the big gong rang, there were delicious meals where everyone came together. In the evening, we dressed for dinner, the men and boys in black and white and the girls and women in traditional *dirndls* from the great cupboards in the hall, and we gathered in the sitting room with the windows overlooking the valley for drinks and talk.

And we were included.

Jean wore history lightly. Over 80 and only recently 'retired', he was in the process of starting a new metal-recycling business. He was funny, witty, deadpan, and delighted in making puns across from French into English or German mid-sentence and back again. He also seemed to be the Schloss handyman, fixing things in his workshop overlooking the courtyard as guests and children and grandchildren came and went or cooled off in the fountain down below. He was thoroughly at home and full of stories.

At the swimming pond he noticed me looking at the lattice of silver scars that scored his body. 'That was the invasion of Belgium

– 11 May 1940.* I held off the Germans for a whole ten minutes,' he laughed (and had spent the rest of the war in hiding, injured, the last operation of many only in 1965).

The Second World War had also marked the house and the gathering: we too were its product. The one thing we all had in common was that none of us lived in Austria – instead, it was Belgium, Italy, Switzerland, England, America; it was no coincidence. The Schloss itself had been commandeered by the Nazis to house the officers of the nearby concentration camp at Mauthausen and when the Russian army of liberation arrived, their boots were so worn out, so the story went, that they cut up the Persian carpets of the Schloss to make replacements.**

Erla – the stairs.

Jean took us round the house. He showed us room after beautiful room, with painted cupboards, carved bedsteads, antique bathrooms squeezed into medieval corners, inventive plumbing, a picture framed in a lavatory seat, a shower room next to the chapel wall – chuckling, 'Where else can you have a shower and listen to the mass at the same time?'

---

* The day before his cousin Clemens was arrested in Edinburgh.
** Listed as Belgian rather than Jewish property, when the war was over, Jean's father Herman (like mine in Schwaz) had come back to see how the house had fared ... there's an excellent story about how he got it back.

The library.

He took us down to the vaulted undercroft that housed the ping-pong table and round the cloisters, and passing the entrance gate we glanced into a whitewashed room with scrubbed floorboards, a chair and an iron bedstead. On the wall hung a portrait of a young man in a white military jacket with green collar. He looked familiar, with his large forehead – a bit like Jean even.

'Who's that?' I asked.

'That? That's Fritz,' said Jean, 'Your grandfather.'

Further on, in a room full of painted furniture, he stopped at a gilded frame containing a black-and-white photograph of an old man with a beard and two white-blonde children on his knee. 'Do you recognise them?' Jean was twinkling.

Would I know?

'That's your mother on his knee and Beate behind and he's our grandfather, both theirs and mine, Josef Schey [the professor of law]. This [dark and ornately carved] was his desk.'

It was very strange. Here suddenly was another life; and the men we'd never known. The place was full of them.

The Erla portrait of Fritz Schey von Koromla, our unknown grandfather.

His father Josef Schey von Koromla, Professor of Law, with his granddaughters
Beate and Inge.

Trees

To finish the tour, Jean took us up a series of rickety wooden ladders to the top of the bell tower and a view over the fields and woods and all the way across the River Danube to the Czech Republic. The bells were huge and black and a flock of pigeons, startled by our arrival, wheeled around our heads.

On the way back down again, he turned at the foot of the ladder, unlocked a dusty door and led us into the nuns' private gallery of the Schloss chapel which, through its door to the village street on the other side, also served as the village church.

On the side altar was a striking medieval sculpture 3m high in carved and painted wood. It showed a man with a long beard lying on his side with a great tree spouting out of his groin (obscured by a strategically placed *pietá* on the altar), its branches full of smaller figures – David and others – sitting among the leaves like fat fruit.

'That's the stem of Jesse,' said Jean and added with a smile, 'Jesse, Ysaye, Schey?'

The Stem of Jesse from the chapel at Schloss Erla.

It was a wonderful piece, life springing out of a man's groin — a 'family tree' in the most literal sense. And, with the exception of the Virgin Mary holding her infant son in a blaze of carved Holy light at the top of the tree, all the figures on the branches were men.

'And there shall come forth a rod out of the stem of Jesse, and a Branch shall grow out of his roots,' says the Book of Isaiah (11:1). Jesse, who farmed sheep and lived in Bethlehem, Jesse also spelt 'Isai' or 'Yishai', the father of King David, who defeated Goliath and wrote the Psalms. It's in the Torah and the Qu'ran too. And, sure enough, there is David with his harp on the second branch up. Forty-three generations later, so the Catholic version of the story goes, comes his descendant Jesus Christ — and there he is, riding at the top of the tree in his mother's arms.

The convent of Erla, 1672.

The Jesse tree, I read, is an image that first appears in 1086 and reaches a peak of popularity in the twelfth century, just when Otto von Machland was founding the abbey at Erla for his sister, the first abbess (in 1152). All over Europe, the tree appears in illuminated manuscripts, psalters, carvings, embroidery and stained-glass windows, among them Chartres (1140), York Minster (1310), Bath Abbey and Wells Cathedral.

Some say it originates in Bohemia – and Bohemia, renamed the Czech Republic just a year before our visit, was the land across the Danube that we'd just been admiring from the top of the bell tower that afternoon. All agree it is the start of the family tree idea.

It reminds me. Not just of the great copper beech tree that stands outside the Schloss here, where we shelter in the shade during the day and sit and talk long into the evening, or of the branches of the London trees I sat and read in as a child, but of another great tree from Sumerian literature, 3,000 years BCE, its branches touching the heavens, its roots drinking in the seven rivers of the underworld. They were potent things, trees, sources of connection, not least family ones, things growing out of the groin.

As for the generation after generation of men on their branches, how to pick your way through – and was I even interested?

Supper time on that first visit to Erla. We're eating at a long, long table, itself made of a single huge plank of oak, in the great, panelled hallway. It feels dim after the sunshine outside. There are seventeen of us, from Belgium, Austria, Italy, England, America and Switzerland, among other places, and most of them are new to me, but all, apparently, relations or family friends. The conversation, in French, runs and laughs and leaps across into English, German, Italian, Flemish and back again. I'm sitting opposite Jean and by this time, he knows I like his tales.

'This one you must know,' Jean says.

He points up at a dark oil painting in a gilded frame, the head and shoulders of a man with a moustache, which hangs on the wall above the table among the antlers and hunting trophies, a boar's head, a stuffed capercaillie.

I don't.

'That's Friedrich Schey,' Jean says. 'My great-grandfather, your great-great-grandfather. Pass the potatoes.' And he goes on, 'Now there's a story'.

And he tells me how Friedrich Schey, a Jewish boy from Hungary, came to Vienna with nothing at the age of 18 in the early part of the

The grandfather's grandfather, the Erla portrait of Baron Friedrich Schey.

nineteenth century. How he started work. How, by the time he was 28, he was a partner in his employer's firm, married to his employer's daughter. When he was 38, he started his own bank, 'Friedrich Schey of Vienna'. By the time he was 48, he was rich, a banker to the Austrian imperial family, the Hapsburgs. How he collected books and paintings, was 'raised to the nobility', became Baron Schey von Koromla and built himself a palace on Vienna's celebrated Ringstrasse. How he had eight children. How, when he was 58, he lost most of his money. Eight years later, he was dead.

'I think that painting must be after he lost his money!' Jean spreads his hands and laughs and the man in the brown portrait looks solemnly down at us all laughing, eating, talking, spread out along the long table; descendants from all over the world, but somehow still in touch, five generations later, despite everything the twentieth century could contrive in the way of world wars, Holocaust, dispersal, distance.

I look up at the picture and wonder, is that the trace of a smile?

12

The Grandfather's Grandfather

I might have left it there. It wasn't so different to the summary my mother had given us of rags to riches, Dick Whittington comes to Vienna – with a little bit more and a sting in the tail. The idea of grappling with official history, archives, genealogy and the male line didn't particularly interest me. But, of course, I couldn't quite leave it alone. And it just so happened that this was also a period when, bit by bit, more was emerging, a new history of Austria's uncomfortable past was being assembled.

Baron Friedrich Schey von Koromla 1815–81.

Then in 2004 a family friend in Vienna* sent me an article about the Schey family – a historical essay by Margit Altfahrt, entitled '*Die Jüdische Familie Schey* –The Jewish Family Schey'.[1] 'You might be interested?'

My German creaked. Three years later, a small exhibition of the same name was held in a former gasworks on the fringes of Vienna.[2] The material came from Vienna's city archive and confirms both Friedrich Schey's dynamic rise and fall and the large number of Schey descendants, and more about his mercantile, political and cultural influence. Here is the founding father of one of the Viennese *Zweiten Gesellschaft* families, the rising nobility of nineteenth-century Austria, a man of influence and culture. Later generations are dismissed as decaying, scattered, failing in influence.

The timing of the exhibition was significant, coming soon after Austria had finally in April 2006 – fully sixty years after the end of the Second World War – acknowledged responsibility for the first time for its part in the crimes of Hitler's Third Reich. Under the Washington Agreement of 2001, Austria had also been placed under an obligation to return looted art and to include and preserve Jewish heritage. In the circumstances, using the old gasworks as the venue seemed an ironic touch. It was also telling that nobody had made contact with the Goldschmidts at Erla or visited the library there. Inevitably, some of the information was incorrect. But there was lots there.

Friedrich Schey makes other appearances: he flits in and out of the history books and through theses, websites and other studies, many of them picking up on Margit Altfahrt's work. The palace he built, the Palais Schey, next to the Hofburg Gardens on the Ringstrasse, features in the coffee-table books.[3] There are cartoons of him. He cuts a figure in the landscape of nineteenth-century Vienna and is part of the revised foundation story being hastily reassembled at the end of the twentieth century, characterised as a model of successful Jewish enterprise.

When I had lived in Vienna as a teenager, I had no idea about any of it. Nor interest. Nobody mentioned Friedrich or the Palais Schey. Not to be remembered? A dislike of pomposity? Avoidance of anything Jewish? Was

---

* This was Eva Badura-Skoda, the distinguished musicologist and wife of the pianist Paul, who had played the piano to me in 1953. Both welcomed me when I came to Vienna in 1966.

it to be moved on from in the same way as our life was not to be tainted by the war? Or was it just a chapter done and closed? It was as remote as any history book and history books held no attraction at the time.

When we cleared my mother's house, though, one of them came to me. This was a book written by another of her first cousins, Alexandra Byers-Schey. The daughter of our grandfather's brother Witold and his wife 'Tante Gretl' (in whose flat I had lodged for the last part of my time in Vienna in 1966), she had come to England with her parents as a child during the war and, like my mother, had gone on to marry and remain here. Her book, *The Family Schey von Koromla: A History*, was privately printed, elegantly bound and written with considerable pride in the family heritage. It contained a wealth of information.

I am no historian, and for me there was little enough flesh on these bones. There was something else, too. Somehow, it weighed heavy, this Schey stuff. I recoiled from the idea of glorious legacy or any hankering for the past. I found myself reluctant to get into all the 'grand days of Vienna' thing – haven't I done enough about Mutti and Fritz and Robert von Lieben? All these lists, the honours, medals, distinctions – they leave me cold; besides, they're on the record already.

I wonder how far this reluctance might have been inherited. My mother's dismissive 'take no notice of that stuff' might also have been a response to the discomfort of her own father's desertion, absence, divorce; that, and her own instinctive egalitarianism. This stuff is not for us. Take no notice. Move on. Live!

The context, on the other hand, might be interesting. I waded on.

Vienna, 1815

Here, the clocks run even further backwards. The story of Friedrich Schey starts in the early 1800s, almost a century before Mutti and Robert Lieben and Fritz (his grandson and namesake) appear in Vienna. We are back with the grandparents of the grandparents, the era of 'Julius von der Traun', Julius Alexander Schindler, Mutti's Liberal politician and poet of a grandfather. Beethoven and Schubert are still alive. It's a world that's hard to imagine.

The hardest thing to grasp of all, bound in the head as I am by assumptions of nationality and country, is the nature of the Hapsburg Empire itself – that enormous entity apparently not based on nationality, language or even geography. How do you think about the world without those things? It was a dynasty, say the experts, and dynasty was a way of uniting and overriding all those other claims. 'No other European state,' writes Martin Rady, 'with the exception of the Ottoman Empire and Tsarist Russia, had so many national groups and in such abundance.'[4]

The idea was that shared loyalty to the emperor and his family enabled everyone to belong, regardless of which part of the empire, which language, people, religion or place they were from. As A.J.P. Taylor put it in *The Hapsburg Monarchy*, 'Austria was an imperial organisation, not a country, and to be Austrian was to be free of national feeling – not to possess a nationality.'[5]

The result was quintessentially cosmopolitan. 'Cosmopolitan', the word itself only comes into use at the end of the 1700s, its meaning full of people and places at ease with different languages, countries, cultures – literally 'citizens of the world'.

Is this the clue? The bit I've been clawing around for? Was some vestige of that what informed my free-range grandmother and my mother in their approach to the world? Was this what we needed to understand?

It was 5 March 1815 when Friedrich Schey was born in the town of Güns,[*] 80 miles from Vienna, on the edge of what is now Hungary but was then right in the middle of the Austro-Hungarian Empire. This was the year Napoleon was finally defeated at the Battle of Waterloo. Europe was exhausted after twenty years of war, and Vienna, the imperial capital, was headline news for the 'Congress of Vienna'.

The big five powers – Russia, Prussia, France, Great Britain and Austria – had gathered there the previous autumn to redraw the boundaries of Europe and redistribute territory in the name of stabilising the continent and preventing future war. (With 216 heads of

---

[*]   Now Kőszeg in Hungary.

state and 20,000 officials, they were, by all accounts, doing a lot of eating and dancing too. It was quite a party.) Austria's foreign minister and state chancellor, Prince Clemens von Metternich, was in charge, architect of the new 'Concert of Europe', and in the years that followed, he maintained it on behalf of the Emperor Franz I with an iron hand, ruthlessly crushing dissent, suppressing liberal ideas, restricting the press, ruling by decree.

Unlike Mutti's grandfather, who was a relative and contemporary of Metternich and part of old Austria, the Scheys were outsiders. They were Jews and they had come to Güns from Lackenbach, about 25 miles away (now in Austria), and before that from Moravia. Güns was one of the imperial royal towns and a good place to trade, but Jews were not allowed. It was hard to get a toehold. It had taken Friedrich's grandfather, Moses, many setbacks and years of persistence to get established there but, by the time Friedrich was born, the family was settled, the business was prospering,[**] and their commitment to the Austro-Hungarian Empire was clear. For the second generation now, the children had been given German rather than Hebrew names: no more Moses and Israel, now they were Friedrich and Alexander, Karl, Anton, Helene, Charlotte … They were moving with the times, their loyalties clear.

It was a concerted effort, this making of a reputation. Family was central, and the household, which included teachers and other employees as well as family members, was the hub. Friedrich's father (another Josef – these recurring names only add to the confusion) was one of six children. His brother Philip was an important businessman in the town and now Friedrich, the first boy to be born in the new generation, had expectations to fulfil. For, if Güns was progress, Vienna, the magnet at the heart of the empire, home of the Hapsburg imperial family itself, was better still.

Friedrich was no barefoot boy then. The family were doing well. He was educated at the *gymnasium* (grammar school) in Güns and then the juridical *lycée* at Oedenburg. Then he was sent to Vienna, aged 17,

---

[**] 'The prosperity of the Schey family may be traced far back. At the beginning of the nineteenth century, it developed into actual wealth, thanks to highly astute financial transactions with debt-ridden Hungarian aristocrats.' (Arthur Schnitzler, *My Youth in Vienna* (1970), p.12.)

to complete his education and get experience at the Wertheimstein Bank before returning to the family business in Güns. At 20 he left for Vienna again, this time for good. It was 1835, the year the Emperor Franz was succeeded by his sickly son, Ferdinand. Metternich remained in charge.

Three Sisters

Vienna, when Friedrich got there in 1835, was nothing like the grand capital enjoyed by his grandchildren (Fritz, Mutti or Robert Lieben) at the start of the next century. It was still relatively small, with a population of just over 300,000, cramped medieval streets hemmed in by the ramparts of the city walls and an insanitary sprawl beyond. But more and more people wanted to be there.

Jews were not welcome. To stay overnight, an 'Israelite', as they were called, had to report to the Jews' Office of the police and pay a stamp tax of 30 guilders a day. There were, however, exceptions: a small number of 'approved' Jewish families who, in return for meeting stringent financial conditions, had been granted the coveted 'toleration permit' and allowed to conduct their useful business as traders and dealers in money (all other occupations being forbidden to them). It was a necessary service for the money-hungry imperial administration.

Josef Landauer, the merchant Friedrich went to work for, was one of these 'tolerated' Jews and Friedrich was duly inscribed in his 'family list'. The household included all sorts of relatives and employees, but once again, family was the core. Landauer and his wife had thirteen children – and in the following years their careful connections through marriage and business were to create a family network that stretched across Europe – from the Worms family in London, to the Morpurgos and Perugias in Trieste.[6]

Friedrich was soon at the heart of it. He worked hard, did well and when, a few years later, he was in a position to marry, he went to Josef Landauer and asked for the hand of his eldest daughter, Emilie.

Here was a fine young man who looked set to do well in the world. He came from a good Jewish family. By all accounts, he was not only astute but had a great deal of charm. 'Yes,' said Landauer, and, in 1839, when Friedrich was 24 and Emilie was 22, the marriage went ahead.

Soon she was pregnant. On 17 April 1840 she gave birth to a daughter. On 19 May, she was dead.

A little while later, Friedrich went back to Landauer and asked for the hand of his next daughter, Charlotte. It made sense: Friedrich needed a wife, the baby needed a mother, who could be closer? So, in 1841 Charlotte and Friedrich were married in their turn. And what happened? She became pregnant and nine months later, in March 1842, both she and their baby died.

For the third time, so the story goes, Friedrich went back to Landauer and this time he asked for his youngest daughter, Hermine. This was too much for Landauer. 'Enough!' he said. 'No! Two of my daughters have died already. You can't have this one too!' And that would have been the end of it. But the youngest daughter had ideas of her own and she was a force to be reckoned with, 'Please Papa, I wish to marry him', and, by the way, 'If I can't have him I won't have anyone else!'[7]

In 1846, Friedrich became a partner in the Landauer firm and that December he and Hermine were finally married. This time, all went well. By the time Hermine gave birth to their first child, Stefan, safe and sound, it was February 1848. Revolution had broken out in Italy and France and was spreading fast across Europe.

1848

The Austro-Hungarian Empire was ripe for revolt. Metternich's rule by imperial decree, with its police state and networks of spies and informers, its impoverished peasantry and general repression had not succeeded in eliminating liberal and nationalist ideas, or the radical intelligentsia. Besides, it was proving to be a financial disaster. The army was weak; there was widespread unrest, agricultural depression and hunger.

By March 1848, revolution had arrived with peasant uprisings in the countryside combined with riots and student demonstrations in the city. In Vienna, a relatively peaceful demonstration of students and citizens turned into a running battle in the street after the commander of the troops protecting the Imperial Palace ordered his men to fire into the crowd. Out in the suburbs, factory workers rose up and set the place on fire.[8]

Their demands were clear: emancipation of the peasants, universal suffrage, an elected assembly, freedom of movement and legal rights for all. Metternich fled to London in disguise, and when in October the Minister for War was hung from a lamppost, the imperial court fled the city too. In November came their next move: the Emperor Ferdinand I (who suffered from epilepsy and water on the brain and was variously described as 'feeble minded' or an 'imbecile') abdicated to make way for a new emperor. His name was Franz Joseph I and he was 18 years old.

In the Hungarian crown lands, many landowners and members of the aristocracy joined the revolt of the peasants, students and workers against Austrian rule in a threat so severe that it could only be brought under control with the help of Russian forces. But the Scheys were not among them. They took a different course. They had made their alliances and they backed the Hapsburgs and the empire. Friedrich's Uncle Philip, back in Güns, was prominent among the supporters.

The new emperor was swift to make concessions, granting individual liberties, emancipation of the peasants and, for the first time, giving Jews the right to own property (it didn't last – in 1851, that right was rescinded, and in 1853 ended). Then, in a strategic swerve, a new constitution was introduced in March 1849, reclaiming Hapsburg power. The danger to the imperial grip had been fended off for now, gradually control was reimposed, a new absolutism prevailed.

It reads like a balancing act, the imperial strategy, or one of those dances of the time – a quadrille, perhaps: give way here, take back there, now stepping back, now advancing. It took nimble footwork to retain power, and reliable friends were invaluable.

A New World

Things were changing. With the peasants now freed from tied labour on the land, more and more people were leaving the countryside for the cities. By 1850, Vienna's population (at 431,000) was more than a third larger than when Friedrich Schey had arrived, fifteen years before, with all the attendant issues of overcrowding, public health and sanitation. The tidal wave of industrial and technological change unleashed by the Industrial Revolution was slow to reach Austria but it was now on its way and Friedrich Schey, it seems, was ready to ride it.

Gas lighting had already been introduced and the first railway had been built from Vienna to Wagram in 1837; with the passing of a railway law in 1854, a railway boom followed. Friedrich Schey was there. Jews might be forbidden the traditional trades but here were new kinds of production, cotton and silk manufacture to be developed and factories to be built. Friedrich Schey was there. Above all, with unrest to contain, wars to pursue, armies to pay and infrastructure to build, the Hapsburgs had an insatiable need for money. And Friedrich Schey was there, too. In 1855, he founded his own company, *Friedrich Schey kk Priv Grosshändler**, and then his own bank. He was elected vice president of the Vienna Stock Exchange. He became banker to the short-sighted (and highly conservative) Archduke Albrecht, Governor of Hungary, one of the richest members of the imperial family. All that and more.

Europe's old cities were bulging at the seams. In France, Napoleon III had set Baron Haussmann to work restructuring Paris, demolishing the crowded medieval neighbourhoods that had made it so hard to control the revolutionary mob and replacing them with airy squares, brand new aqueducts and sewers and boulevards wide enough to march an army along. In 1857, Emperor Franz Joseph followed suit, decreeing the demolition of Vienna's old city walls and ramparts (to the dismay of his generals) and their replacement with a grand new avenue to be known as the Ringstrasse – the Ring – wider even than the French boulevards. It would soon be lined with brand-new buildings of every architectural style – a showcase for the splendour of the Hapsburg Empire.

That empire was in trouble, though. The economy was in crisis and there were external threats, political and military problems to contend with. Nationalism, the idea that different peoples within the empire should have their own nation states, was on the rise. There were expensive campaigns and armies to be provisioned. Friedrich Schey was there too.

---

* 'kk' stands for *Kaiserlich und Königlich* ('imperial and royal'). *Priv Grosshändler* is 'private wholesaler'.

The Court Opera under construction on the Ringstrasse, 1863.

The Italian Campaign of 1859 proved a disaster when the Imperial Army, led by the emperor himself, was heavily defeated by the King of Sardinia and the French in a bloody battle at Solferino. Schey was not only part of the emperor's financial and logistical support but turned over his country house at Lainz to be a military hospital.

The Italian defeat had consequences. Things in Hungary, in particular, were not going well for the Hapsburgs, with rebellious landowners said to be conspiring with Prussia against them. The emperor needed all the support he could get. Was it a coincidence that it was the same year, 1859, that Friedrich and his uncle, Philip Schey, a major figure in Güns, became the first Hungarian Jews to be raised to the nobility?[*] Loyalty was to be rewarded, as the citation for Philip read:

He [Philip] always and even in the hardest of times proved himself the most loyal of our subjects, especially during the Hungarian trou-

---

[*] Philip and his wife Franziska were childless and since the honour was a hereditary one, his nephews were included.

bles of 1848 and 1849 when he displayed his true devotion to ourself and our Imperial house openly and fearlessly for days ... and rendered many services to our troops.[9]

They took the title Schey von Koromla, the prized 'von' lifting them to a new social level. And Koromla – those peaceful fields I walked in – it seems possible that Philip Schey's Csatka lands, where Koromla was, were among the estates forfeited by Hungary's rebel landowners after the revolution of 1848.

The nimble imperial footwork continued. After the defeat of Solferino there were more concessions, among them – at last, twelve years after the demands of the revolution – a limited elected assembly.[**] Despite the rumbling economic crisis, the Ringstrasse project continued. In February 1860, a new decree allowed Jews to own property; not long afterwards, building plots on the Ringstrasse were put up for sale to private bidders. It was one way of funding the public buildings.

The site Friedrich Schey bought, midway between the Opera and the Imperial Court and right next to the imperial family's Hofburg Gardens, was a prime location and some indication of his standing and influence. He commissioned architects Romano and Schwendenwein (who had made their name building Metternich's palace in 1848) to build the Palais Schey there at Opernring 10, and in 1864, the Schey family – with six children by now and two more to come – took their place among the new bourgeoisie of the Ringstrasse, beside the Ephrussis, the Todescos, the von Liebens and many others, in time for the emperor to declare the Ringstrasse officially open in 1865.

Institutions were being created as fast as buildings – and Friedrich Schey was there too. He founded Vienna's Banking Institute and in 1862 he co-founded the *Wiener Handelsakademie*, the Vienna Academy of Commerce, and there are whole lists of other institutions, founder memberships, as well as distinctions and chests full of medals and awards from as far afield as Mexico, France, Brazil, Russia. The man's personality and energy sound prodigious and the honours kept coming. In 1863 the Scheys were raised again, this time to the *Ritterstand* – knighthood.

** This was the assembly Mutti's great-grandfather, Julius Alexander Schindler, was elected to in 1867.

The Schey Palais.

The Schey coat of arms ...

The gate to the courtyard.

... and the wolf at the door.

For Friedrich Schey, like many of the new bourgeoisie, life was not only about money and business but the legacy of the Enlightenment – science, art, music, culture. It was about creating a new world where reason could prevail, and scientific enquiry, literature, music, painting, sculpture and theatre would lead the way. The palaces were not just testimony to their owners' wealth and status but to their taste and understanding of the arts, and Friedrich Schey was as eminent in this as in his business life. He ensured that his new palace had not only business premises on the ground floor and family quarters above but, on the top floor, a dedicated 'writer's flat', a *Freiwohnung*, whose first occupant was the playwright Salomon Hermann Mosenthal.

Friedrich Schey was an accomplished violinist. A voracious reader, he collected paintings, books, musical manuscripts, instruments and more. He sponsored a polar expedition, was one of the founders of the Musikverein concert hall, the Künstlerhaus, the Austrian Museum and, as the city sprouted memorial statues to all the greats, he was involved in the Schiller memorial and joined Brahms and Liszt on the committee for a monument to commemorate Beethoven's centenary.

When his friend, Heinrich Laube, was ousted from the imperial court theatre, the Burgtheater, in a typically Viennese intrigue, Schey got together with a group of other investors to found a new theatre –

Friedrich and Hermine Schey.

the *Stadttheater* – with Laube as its artistic director and himself in charge of the finances. First chairman and then president of the governing council, before long Schey was so thoroughly involved that, night after night, he read dozens of play scripts and increasingly wanted to be involved in casting, while Laube wanted to determine financial policy. It was the end of the friendship.

In the background, the empire's military troubles continued. In 1866, war with Prussia brought another defeat (Königgrätz) with the Prussian Army so close to Vienna that the court had to flee to Budapest

Cartoon of Baron Schey with the theatre director Heinrich Laube.

and the emperor had to make his peace with the dissenting Hungarian aristocracy. The result was the *Ausgleich* ('Compromise') of 1867 in which the empire became a 'dual monarchy' (with the emperor as king of both), with two capitals and two elected parliaments. It also brought a new Liberal Constitution, which finally granted personal freedom and the legal emancipation of Jews. The liberal era had begun.

This was the year the Scheys' last child, Moritz, was born and their first, Stefan, joined the family firm. In 1871 they were honoured again – raised to the *Freiherrstand*, Philip and Friedrich became barons.

What followed were the boom years, a time of massive expansion and speculation known as the *Gründerzeit*. It sounds feverish: the railway network doubled in size, more than 1,000 new stock companies were set up, and seventy new banks were founded between 1868 and 1873. Friedrich Schey was heavily involved.[10]

In Vienna, the new Danube Canal was built and roads, sewers and cemeteries. The three years to 1873 alone saw the construction of five new bridges, six major railway stations and the first spring-water pipeline. As the city grew into the splendid capital his grandchildren were to enjoy thirty years later, Friedrich Schey was in there, rising like a bubble in a glass of champagne.

Was there no limit?

The World's Fair

The year 1873 brought the Silver Jubilee of the Emperor Franz Joseph I and Vienna's opportunity to host the World's Fair for the first time. It was Austria's chance to show itself as good as France or Great Britain. Friedrich Schey had been awarded a medal for silk manufacture at its predecessor in London in 1862: who better to be on the committee?

It was an ambitious project and the theme? *Kultur und Erziehung* – 'Culture and Education'. The fair would celebrate the new era, its culture, industry and technology, and be a showcase for the riches and achievements of the Austro-Hungarian Empire.

The site was large, the pavilions numerous, there were 53,000 exhibitors from thirty-five countries. There was a Palace of Industry, a Hall of Engines and, at the heart of it all, a gigantic Rotunda, 85m high, with a gilded replica of the imperial crown on the top. Money was no object: the turnstiles would soon be ringing and the crowds would more than compensate.

On 1 May, His Imperial Royal and Apostolic Majesty the Emperor Franz Joseph I opened the Vienna World's Fair with great pomp and ceremony. The weather was uncooperative. It rained and it went on raining. The Danube flooded. An outbreak of cholera turned into an epidemic. Attendance was disappointing.

Eight days later, on 9 May, the Vienna Stock Market crashed. As shares plummeted, the National Bank didn't have enough reserves to step in and stop the panic selling. Many of Vienna's new businesses, companies and banks went bust. Friedrich Schey was there too.

The Rotunda, centrepiece of Vienna's World's Fair, 1873.

It was an economic reverse that soon spread out across the world and with the long depression that followed came recrimination and hostility. In Vienna, the fragile mix of different nationalities and languages, classes and religions curdled and separated – and the old antisemitism intensified once again. Of course, for small investors hurting from their losses, it was the Jews who'd been allowed into society, the Jews were to blame.

Unlike many, Friedrich Schey's bank and his business survived, though he lost much of his money. Then, in 1880, his uncle and business partner, Philip Schey, died childless, leaving everything to Friedrich. His will was a reminder of what had been involved:

Through ceaseless hard work, through restless action I have earned this fortune, which I leave to you with my blessing and the hope that you will honour my memory. Never forget that its acquisition cost me many bitter hours, sleepless nights and a life of constant care … It will make it easier for you to further and secure your and my good name which I have always tried to keep spotless.

But time had run out. Within months, Friedrich too was dead.

Philip was buried in the Jewish cemetery in Lackenbach beside his brothers and sisters and previous generations of the Scheys. Friedrich, on the other hand, became the first occupant of a grand, new family vault in Vienna's Zentralfriedhof. The Scheys had arrived. They were now definitely Viennese.

A year or so later, Friedrich Schey's business was wound up, the Palais Schey and the paintings, the Rembrandt and the rest, were sold. But the job was done. The family was established, the name respected, the title was hereditary, and his eight children were as deeply committed to greater Austria and the life of culture and knowledge as their eminent father, with music running through them all. They married into other families of wealth and influence – the Worms, Przibrams,

The Schey tombs at Lackenbach. Philip's is on the right with the pillars.

Friedrich Schey's family vault, Zentralfriedhof, Vienna.

Ephrussis, von Liebens, their own cousins the Landauers, and more – and went on to lead affluent lives among the Viennese bourgeoisie, despite the darkening times.

The Exception

Friedrich meant his five sons to follow him into the family business, just as he had followed his father and his uncle a generation before. Stefan, Paul and Vincenz were already working with him before he died and the youngest, Moritz, 13 at the time, also went on to be a merchant banker as well as a composer, Consul General in Madrid and Austria's Imperial Ambassador to Britain before the First World War. In due course, they inherited Philip's Hungarian assets.

The exception was Josef, the second son, and the one in the black-and-white photograph at Erla with my infant mother and her sister on his knee. As the son of one Friedrich and the father of another, our grandfather Fritz, he too was meant to follow in his father's footsteps, but Josef decided he was not suited to it. Instead, he went for the other option open to Jews of this generation: the professions, in his case law and study, research and the academic life.

Josef Schey was, according to his granddaughter Alexandra,[11] a gentle and modest man who never raised his voice, high principled, intensely hard working, brilliantly clever and a fine musician, but he was not particularly interested in money or material wealth. He studied law at Vienna University in the high days of the 1870s, then in Bonn and Berlin and, specialising in modern (Roman rather than German) law, he was eventually appointed professor of law at the University of Graz at the age of 32, a position which at last gave him the means to marry his fiancée Henriette Lang after a ten-year wait. They went on to have six children – the eldest boy, our grandfather Fritz – and fifteen years later, moved to Vienna on his appointment as professor at Vienna University and dean of the law faculty. There they lived in a flat in Wipplingerstrasse for the rest of his life.

Josef Schey's professional achievements were many. He wrote the 'Mainz' edition of the Austrian Civil Code, and in 1907 was

Josef Schey, jurist and Professor of Law.

appointed to the *Herrenhaus* – the upper chamber of the imperial legislature – for life, where he joined his brother-in-law and mentor, Joseph Unger. From then on, he concentrated on the massive revision of the Austrian Code of Civil Law – the *Algemeine Bürgerliche Gesetzbuch* (ABGB) – and continued to advise both the emperor and, after the First World War, the Austrian Republic. He was also, no doubt, the worried father of the feckless Fritz.

But he was still a Jew, and the climate in Vienna was turning sourer during the depression that followed the market crash of 1873. Antisemitism was rife among the student fraternities of the university. As dean of the law faculty and one of its most distinguished members, when he was proposed for election as vice chancellor, the German National and Christian Socialist fraternities opposed his appointment because he was a Jew. The faculty said they would support him unanimously but only if he promised to resign straight afterwards.

He refused, was nonetheless elected by a majority, and then, as he had apparently always intended, 'declined to accept' the post.

Assimilation

The story of Friedrich Schey, says Margit Altfahrt, is representative of Jewish success in nineteenth-century Vienna, and others echo the refrain. But was that how the Scheys saw themselves?

They were indeed Jews and unashamedly so. 'They neither tried to hide nor highlight their Jewishness.'[12] Their families, their marriages and many in their social circle were also Jews but this was to some extent incidental. In this, the liberal era, they were primarily the loyal subjects of the emperor, a proud part of Austria and Vienna's cosmopolitan society. The objective was progress. It was time to overcome the limitations of the past, put superstition aside and build a new world to the glory of that empire in which reason prevailed and culture, advance, scientific enquiry (the ideas of the Enlightenment and German Humanism) and, above all, the arts in all their forms were the most important things of all.

Religion was something else, it belonged in the private sphere; and Judaism was a religion. That others didn't see it that way was another matter.

It's hard to recapture these ideas, swept away as they were by the racism of the Nazis and their Nuremberg Laws and further obscured since the Second World War and the Holocaust by the need to affirm and restore Jewish history, but this is certainly the set of values that filtered down to us a century later. It's generally described as assimilation and often decried as an attempt to escape or become invisible in a world which was full of disadvantages for Jews. But it seems to have been subtler than that. The process played out down the generations.

While the Schey family in Hungary were practising Jews, and Philip Schey expressed the hope in his will that his descendants would continue to be, the move to Vienna marked a change. The playwright Arthur Schnitzler, writing about his childhood in Vienna in the late 1860s, recalls that his Schey grandmother, a cousin and contemporary of Friedrich's, observed the Jewish Day of Atonement but little else:

The Feast of Tabernacles even the Sabbath, were not celebrated in my grandparents' house; and the generation which followed, in spite of all stubborn emphasis on racial solidarity, tended to display indifference to the spirit of Jewish religion, and opposition, sometimes even a sarcastic attitude to its formalities.[13]

Family recollection bears this out with the anecdote that great-grandfather Josef – Friedrich's son, the distinguished jurist and part of that 'generation which followed' in the second half of the nineteenth century – never went to synagogue. If he did have to attend a funeral or something, said his grandson Jean, he always made a point of taking a science book in his pocket.

Another cousin, the eminent biochemist Edgar Lederer[*], wrote in his personal recollections:

For my family, entirely assimilated for nearly two generations, being a Jew was not based on any religious belief, but mainly on other people's attitude. There was a deep feeling of solidarity for our kinship and we had a strong incentive to work hard and do better than the more or less different or hostile 'others'... The interest in foreign languages and the ease to learn them was quite usual in our Viennese society.[14]

By the start of the twentieth century and the next generation, that of Josef's children, while languages remained essential, religion had become a matter of personal choice. All his sons converted and several married non-Jews, our grandfather Fritz being the first to do so. Some became devout Catholics. Others found their spiritual home in Protestantism (Cousin Victor became dean of Canterbury Cathedral.) The majority were agnostic or avoided religion altogether.

These were not forced conversions like the one required of Gustav Mahler before he could become director of the Vienna Opera. They may have made life in an antisemitic world easier, though the antisemites were as caustic about converts as about Jews, and they

---

[*] Lederer's mother, Frederike was the daughter of Charlotte Schey, our great-grandfather Josef's older sister.

were certainly more consistent with the milieu of society they saw themselves in. The days of racial definition were over, surely?

There was something else going on too – a matter of class. Throughout the nineteenth century, large numbers of poorer eastern Jews with their Orthodox rabbis had poured into Vienna from the *shtetls* of Eastern Europe. As Ernst Gombrich said:

> If the truth is to be told, Western Jews despised and crudely ridiculed the Eastern Jews for their frequent failure to understand, adopt and assimilate the traditions of Western culture.[15]

It was important to establish a distinction.

By the time of our grandparents, the shift was consolidating. When Beate was born in Vienna in 1917, her birth certificate came from the registry office of Vienna's Israelitische Kultusgemeinde, the Jewish religious community, but when Inge was born in Innsbruck three years later, there was no such registration and two weeks later she was christened as a Protestant. Her christening took place in the house of William Adler, a Jewish merchant, who later died in Auschwitz. It was only the following February that Beate, by then nearly 4, was also christened Protestant in the Christuskirche in Innsbruck.[16] On both certificates Fritz was described as *Konfessionslos*, or 'non-denominational', the same term Anny had used on her marriage certificate after leaving the Catholic Church, though for these christenings she declares herself Protestant.

By the time my mother was grown, the attenuated connection with Judaism meant they were now not only second-generation converts or sceptics but 'didn't want to have anything to do with all that'. She had us christened and took us to church for some years but made it clear there were other values of equal importance, above all culture, music and the arts.

> That ideal of culture which indeed replaced religion for many members of the middle class, whether Jews or non-Jews, took Goethe as its model. Not the poet but the free spirit who had no use for established religion, and who was always open to the achievement of other cultures and to all the arts.[17]

It was all in the past. If your antecedents had chosen other religions, or none at all, what did any of this have to do with you? The shock of the Nazis' obscene persecution by bloodline must have been all the greater.

The process ran to its logical conclusion in my mother's brother, the disappearing uncle of Chapter 9. Apparently, he never told his children of any Jewish connection at all (had he forgotten or denied it himself?) and he disliked mention of anything Jewish. He did, however, choose to dust off the obsolete title and call himself Baron Clemens Schey von Koromla – no doubt a useful mark of social position in Argentina. This was a country where many Nazis had gone to ground after the Second World War, also hanging onto their titles, and it was they as a group who were usually associated with the 'von' tag. The irony of that became painfully clear when, sometime in the 1980s, Clemens' son John went for a job with a Jewish taxi firm in Buenos Aires and was asked to fill in a form. He got as far as writing his surname 'Schey von K …' at the top when the proprietor across the desk jumped to his feet, trembling with rage. He slammed his fists down on the desk, 'No one with a name like that works here!' he shouted. 'Get out!'

And John had no idea why.

For us, the link remained a cultural one: we were proud of it but disconnected – not Jewish enough to be Jewish, not Jewish at all perhaps, but at the same time not quite English enough for the English, or anything else much either. Ours was the inheritance of assimilation: we were hybrids, we were Europeans, we were Londoners, we were independent, we were other. And the only home was family.

13

Ten Minutes in Kőszeg

There were more visits to Erla after the first, including a splendid 90th birthday celebration for Jean with the family, the village and the fire brigade band. Then death did it again.

Cousin Jean (born in Austria, living in Brussels), made it to 96 years old and, in one of those coincidences momentous to the family around him, died in March 2011, two days before his grandson, Sebastien, was to be married. It was a life complete, and one of those moments when you can almost hear the generations shifting, a watershed.

The funeral followed swiftly on the registry office wedding and it was four months later that the clans prepared to gather again to celebrate the marriage at the Schloss by the Danube, where Jean had been born and where he had kept the doors open every summer for the scattered family to come back together. It was the first time without him: *Le roi est mort! Vive le roi!*

Jean was not only the keeper of the memories, teller of tales, stories and jokes in five languages, in a very real way he held the family together after the turbulent events of the twentieth century and kept a place where all the far-flung tribe were welcome. To him we owed our inclusion – from far out on the margins in the UK – and the gift of a whole lot of stories about people we never knew. For Sebastien and his sister, whose own father had died suddenly when they were still young, their grandfather had been a constant presence. I felt for them.

So, here's the wedding: what to do about a present? Bogged down in London, wondering what to give the young couple and pondering the passing of the big man, it came to me that maybe a map of the shared family tree – deaths, births, marriages – would be the thing. It had a certain symmetry, the spirit of the moment, a way of celebrating them and Jean too and trying to capture the information we could no longer assume someone else knew.

It couldn't be that hard, surely? I was no expert but with a couple of phone calls, emails to the cousins in North and South America, Belgium, Switzerland and the UK, and a computer to stitch the thing together, it shouldn't take long.

There was a precedent, too. My first attempt at any kind of family tree had been on our first visit to Schloss Erla. Our children had been complaining for some time that, despite having two perfectly good aunts and two uncles, unlike 'everybody else', they had no cousins. Now, confronted by people who were all apparently related, the subject came up again.

'Well, here you are. These are your cousins.'

You could see the disbelief as they considered these big strangers who were racing around speaking French. 'Really?'

And so, one warm evening after supper, sitting under the big copper beech tree that shaded the terrace, Jean's daughter, Cathou, and I set about drawing a diagram. With much laughter and eventually a headlamp as the dark grew thick, we found them an assortment of twenty-three Schey second and third cousins, at least ten of whom were in the house at the time, talking, reading or playing ping-pong in the vaulted cellar by the courtyard after a day spent riding bikes, roaming in the park above the Schloss or swimming in the tree-hung pond down the fields.

So now, ten years later, all I had to do to complete the map of what linked us all was to add a few other sources. Alexandra Byers-Schey's book, published privately, had a family tree in meticulous, minute handwriting in the back. Yet another cousin who I'd met at a funeral knew about a different branch. Finally, my sister produced from her loft a large, handwritten chart she had from our (known, English) first cousin David Mayor, Beate's son, who had had a passion for these things sometime in his teens and we had all thought a bit of a nerd for his interest. Now it was my turn to be the nerd.

By the time the thing stretched across five close-typed, landscape sheets I was cross-eyed, the wedding celebration was two days away and time had run out. But there it was: the family spreading down from great-great-grandfather Friedrich Schey (1815–81), the Dick Whittington of Jean's family yarns – with all of us, spread out across the world, sitting on the branches like the figures on the chapel's Stem of Jesse.

There was even a bit before Friedrich, a string of names from the 1700s at the top of the handwritten tree: Israel, Lipman, Moses, it said, and their dates. I'd never heard of any of them but they added gravitas. I stuck them on a flap, folded the whole thing up and trapped it in covers, tied with a ribbon.

The glue was still drying as I packed my bag and headed for the airport. The present was safely in the suitcase, and in my pocket, snatched up at the last moment, was the dog-eared, drawn-on, rough-draft copy, just in case. There were bound to be babies I didn't know about or dates to be added.

After the main events were over, the gift was opened and spread out on the table in the hall below the portrait of Friedrich Schey, who looked down through the brown varnish as the fifth and sixth generations of his descendants drifted in and out in summer dresses and shorts, passed the map of time and drifted off to play football or dance under the trees.

Past, present, future: here, there, all over the world – and still a connection. It seemed pretty special to me.

A Brief Stop

It was a bit of the same (doffing my hat to Jean and the past) that prompted me to stop on my way to visit friends in Hungary after the wedding. I'd never driven that way before. Though it was nearly twenty years since the end of the Cold War, the countries of the former Soviet Bloc were still largely unfamiliar, part of the 'unknown East', beyond my languages, off the map.

The story in which the great-great grandfather of the brown portrait set out to seek his fortune from Güns in the Hungarian part of the Austro-Hungarian Empire had always sounded very exotic, and immeasurably far away, and so did this. Now it seemed Güns was a place called Kőszeg in Hungary, close to the border with Austria, just inside the former Iron Curtain and little more than two hours south of Vienna. I might as well drop in on the way. No, nobody I asked had ever been there.

Hungarian was a challenge; my map was inadequate but the guide-book's brief two pages on the place should do for a quick stop. Besides, there were other, more important places to look at. The *Rough Guide* sang the praises of Sopron, 'The most historic town in Hungary', 'as well as one of the most attractive', adding that the Esterházy Palace, at Fertőd, down the road, was not to be missed. About Kőszeg it had less to say.

I thought I'd do as it suggested, look at the good bits first, get a sense of the area, some background history. I crossed the border and after a comic first encounter with a Hungarian parking meter, walked down crooked streets into the heart of Sopron's old town. Medieval, gothic, baroque – and empty, despite the height of the tourist season.

There were building works here. The streets of the old town were dotted with stacks of new cobblestones. I went into the Church of the

The Church of the Goat, Sopron.

Goat and found it contained as many towers of scaffolding decorated with workmen as altar pieces decked with angels, and in the centre of its nave, surrounded by plastic sheeting and trailing cables, two men in t-shirts stood in a hole in the floor with a large pneumatic drill while another pushed a barrow load of cement past a newly gilded seraph propped up against the wall.

The new faith of conservation was in action.

Outside, the twisted pillar of the statue of the Holy Trinity was also under siege, its angels/cherubs peering up from a shroud of green netting, against the backdrop of a huge crane. I headed for the Firewatch Tower, famous, according to the guidebook, for its stunning view, only to find that it too was closed to visitors and scaffolded for repair. It was a spectacle. A lot of money was being spent, as if the place was preparing for something. Expectant.

But July was already here. This was the holiday season and there were only a handful of us tourists loitering in the sun. Perhaps they weren't any more in the mood than I was.

I gave up – the baffling parking permit was about to expire – and drove out to Fertöd and the Esterházy Palace. The road trailed through flat countryside and unremarkable villages until it arrived at the kind of large cinder car park lined with gift stalls that mark out major tourist attractions everywhere. There was a handful of coaches, the latest releasing a fresh group of visitors to stretch and yawn under the trees. I followed them as they straggled across the road and into the great horseshoe of the palace courtyard – Prince Esterházy's rival to Versailles – to find the ticket office shut, the promised tours suspended and the palace itself closed to visitors while the grand interiors were also restored, regilded, repaired.

There was still the outside, and the overgrown formal garden. Mainly because it was there and so was I, I took a walk then climbed the sweeping exterior staircase to peer through the windows into the empty halls – no signs of work in progress. What was I doing here? What were any of us doing here? Was this how Haydn felt as he churned out nearly 100 symphonies, operas, songs, trios, quartets and pieces for piano during the twenty-three years he spent here at the court of the Esterházy family, miles from anywhere? What was it doing here in the middle of nowhere?

The palace ignored us: silent, eyes shut, uninterested. The only signs of life came from the bravura display of hundreds of swallows swooping in and out of the nests they'd hung under every eave and window round the whole huge horseshoe, like the decoration in an aria.

I wasn't expecting much from Kőszeg.

⟡

The map was useless and the cross-country route an adventure but eventually, tired and impatient, I found the place, ducking past the huge signs for Tesco on every lamppost. I left the car in the town car park and scanned the guidebook. This wasn't going to take long. Ten minutes should be enough.

Kőszeg's claim to fame, it seemed, was that this was the town where, in 1532, the relentless advance of the Turks under Grand Vizier Ibrahim was finally brought to a halt by a small garrison of 400 men in the castle led by a Croat Captain Nikola Jurišić, who somehow held off the 80,000 Turks who besieged them for nearly a month. 'After nineteen assaults the Sultan abandoned campaigning until the following year, by which time Vienna was properly defended.'[1] Or so the story goes. The Turkish spin doctors of the day described the fort as huge, high, inaccessible, impregnable. And there it was in front of me: rising out of the grassy moat beyond the car park, barely the height of a two-storey house, with the fort above a single storey more. How slippery is history. That must have been quite a siege.

Of the more recent past – the forty years of communism behind the Iron Curtain – there was less said. Some 5km outside the town, a huge, glass-faced border post squatted above the road, empty now, mothballed but not dismantled. Kőszeg seemed to stand on one of history's fault lines.

It was late afternoon by now, and thoroughly jaded by the day's sightseeing, I set off for a quick 'I was there' stroll before heading on south to my friends'.

It was a pretty place. I turned down a street towards the centre of the town, past a stone saint who stretched his hand out towards mine from a niche in the yellow wall. The tarmac ended. The road had been dug up. Was there anywhere in Hungary that wasn't being rebuilt?

Kőszeg, 2011.

More great infrastructure works were clearly underway (a libation of 1.5 billion Euros-worth of EU money being poured over the town, as it turned out) but work had stopped for the day, there was almost nobody about and the uneven surface of mud and earth lent the houses a strange, timeless feel. The imagination didn't have much left to do. The markers of the present had gone. It could have been the middle ages or any time since. And as the street wound and curled, wider here, narrower there, it got me.

Every corner I turned, every new view, was more attractive: angles, alleyways, houses with stucco fronts, no two the same, stone archways, red roofs, and, rising above them, green onion domes on church towers; whichever way you looked, they seemed to group themselves to please the eye. It was really very pretty.

So, this is where he came from, the great-great-grandfather of Jean's story. How pleasing. This was the place he'd left for Vienna in the 1830s. Suddenly there was the possibility of time even before him, real people in a real place: a Jewish family in the early 1800s – here on these streets. It couldn't have looked very different. What would that have been like? Where would they have walked and talked? I knew precisely nothing.

241

I tried the guidebook. It mentioned a 'former synagogue ... which can only be viewed from the street'. It had only been built in 1859, well after he had left, but I walked past anyway and, sure enough, there it was, behind rusting bars at the far end of a long plot, an abandoned castle of crumbling red brick with a crenelated tower on either side, their plaster surfaces long since fallen off. The gates were locked with a rusting padlock and chain. 'A sad reminder of the provincial Jewish communities that never recovered from the Holocaust,' said the guidebook. The Jews of Kőszeg had been sent to Auschwitz in 1944 and they hadn't come back.

It was getting late. The town was peaceful. The cafés on the square looked pleasant and the whole place worth another look. Perhaps I hadn't stayed long enough in Sopron, hadn't given it a proper chance. Maybe this time, I should try harder. Spoil myself.

I took a room above a café on the main square with a view to the front over the square and from the bathroom another across red roofs towards the green onion tower of the old church. Really an extremely pretty place. Starting to feel like a treat.

There are times when your brain is just freewheeling – like this downtime after the wedding – easy, switched off – and then, kerpow! Like being caught by a surf wave. *Beshert* is the word, says my friend Margaret. Something that's waiting to happen.

The synagogue, Kőszeg.

It was a warm night. I went down to the café for something to eat and found a table by the open door. At the next table a young woman was busy on a laptop. We smiled and nodded. She typed. I browsed the book some more and then, being nosey, noticed she was typing in English. And we began to talk.

'The internet's down. This is the only place I can get a signal tonight. And you?'

'I'm just passing by – curious, a remote family connection with Kőszeg. Thought I'd come and have a look on my way through. But it's such a lovely town. Do you know it well?'

'I've been here for a year. Doing a master's degree.' And so we talked.

Her name was Jenna Goodhand and she came from Canada. She told me about Kőszeg's Institute of Social and Economic Studies and its international master's degree courses and I wondered aloud about what life might have been like for Jews there in the late eighteenth century and whether there was anyone who'd know about such things.

'I can ask my history tutor if you like,' she said and, fingers faster than speech, fired off an email. The reply came back within minutes. The person who could help is Imre Söptei, at the town archives. He speaks a little German but no English.

We said goodnight and went our separate ways.

Next morning the sun was shining and the view from the window, already familiar, looked even better, if that was possible. I was enjoying this. Maybe I should stay another night. After all, I wasn't likely to pass through Kőszeg again anytime soon, if ever.

At breakfast in the café, I asked if I could keep the room. The manager went off to consult his book. He came back shaking his head. 'I'm sorry, but we're fully booked tonight.'

'What a pity.' My first cloud appeared. 'It's very nice here.'

A man having coffee at a table nearby looked up. 'I have a guest house in the mountains,' he said. 'It's about 2km outside the town. If you'd like to stay there, I can offer you a room.'

'Well ...'

We chatted.

What was I doing here?

Just a tourist, passing by, vague family connection, long time ago, curious. What a lovely town. I thought I might try to find out a bit more about its history before I left, maybe visit the Jewish cemetery.

'It's on the way to my place.' He drew me a map on a piece of paper. 'I've been given the name of Mr Söptei, the town archivist.'

'I don't know him,' he said. 'But it should be possible.' He picked up his mobile and, clearly busy, went back to his table to make his phone calls. I ordered some breakfast and talked to the manager.

The other man finished his calls and came over again. 'You have an appointment with Imre Söptoi at the town archive at eleven o'clock. He has a meeting first but he'll see you then,' he said, and he told me how to find it.

Archive

The archive wasn't far. I followed directions: round the corner past larger-than-life Saint Janos reaching out from his niche in the wall, next to the Szigma advertisement and under the arch of the huge tower (medieval, built in the 1930s – a monument to Hungary's reviving national pride, said the guidebook) into the market square. At the far end were not one, but two churches, close beside each other, and in between the rumpled ground was dotted with piles of ballast and pallets of paving stones waiting to be laid.

It had started to rain. I turned right along an arcade, dodged another hole in the ground cordoned off with orange netting and found the door marked for the archive. It led up a white-walled wooden staircase to where the office, lined with books, looked out onto the square.

I was early. I sat and waited, suddenly aware of the difficulty of what to ask or how to turn what did I want to know, who were they, what would life have been like into the kind of thing that could be answered by a historical archivist in a language I didn't speak.

I was jotting in my notebook, 'When did the Jews come to Güns – Jewish community since when?' when the archivist appeared. He was youngish and obviously busy and spoke even less German than I did. I thanked him for making time to see me, and we stumbled into a halting exchange.

'*Geschichte der Juden in Kőszeg?*'
'*Meine Familie.*'*

---

* 'History of the Jews in Koszeg?' 'My family.'

St Janos and the main square.

He looked faintly bored – how many visitors must he have who were after this sort of thing? It was looking as if we were going to have to use sign language when I remembered the draft of the family tree still stuffed in my bag and pulled it out. I pointed to Friedrich at the top.

'Kőszeg,' I said, and myself among the ruck of descendants five generations below – 'London.'

'*Familien Name?*'

'Schey.'

'*Ein Moment.*'

Mr Söptei left the room. A minute later, he came back holding a large book with a glossy cover. He handed it to me, open at the start of a chapter, and pointed. It was all in Hungarian. This was impossible. I stared politely and eventually recognised his name on the page – this was obviously something he'd written – I smiled a compliment – but the rest? The chapter title alone was incomprehensible: *A Schey család Kőszegen, 1794–1883*. But hold on … Was that Schey? He beamed.

Imre Söptei had written a chapter in the academic book *Lectures on the History of Vas County* called 'The Schey family in Kőszeg 1794–1883'.

Amazing! They were here!

In front of me was somebody who knew about a raft of origin I scarcely knew existed. Were language problems to be allowed to get in the way? We struggled on and slowly information trickled through. It was tantalising.

The Scheys, Mr Söptei told me, came from Lackenbach, 25 miles away in what is now Austria. Before that, they came from Morvaorsszag/Mören, which turned out to be Moravia, now in the Czech Republic. The first to come, sometime in the mid 1700s, were Israel and his son, Moses Schey, my great-great-grandfather Friedrich's own grandfather and great-grandfather. The ones on that extra flap of paper in the family tree I'd made.

Israel, a *Kleinhändler*, or small trader, appears in the records as being fined and having his goods confiscated in 1785 and a little later being thrown out of the town altogether. For where Jews were allowed to live in Lackenbach, Kőszeg/Güns was one of the royal imperial towns – no doubt the reason it was a good place to try and trade – and Jews were not permitted to live or own property in the imperial cities. For the same reason, maybe, they were not buried here but in Lackenbach, he told me.

And why did they choose the title Schey von Koromla? What was Koromla?

'*Csatka*,' said Imre Söptei, and '*Csatka Komarom Komitatz*'. I wrote it down with no idea what he meant.

Of Friedrich, or Frigyes, as they called him here, there was little information, though his later reputation was well known, but then he had left Kőszeg as a young man. No, Fülöp Schey was the name Mr Söptei kept coming back to. I recognised the name, of course, as 'Philip' in German – this was the uncle and business partner of great-great-grandfather Friedrich, the one who was raised to the nobility at the same time; the first Hungarian Jews to be so rewarded. According to the text, at the time he was cited not just for his loyalty to crown and emperor during the revolution but for 'his services to suffering humanity, regardless of creed'. And here he was.

Information came through staccato, in little nuggets – with a powerful hunger for meaning. Fülöp, Mr Söptei told me, business man. Philanthropist in Kőszeg. Important here. Many charitable works. Founded a kindergarten. The first kindergarten in Hungary, on condition it took children from all religions. Founded an institution for the poor to support Jews, Catholics and Protestants alike. Imperial police. Other charities. He founded the Jewish cemetery here in memory of his father Moses. And then ...

'*Szinagogat*,' he said. And '*Szinagogat*' again.

'*Szinagogat Fülöp Schey gebaut.*'[*]

Amazing. Nobody had ever mentioned any of this, not even the exhibition in Vienna. There was only that bare sequence of names at the top of the tree that I'd tacked on at the last minute. But here, little more than two hours from Vienna and three or four from Erla, here it all was and had been all along, and none of us knew. Because of the war? Because of the Iron Curtain? I suddenly understood – a realisation, an education – just how much the twentieth century had got inside our minds and formed them. In the case of those of us born in the West halfway through that century, spared the devastation of the two world wars and lucky enough not even to have to think about survival, it had cored them with a huge ignorant hole.

_____

[*] 'The synagogue. Philip Schey built the synagogue.'

Imre Söptei presented me with a copy of his article. In return, I held out the draft of the family tree – would he like to copy it for his archive? As he hummed away on the photocopier in the adjoining room I thought of the shadows of the dancing wedding guests, the cousins in South America, North America, Belgium, France, Italy, England swirling around me, about to take their places in the archive of a small town none of them had heard of.

Mr Söptei and I shook hands and said goodbye – a helpful archivist, a satisfied tourist – and I walked down the stairs and out under the arches into the square with a new take on the world.

So, Philip Schey had built the synagogue here. That locked and ruined synagogue. Imagine.

In 1859 ... hold on, it's that year again: a decade after the revolution, the year of the Italian Campaign fiasco, the year Philip and Friedrich Schey were 'raised to the nobility'. At a time when Jews were not allowed to own property, this must have required special concession. Was this part of the thanks for 1848? According to the dog-eared family tree, Friedrich was already a big figure in Vienna by this time, his second son, our great-grandfather Josef, 6 years old. Here was a parallel life – a new thought, new life on the old tree. Did Friedrich and his family come to the inauguration?

I walked slowly across the square, dodging the piles of sand and stacked drainage pipes and tried to take it all in. The rain had stopped, the sun was out and the painted house fronts – medallions, cherubs and the sgraffito house looked lovely. I stopped to look into the two churches of St James and St Imre that pressed up against each other at the far end of the square and admired their baroque altarpieces and faded frescos from the 1200s. It was time to go and find out about the room in the guesthouse in the mountains and to take in the Jewish cemetery on the way, the cemetery Philip had built, even if he wasn't buried there. The biro map of the route was in my pocket, with the cemetery marked as a circle on the way. I thought about Moses Schey and his trading, Philip Schey and his charitable works and, wandering up one alleyway and then another, decided to take a little detour to pass the synagogue – his synagogue – again.

There it was, derelict and abandoned as before. But this time, astonishingly, the rusty chain was dangling. The gate was ajar. A painter in overalls was setting up his trestles and preparing to paint one of the two low buildings that flanked the path immediately inside. Of course I couldn't resist. I pushed the gate open and went in.

Szinagogat

I had hardly gone two steps down the path when a large woman came, smiling, out of the house on the left, stretched out her hand and asked for 400 forints. 'Museum!' She pointed at the door she'd come out of.

I dug around for money in my bag and found again the dog-eared envelope with the draft family tree in it. Why not share my new discovery? I took it out, pointed down the path at the synagogue – '*Meine Familie*,' I said, still surprised at the thought, and unfolded the concertina, 'Schey'.

The effect was dramatic. She pushed aside my money and ushered me into the little rabbi's house with smiles of welcome and real pleasure. We talked. Of course she knew the Scheys. Her German was good.

Mrs Beres and the rabbi's house.

'I am not Jewish,' said the woman in the little house at the entrance of the Kőszeg synagogue, 'but my grandfather was. He died in the camps.' Her eyes rim with tears, this large, smiling woman with the round, red cheeks and the smile. 'I bought this place five years ago. It was the rabbi's house and the schoolroom, and everything here I have collected.' We speak in broken German, hers Hungarian, mine English.

The two small rooms are full of things: candlesticks, carvings, books, pictures, cushions, Jewish memorabilia she has gathered from markets and sales and goodness knows where and brought back here to safety. Her name was Anikó Beres. She clears away some things on a sofa and on the windowsill to point out the scratched wood, initials scratched and carved into the sills by the rabbi's bored pupils. 'They're my favourites.'

And on the top of a large, brown bookcase, in pride of place, is a portrait engraving of a man with a jowly face. 'That's Philip Schey,' she says proudly.

The house was derelict, but she has restored it, and today she is there because the painter is painting the outside walls in the small miracle that has the gates unlocked and me passing by. The walls are plastered, the

Philip Schey.

windows glazed and the heavy, wooden front door, a new one, has, she shows me proudly, the Schey coat of arms etched on its two glass panes.

On the sofa, a carved wooden version of the same coat of arms ('It's not old. I had it made.') leans against a small painting of a man with dark eyes.

'Who's that?'

'That's my grandfather', and again the sadness.

The contrast with the synagogue at the far end of the plot is striking, I say.

'Ah the synagogue,' she sighs. 'That's another story.'

Where the two small buildings at the entrance gate which she owns, the rabbi's house and the ritual bath opposite, are spick and span, the larger building totters. The pale stucco has fallen off long ago and the exposed bricks are the colour of dried blood, the surface rough, the mortar half-washed away. With its two towers and the dome in between, it looks like a small and battered castle.

The synagogue.

'It belongs to someone else. He won't repair it. I try and keep the water out.'

He bought it in 1996 – 4 million forints – a property developer, wanted to make it into an Irish pub. But then he went bust. No, he won't sell – first he wanted 10 million forints, at the last count wanted 100 million – impossible. Meanwhile, it falls down. The tale is complicated and I'm not sure I've understood. She pulls open a drawer and takes out a DVD – they made a film about it for TV: *Synagogue for Sale.*[*] But it's not.

'Would you like to see inside?'

She walks me down the path. The grass on either side is carefully mown and stones inscribed in Hebrew lean against the wall, some new, some old. (With much miming, she explains that one of them is an inscription of the ten commandments she has bought from somewhere recently.)

We go in under the porch – tiled floor, tall, rusting iron candelabra, an old-fashioned bicycle, two small wooden wagons. To the left, a door to a broken flight of stairs (to the women's gallery) is hanging off its hinges but straight ahead of us a larger pair of carved wooden doors let us in through a stone arch.

And I'm stopped in my tracks.

A space. A silence. A hole in time. Totally unexpected.

It was one of those places that takes your breath away. Hard to say why. It wasn't big. It was circular and full of light and very, very quiet, as if time itself had stopped and the Jews of Kőszeg, seventy years dead, had just stepped out. It was beautiful and abandoned and full of feeling. Beautiful and sad. The high, domed ceiling, quartered with painted flowers and medallions where the plaster hadn't fallen off, soared up to a round lantern window at the top, full of light and space. There was scarcely a right angle in the place – it was all a sweep of curves.

But if time had stopped, decay had not. The wooden gallery that ran round half the circumference was carved and fringed along its lower edge but light flickered through its rotten floor, small timbers dangled and wooden props supported the far end. The faded trace of painted

---

[*] Zsuzsanna Geller-Varga made two films about Kőszeg – *Synagogue for Sale* and *Once They Were Neighbours*, about the town's Second World War concentration camp.

arches, decorative detail, scrolls and flowers were still there on the walls – and so was the grace of the whole idea. Light floated in through round windows and arched ones in the half-domed bays on four sides, and at the front, a single shaft of sunlight beamed through encroaching ivy onto the dark wooden ark where the Torah scrolls had once been kept.

Inside the synagogue.

253

Built to the glory of God by Philip
Schey von Koromla.

Mrs Beres pointed up. There, painted in a medallion on the ceiling was an inscription, 'Built to the glory of God by Philip Schey von Koromla'.

I walked around – amazed would not be too strong a word. The inside was so different to the raw, red fortress of the exterior. There was a grand piano to one side, covered with a tarpaulin. 'The sound here is wonderful,' she told me, and pointed out a visitors' book on a table, and arranged on the platform in front of the ark she showed me a series of flat, terracotta tablets, each with a name in Hebrew pressed into it.

'I make those,' Mrs Beres said. 'They are the names of the people from Kőszeg.'

'The ones who died in Auschwitz?'

'Yes.'

She brought a floodlight, switched it on and plugged in a tape recorder which played slow klezmer music and then she left me. Lost in time and thought and silence, I must have spent an hour or more just looking and when I came out, the painter was clearing up his pots and ladders and Mrs Beres had gone.

It seemed very wrong to leave without saying goodbye or half the thanks I felt, but I did, with a strange ache in my heart, my head struggling to catch up.

The Road to the Cemetery

It was afternoon and I hadn't even started on the walk to the mountains or the Jewish cemetery on the way. I stopped for chocolate cake at a *Café-Konditorei*, by the castle walls, then set out along the road out of the town to walk it all in.

Gradually the houses spaced out after the medieval jumble of the centre and soon, for no apparent reason, little tables began to appear on the pavement with bunches of garden flowers in jars and hand-written price tags, 100F, 200F, next to honesty boxes for the money. I thought of Mrs Beres: I would like to take some flowers to thank her – maybe on the way back? She moved me with her smile, with her mission, with her solitary attempt to remember, put things right, keep vigil, take care of a stricken building. Even to welcome me.

The reason for the flower tables became apparent when the town's main cemetery sprang up on my right – a big, walled place, full of fine gravestones and marble plaques and flowers in vases and neatly kept paths. It seemed to go on and on, eventually ending with a roadside shrine containing a white marble pietá – the Virgin Mary holding the body of her dead son Jesus across her lap and with it the sorrows of the world. I thought of Mrs Beres again.

The town thinned out further and a bend in the road appeared where, according to the sketch map in my pocket, the Jewish cemetery should be. There was no sign of it, just some dark trees, what looked like a door to an electricity substation and a turning off to the right. The many-headed signpost at the junction included a rather vague pointer marked for the cemetery. I followed it up the road.

Kőszeg's Catholic cemetery.

Round the corner the trees gave way to brand new villas set back behind metal gates. They were big and brash, each one different: ranch-style mansions with sweeping roofs and paved driveways, Hungarian flags flying behind iron railings tipped with gold. The new wealth of the post-communist market economy was everywhere.

As one huge new house followed another, there was still no sign of the Jewish cemetery. I took a detour down a side road – could it be hidden behind these monsters, round the back? The construction sites and villas gave nothing away. I went on up the hill looking for something old but all I could see was a small business estate with a large tooth in neon lights, marking yet another booming dental practice (not only the British but the Austrians came to Hungary for their teeth) and a playground and park with another new building that looked like a spaceship. Its signboards proclaimed, 'The Istvan Bechtold Nature Conservation Visitors' Centre'. They would be bound to know.

I went inside to find a spectacular round building with interactive exhibits and an impressive display of ornithological information in several languages. No expense spared. I wandered and admired the presentation of high-level science and clear explanation for all ages. It was the best I've seen anywhere.

'*Jüdische Friedhof?*'*

---

* 'The Jewish cemetery?'

The girl in the gift shop didn't speak enough German to tell me how to find it. She fetched the manager and I tried again.

'It's down there.' She pointed back the way I'd come.

'OK. But where?'

'See that truck?' A fire engine was crawling up the hill past the first of the mansions. 'There.'

I was none the wiser.

'But you won't be able to get in anyway,' she said encouragingly. 'It's always locked.'

I headed back to the main road, resigned to not finding it, down the hill, past villa after villa and one new wall after another. I had nearly reached the turning that would put me back on the road into the mountains and had pretty much given up – the Scheys weren't buried there, after all – when I saw ivy. It was growing thickly over the wall beyond the last house before the corner with the dark trees of the turning thick behind it. Ivy? On *these* new houses?

I crossed the road and looked over the wall. On the other side, the overgrown trees squeezed close together and under them, in the dry half-dark, tombstones leaned at drunken angles between their trunks, engulfed, overshadowed, abandoned. This time, unexpectedly, it was my eyes that filled with tears.

On the main road, the unmarked door to what I'd thought was an electricity substation was locked. On that, everyone agreed.

The Jewish cemetery, Kőszeg.

The door to the Jewish cemetery.

Ambush

I carried on. Thoughtful.

'*Putzi, Putzi, Putzi.*'

On the other side of the road a woman pushing a baby in a buggy is smiling, playing, talking to the child. '*Putzi, Putzi, Putzi, Putzi,*' she laughs.

And suddenly, I am ambushed. Falling into a place almost before memory, where my mother is babbling those very same nonsense words to me and I am too small to remember anything else. I'd never heard them since. There are strange connections here. Is the woman babbling in Austrian? Did my mother ever come to Hungary or is this part of the language map of that previous, connected central Europe, another unknown heirloom, drifting down?

The road led on into the national park, through forest and along a valley with small wooden huts and summer houses scattered among the trees on either side. It was further than I expected. When I finally arrived, there was nobody about. I climbed the steep path to a cabin in the woods and someone staying there rang the helpful man.

'He's on his way back from town on his bicycle but he says the room has been taken now. He thought you'd changed your mind.'

&

It was late when I finally got back to the outskirts of the town. I walked back through the Catholic cemetery, past its rows of marble statues and tended tombs, and listened to the bells ringing. It was too late now for flowers. I would need to start for the south soon if I was going to make it to my friends' tonight but I still wished there was something I could leave for the woman at the synagogue to thank her for her kindness. The early part of the family tree might have been nice for her museum.

As I reached the centre someone called my name.

It's late afternoon, the streets are deserted. I am in Hungary, in a place where I don't know anybody and I don't speak the language. And somebody's calling my name?

'Kathy!'

But I am a stranger.

'Hi Kathy.' It's Jenna Goodhand, *dea ex machina*, on her way to a party. 'How's it going?'

Where to begin? I thanked her for the archivist's name, told her what had happened.

'You got into the synagogue? But that's amazing!'

I told her about Mrs Beres and how kind she had been and how much I'd like to thank her too. 'Do you know if there's a photocopier I could use anywhere?'

'There's one at the institute. If you meet me there in the morning ...'

So that was that. I went back to the café. 'I don't suppose anyone's not turned up?'

'Well as it happens ... '

After supper and an excellent ice cream at a table on the square, I went to bed, head spinning, only to be kept awake until long into the night by the hammering of techno music somewhere too close for comfort. It echoed over the roofs and bounced off the square outside. Even with the windows shut and a pillow over my head there was no escape from it or my swirling thoughts, endlessly rerunning the day.

The Institute

At 9.30 the next morning, I met Jenna Goodhand outside the institute. She looked as fresh as a daisy.

'How was the party?'

'Great. It was my birthday. Everybody came.'

Slowly it dawned on me. 'You weren't playing techno ...?' The disturbed night suddenly seemed perfectly reasonable.

She took me in through a gate into the covered arch of the entrance-way. It was the first time I'd been into one of Kőszeg's old houses – modest in size, when seen from the street, but the covered arch or undercroft (useful shelter in winter) led through to a courtyard beyond with the bulk of the building, invisible from the road, stretching back on one side and turning at right angles at the end of the long plot. Each one a small citadel. This one was beautifully restored.

'This is where we have our lectures and where the offices are. I've been helping the director with administration as a part-time job while I've been on the course.'

Up the stairs and past the student notice boards we came to the office on the first floor. The view here was onto a huge, round building without any windows – next to the medieval wall. She introduced me to the departmental secretary and we admired the view.

We'd just started photocopying the family tree when a man strode in, tall, brisk and clearly in charge. He greeted Jenna and she introduced me. 'This is the director of the Institute.'

'Hello. What are you doing here?' His English was excellent.

'Er ... I'm using your photocopier. I hope you don't mind.'

'What for?'

So I explained: my visit to Kőszeg for a quick look, the Schey family connection and how I happened to find the synagogue open yesterday and had gone inside and how kind Mrs Beres had been and how I was copying the family tree for her by way of thank you.

'You got into the synagogue?'

'I did. And it's stunning. Such a pity. What a thing!'

As we talked I thought to hell with being polite and voiced what struck me most: how affluent the town appeared, how much money was being spent on restoration, the bird-watching centre, those brash new palaces out by the Jewish cemetery. 'It's impressive. It seems as if there's a lot of money kicking around here.'

'1.5 billion euros of EU money,' he said.

'It's all the more striking that the only exceptions are the synagogue and the cemetery – they stick out like a sore thumb. Ugly. Obvious. Still? The Holocaust is obviously a difficult bit of Hungary's history. But the message it gives is still pretty clear.'

'Yes, it's bad. Something really needs to be done.' His mobile rang and he left us to our copying and went into the inner office.

A few minutes later he was back. 'Come with me,' he said. 'We're going to have a meeting with the deputy mayor.'

We left the institute and crossed the street. A man was sitting on a tractor talking to another standing below him. The director greeted them and introduced me. 'That's the mayor,' he explained, as we walked on, 'but it's the deputy mayor we want. He gets things done.'

Another archway led under another long, white building. We crossed its courtyard and climbed stairs under painted ceilings to the deputy mayor's office. He was young – excellent English, fluent German – enthusiastic. And straight to the point.

I explained again: the family connection with Philip Schey and the visit of the previous day and said again how lovely the town was and how impressive the restoration work and how strikingly sad the condition of the synagogue and cemetery were by contrast. That it spoke volumes – and not good ones.

We talked. What to do?

The director of the institute began: we need to set up a project – get funding – from the EU, Norway, other sources, UNESCO. The institute has a UNESCO chair. He talked about 'stakeholders' – we need to make a list of them. There's the town, of course, the institute, the Jewish community? There is no Jewish community in Kőszeg, the Schey family – and here it comes.

Suddenly I, a passing English tourist knowing nothing at all, appear to be the Schey family. A catalyst? A lightning conductor.

'We need to acquire the synagogue, make sure it's restored.'

The director was on to it. The deputy mayor, too. And so, of course, was I.

It was impressive how straightforward it all sounded. These guys knew what they were doing. It all seemed to be moving so fast. How can this be?

The meeting lasted barely half an hour but by the end of it something had happened. A route map seemed to be in place. A network of stakeholders. An intention for the future. It seemed effortless, astonishing. And as totally accidental as my walking into the town in the first place. Thanks to Jenna, who had been taking notes throughout, the minutes would be in our email by the end of the day.

The deputy mayor showed me round their fifteenth-century offices with the beautifully restored painted ceilings. We crossed back over the road and the director showed me round his institute – again, beautifully converted and restored – a lecture theatre carved out of the roof, study areas, a modern educational model in a baroque shell. We went on to visit the sgraffito house I'd so admired from the square, the previous day. Inside, the institute had just opened a new library under vaulted, painted ceilings – every book was brand new and paid for with funding from Norway. I thought longingly of being able to sit and study in that space with the square outside and the bells of the medieval church passing the hours. New books? What a privilege.[*]

When we'd finished, I took the photocopy of the family tree round to the synagogue to leave for Mrs Beres. There was no one there. The gate was locked, the air of desolation undisturbed. The sleeping beauty was asleep again. It was hard to believe that yesterday had ever happened.

And finally, I headed south.

Going Back

The whole story spilled out of me when I reached my friends'. They listened with generous attention and when I'd finished, the first thing

---

[*] And thought of home in London – one of the world's great capital cities, centre of wealth and stock markets, but where the potholes in the road took months to patch and where libraries struggling with battered books and zero funding were being cut and closed.

my host said was 'But who had the right to sell the synagogue in the first place?'

It hadn't occurred to me.

In the next few days, between outings and walks with the children and visits to the vegetable patch and meals with friends, we ploughed through selected parts of Imre Söptei's article, translating as we went. Here was the curve of the nineteenth century: the Scheys from nearby Austria and before that, Bohemia, struggling as Jews to settle in Kőszeg from the 1790s but, always Austria-facing, naming their children and conducting their business in German. They had moved on again within two generations. Like so many others from western Hungary, by the 1880s they had all followed Friedrich to Vienna, drawn by the magnet of the imperial capital – there wasn't a Schey left in Kőszeg.

The exception was Philip Schey: childless, extremely rich in land and business and well connected with the imperial family. Though he now had a flat in Vienna and a country house nearby, he remained involved with the Hungarian crownlands and active in the public life of Kőszeg, a major philanthropist who was granted citizenship and became a councillor.

The article gave details: how his charitable works were characterised not just by loyalty to the imperial family but by a desire to build bridges between different faiths. He founded a hospice to support ten destitute people a year (two protestants, four Jews, four Catholics, it specified) and named it after Archduke Albrecht; the kindergarten (to admit children of all faiths), named after the Empress Elisabeth; there was a foundation for the benefit of the imperial police. Then there was the Jewish cemetery in 1852 and the synagogue endowed in 1859 with a foundation to support two rabbis and a school. The details, and the relish of the historian fastening on documents, were so compelling you almost miss the sidestep, when the precision slips: the kindergarten and its generous endowment was 'given' to the town in 1944. Given? Really? In 1944? There's so much that can't be said.

We were barely halfway through when, one evening, milling around with the children, the phone rang. For me? It was Béla Básthy, the deputy mayor. Would I be able to come back to Kőszeg on my way home? A representative of the Christian Jewish Evangelical Group of Vienna was coming to the town and wanted to visit the synagogue.

It would be good if I could be there too and the local newspaper was interested, would like to take some pictures.

Still trying to piece the story together, there were so many questions that my German ran out. I handed the phone to my host and the conversation switched to Hungarian. When the call ended, he had the details of the synagogue's journey onto the open plains of the new capitalism – and not only had Mr Básthy answered with everything he knew, but he had also picked up the other line and called his father who had been mayor at the time the building was first sold to get the facts straight. The rest of the information came later.

So, now for the twentieth century (the Jewish community in the town peaked at about 266 in 1910) and here's the Second World War again: 1944. The Russians were advancing from the east and driving the Nazis back across Hungary. But though defeat was looming, the Germans' determination to eliminate the Jews – their 'Final Solution' – only grew.

In Kőszeg, the 117 Jews of the town were confined to a house in the street once proudly named after Philip Schey, and their assets, including the synagogue and its generous endowment, were seized. They were then deported to Auschwitz just four days before the Hungarian Government finally gave in to international pressure and stopped the deportations, but not before 80,000 Hungarian Jews had been sent to their deaths.

In the same year, the town saw hundreds more Jews imprisoned in the forced labour camps there and by December, as the Russians continued their advance, 8,000 more were marched in from the east and held in a camp at the brickworks. Many died, and when the camp was cleared in March 1945 those too weak to be marched west to the death camps were gassed in one of the sheds.

When the war ended Hungary became part of the Soviet Bloc. Religion was banned under communism, the synagogue left empty, the little buildings at the gate requisitioned for housing. The Iron Curtain came down just outside the town.

Now for the Cold War. And that's how it stayed for forty-five years.

In 1989, when communism gave way to a new Hungarian Republic – elections, the free-market economy – religious buildings were 'offered back' to their communities. Unsurprisingly, there was no Jewish community in Kőszeg, so in 1992 the building was offered to the town – on one condition – it had to be restored without delay.

'We said no,' said the deputy mayor. 'In retrospect, it was probably the wrong decision. But where was a small place like this going to find the money?' (Hungary didn't join the European Union until 2004.)

So then the synagogue was sold – the property developer, bankruptcy, repossession by the bank. Sold again at auction – all the glories of the free market. And now this owner is also bankrupt and there are creditors. I was struggling to hold onto even half of this.

The story of Kőszeg and its Jews, the Second World War with its ghetto, the town's forced labour camps, the deportations to Auschwitz of 1944 and all that had happened since, under communism and now the new capitalism, would take up an entire book. Besides, the chapters were still being written. The efforts to save the synagogue continued.

But how raw that history is, and how unresolved. Just below the surface, it was something many would have liked to forget and move on from, if only the remains would stop reminding them. In fact, the condition of the synagogue and the cemetery were actually a perfect expression of how stuck it was and how difficult to address. If we ignore it, won't it just go away?

I did go back to Kőszeg on my way home, to an afternoon gathering hosted by Mrs Beres and her husband in the little house by the gate – with drinks and snacks and meeting the other visitors. Our group consisted of a Turk, a Canadian, a Romanian, an Austrian, a Brit and three Hungarians. It was a generous and friendly occasion – almost a celebration. I was made very welcome. 'Best not to say anything about the future,' I was advised before talking to the reporter from the local newspaper. The photographer took pictures of us all inside the synagogue.

It seemed a good time to ask Mrs Beres about the Jewish cemetery: was it possible to get into that too?

'I have the key,' she said, and a search ensued but it couldn't be found. It was a nice party.

I was heading back through the rain to where I was staying when my phone rang. 'We've found it! The key! Come back.' And so, the group of us, the deputy mayor, Mr and Mrs Beres, the Turkish visitor, squeezed into several cars and drove out to the bend in the road where the dark trees were.

It was strange to see the door open. The rain was still falling; the fading evening light seemed to be swallowed by the overgrown cypresses (a screen planted by the town in the 1960s). Everything dripped. Beyond the trees waves of wet ivy lapped up over the abandoned tombstones. And yet it wasn't entirely sad. We pulled ivy from the stones to reveal names and dates – 1936, 1942 – and a strange elation ran through the anguish, as if our being there offered hope. Tonight, they were not forgotten. Things could change? In one corner was a solid memorial to the dead of Auschwitz: 117 names on a slab, 1944.

When we finally locked up and left, the deputy mayor pointed to another stone mounted above the gate. 'Freiherr Philip Schey von Koromla in memory of his father Moses', it read. The Scheys might all have left Kőszeg but Philip was making sure the name was not forgotten.

Now it was properly goodbye – we stood in the road with the car doors open and shook hands, kissed cheeks, moved and strangely sad to leave – a little group of people laughing in the gathering dark. Cars coming in the other direction had to slow down to get round the obstruction, their headlights gleaming on the wet road, their occupants peering out curiously.

The deputy mayor laughed at them and waved. 'Watch out!' he called. 'The Jews are back!'

It was quite a legacy.

The Jewish cemetery, Kőszeg, and its memorials to the 117 who died
in Auschwitz in 1944.

14

What Happened

Home

I was still reeling from the cascade of coincidences that my visit to Kőszeg had unleashed when I got back to London and ordinary life. It was August. The street was dusty, the front gardens overblown, there were gaps among the parked cars and children kicking footballs: the summer holidays were underway. Walking up to the shops, I was reminded of how many of the people who lived here came from other places – Grenada, Israel, Bulgaria, Argentina, North America, Hungary, France, Japan, Bangladesh – and that was just among the people I actually knew. This was London – we were all of a mix.

A few days later, there was some kind of gathering at our house; I forget why, but there was food and drink, friends and neighbours, talk. Towards the end of the evening, our next-door neighbours arrived. We had lived semi-detached for over twenty years; their study was on the other side of the wall from mine and even more heavily loaded with books. Two of our children had been in the same class at school and were still fast friends; they had come to Austrian Christmas Eve at our house, and we went to Hanukkah and Pesach at theirs. Jeremy was a scholar of Hebrew liturgy and the obvious person to tell about a lost synagogue. I told him about the ten-minute visit to Kőszeg that turned into three days, the whole long story of it. There were so many things I wanted to know.

Later that night, when everyone had gone and I was clearing up, the doorbell rang. At 1.30 in the morning? There was Jeremy again with a big book open in his hands – the *Encyclopedia Judaica*. He stubbed his index finger at the page, grinning. 'Here you are. Kőszeg. "The first Jew in Kőszeg was Schlesinger, M", and he was *my* great-great-great-great whatever grandfather.'

We fell about laughing. 'Neighbours then.'

〜❧

There is no end to this account or to the stories that are no doubt still floating around and remaking themselves. There's no limit to the history either. Characteristically messy, it trails in all directions and refuses to be rounded off nicely. New babies are born – grandchildren, cousins – and stories may or may not be told. To be continued.

But despite the scatter and distances between us, the extraordinary sinew of family remains, the thing that links us. There's no need to do anything about it, it's just there, a fact, and most of the time most of us ignore it, but throughout the process of writing this, it has offered a web of connection and brought me to a pick-and-mix of very different people, some unfamiliar, others instantly recognisable, to whom the mere fact of my existence opened the door and for whose generosity I am deeply grateful.

It is striking how the stories from the past have continued to unfold throughout my time here. If the tobogganing grandmother appeared in early childhood, by the time I wandered into Kőszeg I was in my 60s. Asking questions may come naturally, but I never set out to study all this, except perhaps in the last years of trying to understand something of the context they came from. The idea was just to catch what was there, the memory trail of the ancestors.

In the eleven years since that first visit to Kőszeg, much has happened. It began with a number of meetings, visits and discussions about the synagogue, and attempts to raise the funding to buy the building back – but how, then, to fund restoring it? Then, in a further twist to the tale, Ferenc Miszlivetz, the director of the institute in Kőszeg, the person I had met over the photocopier, invited Viktor Orbán, once his student, now prime minister of Hungary, to come and open the

Summer University in Kőszeg and took him into the lost building. This was 2012.

As I heard it, Orbán was so struck by his visit that on returning to his office he gave an order for the synagogue to be bought back by the State Property Agency. At once. No argument.

The last, resistant owner explained he had signed the property over to his son – but where was that son? He was finally traced to his job as a slaughterman in a slaughterhouse in Germany and was obliged to sign the documents of sale. In the two years that followed, Mrs Beres was bought out of the two buildings by the gate, mired in the legal tangles of dividing the site in the first place.

And so, in 2014, Kőszeg's synagogue became the property of the state again; the roof secured, gutters fixed, it was boarded up, locked and left for six years while talks were held and plans were made. Then, miraculously, came state funding and a great restoration, completed in the spring of 2022. As the sound of war rang out in Ukraine and millions of people fled that country, it was ready to reopen as both a religious building and a cultural centre. And, in a town whose Jewish community was destroyed in 1944, a reminder of all those who were no longer there.

Meanwhile in Britain, in a frenzy of hyperbole and spin, the UK European Membership Referendum of June 2016 had resulted in a vote to leave the EU. Brexit. There was a whiff of xenophobia in the air.

For me and many others it was a visceral blow, a dislocation, a loss of trust. It was not just a case of back to border restrictions, passport stamping and bureaucracy – we'd managed that before and could do it again, of course, but in some way it felt like a challenge to our very identity. I cannot *only* be British, if this is what British is. Whatever else I may be, I am a European. For the first time in my life, I didn't want to be part of a country like this. While London remained the glorious, complicated, multicultural tapestry I had grown up in and I didn't know a single person who had voted to leave, shades of the nationalisms and terrors of the past rose again.

A desperate longing to escape came upon me – a return to the child-hood worry-dreams. My bag was packed but where in the world could any of us go now?

In November 2019, my Schey cousins, Victor and Edmund de Waal invited me to join them and their family in Vienna for the opening of an exhibition about the Ephrussi side of their family at the Jewish Museum there. Victor, now in his 90s, had come to England from Austria as a boy refugee in 1939 and gone on to become dean of Canterbury Cathedral, among many other things; Edmund, author, potter, artist, historian, had been born and brought up here as I had. It was a memorable three days of visits, receptions, dinners and speeches with forty-one members of the diasporic family from all over the world, many of whom had never met before.

The media, the mayor of Vienna, the president of Austria and many important cultural and business figures spoke of the importance of the occasion, gladness that the Ephrussi archive had returned to Vienna, shame and regret for what had happened in the past and admiration for what was a very fine exhibition. The generosity was enormous, but still it was hard.

On the last evening, as we adjourned to a Lebanese restaurant, there was one final, unscheduled speaker. Husband of the director of the Jewish Museum,[*] he told us that he was an MP and a month earlier the Austrian Parliament had passed a new law that would come into force in October 2020, giving the right of Austrian citizenship to the descendants of 'persecuted ancestors'. And not only that, but the rare privilege of dual nationality, something Austria does not normally allow. Two months later, on 31 January 2020, Britain left the EU.

By this time, we were in the thick of a pandemic and in March 2020 came the first Covid-19 lockdown. Almost exactly 100 years after my mother's birth in the mountains of Tyrol, in retreat from the Spanish flu pandemic, I found myself sheltering in the English countryside with

---

[*] Martin Engelberg, the husband of Danielle Spera, who was head of the Jewish Museum.

my partner, not far from her grave, staying in, seeing nobody, even washing and disinfecting the food that was left on the doorstep by volunteers and the kind local supermarket.

And was it a surprise? No.

I knew this had happened before. It was there in the stories. As I walked my daily walk through the silent countryside – not a car on the road – I thought about it all again. Symmetry, familiarity.

In October 2020 I submitted my application to accept the offer of Austrian citizenship to the Austrian Embassy in London. It took papers and papers, mountains of papers – my mother's birth certificate, her childhood passports, her parents' marriage certificate, her mother's UK registration book – 'Aliens order 1920' – my birth certificate and more. The research I had done for this book had given me a lot of material, but still there were layers of legacy to peel away.

'Persecuted ancestors'? It was a given fact that my grandmother had not been a refugee, and nor had my grandfather. He had chosen to go to Argentina. He went to make his fortune. They were not victims. They had not been driven out. That's what we had been told. The stories we had been brought up with had gone to great lengths to make a safe world for us. And we believed it. But now it was time for the other evidence.

There was very little. Much of it had been eradicated. And yet ... that 1935 land registry book from Schwaz screaming *'Jude'* next to my grandfather's name? His sudden departure in 1938, which just happened to coincide with the laws which would have meant his death? And his brothers and sisters all leaving at the same time?

Could I supply evidence of his papers on leaving Austria or his papers arriving in Buenos Aires, asked the magistrates in Vienna. I could not. I had never met him. I'd had no contact. Even the cousins I had met in Argentina had no contact.

But others were now turning over this same soil (at last, seventy-five years later) and with the generous help of Eberhard Sauerman,**

** Mr Sauerman had written a biography of Fritz von Schey for the reprint he edited of Schey's novel *Das Preisgegebene Herz* (University of Innsbruck, 2022).

I was able to direct them to a PhD thesis at the University of Vienna. In it was an account of the first meeting of the Committee for a Free Austria, the *Comité Austriaco Austria Libre*, the anti-Fascist association of Austrian emigrants in Argentina, which took place in Buenos Aires in 1941 – and there, among the founder members, was his name.

In June 2021, a large envelope fell through my letterbox onto the floor. Eighty years later. Inside was a folder containing my certificate of Austrian citizenship and a welcoming letter from the mayor of Vienna. Despite the ironies, and whatever my ambivalence about Austria's history and ideology, I was part of Europe once more. It was a strange relief.

And now there is war in Europe again. Can these things really not stop repeating themselves? And which version of the story is right? Who knows?

The fact is that history remains alive and only just below the surface. Prodding at it is like poking a wasps' nest with a stick or sticking your fingers into an electric socket: dangerous. Europe's nineteenth- and twentieth-century history is raw and painful. Yet the stories we inherited were anything but. They were full of life and energy and vigour, sorrows were passed over, dark times ignored.

How do the two things fit together? And how do they fit with the people we knew? Were previous generations so different; were they braver and happier than we know ourselves to be? Or just lucky? A look at the letters is enough to dispel that idea. My father had a huge talent, my mother a boundless energy for life, but I also understood from the beginning how fragile they were underneath.

It is impossible ever to know what actually happened. History can pretend to be organised, a flowing sequence of cause and effect, one thing leading to another, but clearly that's not how oral narrative or memory work. They're more like patchwork, collage, layers or threads in a fabric, and the point at which a story is delivered is often as significant as its content in the way it works on the recipients. That is why this book is not an orderly sequence from the myths of the middle ages to the twenty-first century but an attempt to capture something of the chaos of anecdote and chance encounter in the course of one life.

Like all fiction, stories are a way of managing reality, translating it, shaping it, embedding it in some kind of manageable form in order to pass it down the generations. Above all, they're portable, like languages – this is all-important if you're going to live in different places. They're also a driver. Where surrounding events diverge from the tales that are told, it may be for a reason. Some things are better forgotten. Like silences in music, the things left out are an integral part of the composition.

So why do things get told this way?

Maybe stories are like the smiling pictures on social media, and before that, in the photo albums – life perfectible (though it's interesting to see that people smiled very little in the oldest albums; record was a solemn business). How many of us take pictures of our children when they're crying, angry or in pain, or feel able to keep the results if we do?

It's not about truth in the literal sense then – whatever that might be.

Looking at the maternal edit, what comes through most clearly is that the stories we grew up with were courage tales, tools for going on, fuel for future generations, a kind of buoyancy aid. That, and entertainment. Others, they tell us, mothers – your own others – have been there before; listen and laugh. And, by implication, you can do it too: you can keep going, pick up the bits and take them forward. Events may be horrible, relationships painful, loss devastating, life may go badly wrong, but here's precedent, company and perhaps even consolation. Here's what matters: life is powerful. And you're part of it, not alone but connected to these others.

It's a fragile hypothesis, I know, but I can't think of another reason for the survival of these stories over so much time and distance. Or a better reason for passing them on.

Notes

Chapter 1

1 'RG', writing in a local newsletter here, was Rolf Gardiner who lived at nearby Springhead. Mutti was godmother to his son John Eliot Gardiner. 'She brought me Papageno-Papagena puppets on my 3rd or maybe 4th birthday party,' he writes. 'I adored your grandmother Anny.'

2 Alma Mahler-Werfel, *Mein Leben* (S Fischer Verlag, 1960).

3 See page 61.

4 Stefan Zweig, *The World of Yesterday* (University of Nebraska Press, 1964) p. 23

5 Carl E. Schorske, *Fin de Siècle Vienna: Politics and Culture* (Cambridge University Press, 1981) p. 8.

6 Steven Beller, *Vienna and the Jews 1867–1938: A Cultural History* (Cambridge University Press, 1989) p. 176.

7 Schorske, *Fin de Siècle Vienna*, p. 8.

8 Zweig, *The World of Yesterday*.

9 I heard this story from Sissi Pockels, who appears in the next chapter.

Chapter 2

1 Zweig, *The World of Yesterday*, p. 246.

2 John Keegan, *The First World War* (Alfred A. Knopf, 1999).

3 Maureen Healy, *Vienna and the Fall of the Habsburg Empire: Total War and Everyday Life in World War I* (Cambridge University Press, 2004) p. 41.

4 Otto Kallir, *Egon Schiele* (Crown Publishers, Inc., 1966).

5 Jill Lloyd, *The Undiscovered Expressionist: A Life of Marie Louise von Motesiczky* (Yale University Press, 2007) p. 63.

6 Grandmother Schindler (née Minich) died in 1921 and was buried in Schwaz.

Chapter 3

1 My father had nothing to say about Fritz. It was as if they'd scarcely met. My mother hadn't much to say either: he was tall. He was handsome. He was funny. And he liked playing practical jokes. Like the one when he sent a kipper in a parcel addressed to himself, to a post office where the postmaster in charge was a man he'd fallen out with. And then he didn't collect it. Under post office rules the man was obliged to keep the parcel for three months – three long, hot, summer months as the fish rotted and stank – in the room he worked in. It smelt terrible. What a joke.

Now the joker was 71, he lived in Argentina and had a new-born son called José.

Chapter 4

1 Zweig, *The World of Yesterday*, p. 315.
2 George Clare, *Last Waltz in Vienna* (Macmillan, 1981). My notes from the Pan paperback edition (1982).
3 Fritz von Schey, *Du Allem Ausgesetztes Herz* (Verlag der Johannespresse, 1936).

Chapter 6

1 Zweig, *The World of Yesterday*, p. 248.

Chapter 7

1 Hugo Herbert Jones in a letter to me.
2 www.ushmm.org/outreach/en/article.php?ModuleId=10007695 and en.wikipedia.org/wiki/Nuremberg_Laws
3 Johanna 'Hanny' née Baroness von Buschman.
4 Margarete 'Gretl' née Edle von Mayer Gunthof.

Chapter 8

1 I am indebted to Gini Fletcher for the tribunal letter from her aunt, Marianne Schey.
2 Peter and Leni Gillman, *'Collar the Lot!': How Britain Interned and Expelled its Wartime Refugees* (Quartet Books, 1980).
3 Ibid., p. 72.
4 Ibid., p. 73.
5 Ibid., p. 102.

Chapter 9

1 Gillmans, *'Collar the Lot!'*, p. 206.

Chapter 10

1 From Lloyd, *The Undiscovered Expressionist*.
2 Fuks, Evi and Gabriele Kohlbauer-Fritz (eds), *Die Liebens, 150 Jahre Geschichte einer Wiener Familie* (Jüdisches Museum Wien, 2004). The chapter on Robert Lieben (*Unendliche Gedanken Denken, Robert von Lieben - ein grosser Erfinder*) was written by Hans-Thomas Schmidt.
3 The source for Mathilde's letter is Eberhard Sauermann.

Chapter 12

1 Margit Altfahrt, *Die Jüdische Familie Schey*, 'Jahrbuch des Vereins fur Geschichte der Stadt Wien' (Wiener Stadt und Landes Archiv, 2007).
2 Ibid.
3 In 1980 the Palais Schey was used as the setting for the TV series *Ringstraßenpalais: Eine Wiener Familiengeschichte* (*Palace on the Ring: A Viennese Family Story*).
4 Martin Rady, *The Habsburgs: The Rise and Fall of a World Power* (Allen Lane, 2020) p. 107.
5 A.J.P. Taylor, *The Hapsburg Monarchy*, (Penguin, 1990) p. 25.
6 Altfahrt, *Die Jüdische Familie Schey*, p. 8.
7 This touch of oral narrative is from Alexandra Byers-Schey, *The Family Schey von Koromla: A History* (private publication, 1991).
8 *The Spectacular Rise and Fall of the Hapsburgs*, Mischa Glenny, BBC Radio 4, 20 November 2006.
9 Quoted in Altfahrt, *Die Jüdische Familie Schey*, p. 6.
10 Altfahrt, *Die Jüdische Familie Schey*, p. 10.
11 Alexandra Byers-Schey, *The Family Schey von Koromla*.
12 Louise Hecht, 'Appropriation of "Jewish" space' in *Ringstrasse: A Jewish Boulevard*, ed. Gabriele Kohlbauer-Fritz (on behalf of the Jewish Museum Vienna, Amalthea, 2015), p. 267.
13 Arthur Schnitzler, *My Youth in Vienna* (Weidenfeld and Nicolson, 1971) p. 13.
14 Edgar Lederer, *Selected Topics in the History of Biochemistry: Personal Recollections, Part 2*, ed. G. Semenza (Elsevier Amsterdam, 1986) p. 440.
15 Ernst Gombrich, 'The Visual Arts in Vienna circa 1900: Reflections on the Jewish Catastrophe' (lecture), *Occasions*, 17 November 1996 (Austrian Cultural Institute, London), p. 18.
16 I am indebted to Fritz von Schey's biographer, Eberhard Sauerman, for his research on this.
17 Gombrich, 'The Visual Arts in Vienna circa 1900', p. 16.

Chapter 13

1 Darren Longley, *The Rough Guide to Hungary* (Rough Guides, 2010).

Bibliography

Adler, Jeremy, and Birgit Sander (eds), *Marie Louise von Motesiczky 1906–1996: The Painter* (Prestel Publishing, 2006).

Altfahrt, Margit, *Die Jüdische Familie Schey* (Wiener Stadt und Landes Archiv, 2007).

Beller, Steven, *Vienna and the Jews 1867–1938: A Cultural History* (Cambridge University Press, 1989).

Blackshaw, Gemma, *Facing the Modern: The Portrait in Vienna 1900* (National Gallery Company, 2013).

Broch, Herman, *Hugo von Hofmannsthal and His Time: The European Imagination 1860–1920*, trans. M. Steinberg (Chicago University Press, 1984).

Clare, George, *Last Waltz in Vienna* (Macmillan, 1981; Pan, 1982).

Fuks, Evi, and Gabriele Kohlbauer-Fritz (eds), *Die Liebens, 150 Jahre Geschichte einer Wiener Familie* (Jüdisches Museum Wien, 2004).

Gay, Peter, *Schnitzler's Century: The Making of Middle Class Culture 1815–1914* (W.W. Norton, 2002).

Gillman, Peter and Leni, *'Collar the Lot!' How Britain Interned and Expelled its Wartime Refugees* (Quartet Books, 1980).

Gombrich, Ernst, 'The Visual Arts in Vienna *circa*. 1900: Reflections on the Jewish Catastrophe' (lecture), *Occasions*, 17 November 1996 (Austrian Cultural Institute, London).

Healy, Maureen, *Vienna and the Fall of the Habsburg Empire: Total War and Everyday Life in World War I* (Cambridge University Press, 2004).

Hobsbawm, Eric, *Interesting Times: A Twentieth-Century Life* (Allen Lane, The Penguin Press, 2002).

Hudson, William Henry, *The Purple Land* (Sampson Low, 1885).

Hudson, William Henry, *Long Ago and Far Away* (Eland, 1918).

Kallir, Otto, *Egon Schiele* (Crown Publishers Inc., 1966).

Karpf, Anne, *The War After* (Minerva Paperback, 1996).

Keegan, John, *The First World War* (Alfred A. Knopf, 1999).

Kohlbauer-Fritz, Gabriele (ed.), *Ringstrasse: Ein Jüdischer Boulevarde* (on behalf of the Jewish Museum Vienna, Amalthea, 2015).

Lederer, Edgar, *Selected Topics in the History of Biochemistry: Personal Recollections, Part 2*, ed. G. Semenza (Elsevier, 1986).

Lloyd, Jill, *The Undiscovered Expressionist: A Life of Marie Louise von Motesiczky* (Yale University Press, 2007).

Longley, Darren (Norm), *The Rough Guide to Hungary* (Rough Guides, 2010).

Mahler-Werfel, Alma, *Diaries 1898–1902*, eds Antony Beaumont and Susanne Rode-Breymann (Faber and Faber, 1999).

Mahler-Werfel, Alma, *Mein Leben* (Frankfurt, 1960).

McCagg Jnr, William O., *A History of Habsburg Jews 1670–1918* (Indiana University Press, 1989).

Nicholson, Virginia, *Singled Out: How Two Million Women Survived Without Men After the First World War* (Viking/Penguin, 2007).

Rady, Martin, *The Habsburgs: The Rise and Fall of a World Power* (Penguin Books, 2021).

Roth, Joseph, *Radetzky March,* trans. Michael Hoffman (first published Berlin, 1932; Granta Books, 2003).

Roth, Joseph, *The Emperor's Tomb*, trans. Michael Hoffman (Granta Books, 2013).

Sands, Philippe, *East West Street* (Penguin Random House, 2016).

Schey, Fritz von, *Du Allem Ausgesetztes Hertz* (Verlag der Johanespresse, Vienna, 1936 and reprinted as *Das Preisgegebene Herz*) ed. Eberhard Sauerman (Innsbruck University Press, 2022).

Schindler, Meriel, *The Lost Café Schindler* (Hodder & Stoughton, 2021).

Schnitzler, Arthur, *My Youth in Vienna*, trans. Catherine Hutter (Weidenfeld and Nicolson, 1971).

Schnitzler, Arthur, *Der Weg ins Freie, 1908* (Northwestern University Press, 1992).

Schorske, Carl E., *Fin de Siècle Vienna: Politics and Culture* (Cambridge University Press, 1981).

Söptei, Imre, 'A Schey család Köszegen, 1794–1883' in *Elöadások vas Megye Történetéröl v.*, eds Mayer László and Tilcsik György (Szombathely, 2010).

Snowman, Daniel, *The Hitler Emigrés: The Cultural Impact on Britain of Refugees from Nazism* (Chatto and Windus, 2002).

Taylor, A.J.P., *The Hapsburg Monarchy 1809–1918* (Penguin, 1990).

Waal, Edmund de, *The Hare with Amber Eyes* (Picador, 2010).

Zweig, Stefan, *The World of Yesterday* (University of Nebraska Press, 1964).

Private Publications

Byers-Schey, Alexandra, *The Family Schey von Koromla: A History* (private publication, 1991).

Goldschmidt, Brigitte, *Himmelsforten* (private publication).

Goldschmidt-Propper, Renate, *Kde Domjov Muj* (private publication, 2015).

Lusk, Catherine Goldschmidt, *Erla* (photographs, private publication, 1994).

Radio, TV, Film

Bragg, Melvin, *In Our Time: The Congress of Vienna* (BBC Radio 4, 19 October 2017).

Geller-Varga, Zsuzsanna, *Once They Were Neighbours* (2005) film.aromo.com/once-they-were-neighbours

Geller-Varga, Zsuzsanna, *Synagogue for Sale* (2007) film.aromo.com/synagogue-for-sale/

Glenny, Mischa, *The Spectacular Rise and Fall of the Hapsburgs* (BBC Radio 4, 20 November 2006).

Montefiore, Simon Sebag, *Vienna: Empire, Dynasty and Dream* (BBC4, December 2016).

Koerner, Joseph, *Vienna: City of Dreams* (BBC Radio 4, 27 January 2008).

Acknowledgements

At the beginning of this book is a simplified family tree, stripped back to the essentials to guide what follows. In reality the family continues as families do and the breadth and range of even this small strand of the Schey line is considerable, reaching across the world. With apologies in advance to all the partners, husbands and wives I have no room to name, and the children and grandchildren whose names I have withheld for their own privacy, here's a sketch of where we are at the time of writing - five and six generations after Friedrich Schey, seven since Kőszeg.

I have never managed to make contact with my mother's half brother José, the baby uncle of Chapter 3, in Argentina but I believe he has three children now in their forties, possibly in Canada.

Of my mother's immediate siblings her older sister Beate had two children: Patricia who lives in Spain and has two children and David in England with one son and two grandchildren.

In Argentina her brother Clemens had three children: Karen, Marina and John, (known to all as Maxie). Karen had four children and they in their turn have a total of six children living currently in Mallorca, and Patagonia, Argentina. Marina had one child who now lives in New York with two daughters and a stepson, and John had two daughters who are in in Buenos Aires bringing the total of Clemens great-grandchildren to 10.

Then there are my own children, two in England with two children each and one in Switzerland with one child, making me the glad grandmother of 5.

It is to all of these, their numerous cousins and the future that I dedicate this book.

❧

There are so many people to thank that it's hard to know where to start.

Thanks go above all to my mother, Inge, and my father, Bill, without whom these stories would not have survived, and nor would we;

Then to my sister Tessa, who travelled the same road, for her help, research in Innsbruck and London, wonderful artwork, links to people I didn't know and for salvaging the family records and photographs while clearing the house;

Sara Kidel, who is and always has been our other sister, for her fearless zest for living and the friendship of a lifetime;

Frankie Armstrong for whom I made my first book – *My Song is My Own, 100 Women's Songs* – and who, nearly forty-five years of deep and musical friendship later, led me to The History Press;

John Benington for our great, long conversation and his unwavering encouragement year after year when I was at the point of giving up;

Gill Gorrell-Barnes who listened and heard as I felt my way along;

My partner, Nick Davidson, who has patiently lived with all this and urged me on;

And our children Charley, Dan and Annie, their partners and their children who hold the future in their arms.

Of the many members of the Schey family, particular thanks go to:

Gini Fletcher for permission to quote from her aunt Marianne Schey's tribunal letter;

Victor de Waal, for his kindness and interest, and Edmund de Waal for the 2019 gathering in Vienna;

Jessie Gough in New York and the South American cousins I met in 2007;

Edmund Byers, for the use of his mother, Alexandra Byers Schey's book;

Jean and Jacqueline Goldschmidt and all their family, particularly Dominique Huberti and her children Sebastien and Laetitia, for their hospitality, our wonderful visits to Schloss Erla and their permission to use some of the pictures from its walls.

And to others:

Paul and Eva Badura-Skoda in Vienna;

Hans-Thomas Schmidt for his advice on Robert von Lieben;

Eberhard Sauerman, Fritz Schey's biographer, who gave me vital leads;

Frances Carey of the Marie-Louise von Motesiczky Charitable Trust in London;

Ursula Cornish, who helped me translate my grandfather's 1915 letters;

My neighbours, especially George Blair, fellow hybrid and photographer, and Jeremy Schonfield and his family, on the other side of the wall;

Carol Savage for that last minute photograph;

Margaret Brearley for the gift of a word;

In Hungary, Nick Thorpe and Andrea Weichinger for their hospitality, translation of Hungarian and a mass of help;

Zsuzsana Geller-Varga, for her films, *Synagogue for Sale* and *Once They Were Neighbours*, as well as her helpful advice;

And in Kőszeg, Jenna Goodhand who started it all off; Imre Söptoi, archivist; Anikó Beres who guarded the gate; Béla Básthy, mayor; Ferenc Miszlivetz and his team at iASK (the Institute of Advanced Studies Kőszeg) and the Kőszeg-KRAFT project; Anikó Magasházi; Katalin Galambos; Mónika Mátay; Tamás Fejerdy; and many others; and, back in England, Graham Bell who kept me in touch.

I would also like to say a very big thank you to Laura Perehinec at The History Press for taking it on, Ian Pearson for opening the door and Jezz Palmer, Katie Beard, Anette Fuhrmeister and Helen Richardson for making this book happen.

Permissions

Excerpt from *The Secret Scripture* by Sebastian Barry © 2008 Sebastian Barry, used by permission from Faber and Faber Limited and of Viking Books, an imprint of Penguin Publishing Group, a division of Penguin Random House LLC. All rights reserved.

Excerpt from *The War After* by Anne Kampf © 1997 Anne Kampf, Heinemann, used with kind permission from the author.

Apart from those listed below, all photographs and illustrations in this book are from the author's family or personal collections.

p. 24   Christmas card, courtesy of the estate of W.A. Henderson.
p. 36   The Burgtheater, courtesy of Philippa Helliwell.
p. 53   Map of Austria–Hungary, 1914, based on one drawn by Alphathon, CC 3.0
p. 59   Map of the Republic of Austria, 1919, based on one drawn by Alphathon, CC 3.0
p. 60   *Notgeld*, courtesy of Schloss Era. Photograph by Kathy Henderson.
p. 66   *Sissi playing Mozart in the Rotenturm Schlössl*, courtesy of Tessa Henderson.
p. 68   *The Rotenturm Schlössl*, courtesy of Trauerhilfe, Bestattung Othmar Lechner, Schwaz.
p. 73   Two murals and the painting of the two sisters, by Katherine Eliza Henderson, from her estate courtesy of Brian Moser.
p. 90   The Feldherrnhalle, courtesy of INTERFOTO/Alamy.
p. 105   The *péniche* and the Halle de la Marine, courtesy of Tessa Henderson.
p. 112   Chameleon letter, courtesy of the estate of W.A. Henderson.
p. 136   *Hunting*, by Marie-Louise von Motesiczky, courtesy of the Marie-Louise von Motesiczky Charitable Trust 2023 and Frances Carey.

Every effort has been made to identify copyright holders and obtain their permission for the use of copyright material. If any omissions have occurred, please get in touch with the publisher for corrections to be made in future reprints and editions.

Index

Note: italicised references denote illustrations and the suffix 'n' denotes a note

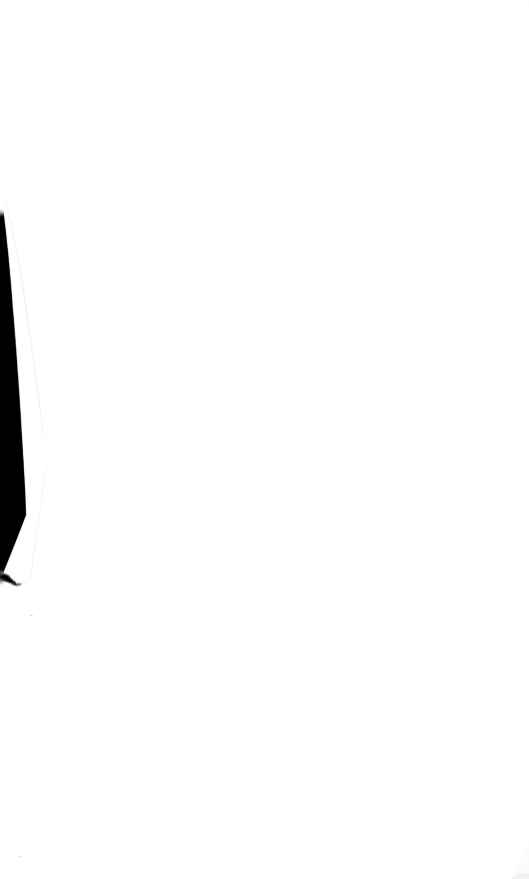